Core/Periphery Relations in Precapitalist Worlds

EDITED BY

Christopher Chase-Dunn
and Thomas D. Hall

Westview Press

BOULDER • SAN FRANCISCO • OXFORD

The cover illustration is a photograph of a Roman coin bearing the likeness of Vercingetorix, a chieftain who united the Gauls in resistance to Caesar; reproduced from Jack Holland and John Monroe, *The Order of Rome* (Boston, MA: Boston Publishing Company, 1986), p. 41, by kind permission of the publisher.

This Westview softcover edition is printed on acid-free paper and bound in library-quality, coated covers that carry the highest rating of the National Association of State Textbook Administrators, in consultation with the Association of American Publishers and the Book Manufacturers' Institute.

Published in 1991 in the United States of America by Westview Press, Inc., 5500 Central Avenue, Boulder, Colorado 80301, and in the United Kingdom by Westview Press, 36 Lonsdale Road, Summertown, Oxford OX2 7EW

Library of Congress Cataloging-in-Publication Data
Core/periphery relations in precapitalist worlds / edited by
  Christopher Chase-Dunn and Thomas D. Hall.
    p. cm.
Includes bibliographical references and index.
ISBN 0-8133-7951-2
  1. Economic history. 2. Economics, Prehistoric. 3. Economic
anthropology. 4. Dependency. I. Chase-Dunn, Christopher K.
II. Hall, Thomas D.
HC21.C649 1991
330.93—dc20
                                                              89-48383
                                                                  CIP

Printed and bound in the United States of America

The paper used in this publication meets the requirements
(∞) of the American National Standard for Permanence of Paper
for Printed Library Materials Z39.48-1984.

10   9   8   7   6   5   4   3   2   1

This book is dedicated to Vercingetorix,

the chieftain who united the Gallic tribes in resistance to Caesar.

CONTENTS

PREFACE

In discussing how we would preface this collection we decided that describing how we became interested in seemingly arcane topics like prehistoric trade and ancient empires would be a good start. We reasoned that a narrative of how our interests shifted to such topics might entice other social scientists to join in our venture. We share values common to all students of social change: curiosity about how the world came to be as it is, what forces and processes keep it that way, and what -- if anything -- might help change it for the better. We were both attracted to, and have become active researchers and writers in, the world-system perspective. Our paths to this common meeting point were distinct, but once crossed they have become increasingly intertwined.

Chase-Dunn began his academic career as a quantitoid sociologist performing crossnational research to test propositions about the effects of international economic dependence in the post-World War II world-system. His encounter with the world-systems perspective led to an effort to formulate an explicit theory of the structures and processes of the modern world-system, which was published as *Global Formation: Structures of the World-Economy* in 1989. In 1986, as he was completing the last chapter of *Global Formation*, Chase-Dunn tried to confront the problem of transformation -- how the contemporary world-system might change its fundamental logic. His earlier work on a world-systems interpretation of the emergence and reintegration of the socialist states led to some tentative conclusions, but he realized that the scientific basis for understanding the transformation problem would be found in the comparison of instances in which whole world-systems had undergone transformations of their basic logics in the past. The provocative essay by Ekholm and Friedman, "'Capital' imperialism and exploitation in the ancient world-systems" (*Review* 6, 1, Summer 1982), stimulated him to write a 140-

page manuscript entitled *Rise and Demise: The Transformation of World-Systems*, which proposed a working typology to determine similarities and differences between stateless, state-based, and capitalist world-systems. Though this manuscript was circulated among colleagues and is cited in some of the chapters in this collection, its preliminary nature has delayed publication. Chase-Dunn and Hall plan to rework and redesign this into a comprehensive introduction to the comparative study of world-systems.

Hall came to world-system theory as a refugee from the "my village separate from the world" school of anthropology. As is typical of graduate student tyros, he did not appreciate that this was a dying tradition. Working on the Navajo Nation in the early seventies pushed Hall into sociology from anthropology and primed him to appreciate world-system theory's promise, if not its delivery, of a globally and historically connected approach to the study of society and change. Many years of study, rumination, a dissertation, and more rewriting than anyone likes to admit, led to *Social Change in the Southwest, 1350-1880.*

Two of that book's major themes are germane to this collection: the reconceptualization of incorporation as something that starts much earlier, and is more profound, than Wallerstein used to recognize and a comparative strategy that examined the impacts of Mesoamerica (albeit briefly), Spain, Mexico, and the United States on ethnic relations and group formation in what became the U.S. Southwest. That comparative strategy was groping toward examining both how the "modern world-system" evolved and how it differed from earlier, precapitalist world-systems. A subsidiary interest developed along the way: How were the nomad/sedentary relations Hall was studying in Hispanic New Mexico similar to, and different from, those that occurred elsewhere in the world, especially on the fringes of China?

Hall and Chase-Dunn crossed paths for the first time on a BART train from Berkeley to San Francisco in the process of getting from cheap digs to the 1982 American Sociological Association (ASA) meetings. Over the years we found an increasing convergence of interests and began to work together. We co-organized an ASA round table discussion on "Comparing World-Systems" in 1986, and then a series of panels and papers at the 1988, 1989, and 1990 annual meetings of the International Society for the Comparative Study of Civilizations (ISCSC).

After organizing the 1989 ISCSC panels we began to think about putting some of the papers together in a collection. Meanwhile, *Social Change in the Southwest* had been finished and was published, *Global Formation* had gone to press, and the out-takes on precapitalist world-systems had been proposed and accepted at Westview Press as *Rise and Demise*. In our original proposal for this collection Chase-Dunn was going to write a theoretical opening and a chapter exploring the idea of stateless world-systems through a study of California Indians, and Hall was going to push his ruminations on Southwestern and Central Asian nomads into presentable form. In order to do that, Hall had to rethink, for the umpteenth time, what a world-system is. To complicate, but tremendously enrich, his ruminating, Thomas Barfield published *The Perilous Frontier* and Janet Abu-Lughod published *Before European Hegemony*, with the result that we merged our theoretical musings into what is now Chapter 1. The discussion of California Indians has been postponed until more research can be completed, and *Rise and Demise* has become a joint, bigger -- and we hope better -- project.

Meanwhile, the Braudel Center's journal, *Review*, has published a somewhat different and considerably longer piece by Andre Gunder Frank and a series of articles thinking about where world-system theory has been and where it might be going (*Review* 13, 2, Spring 1990). A good deal of the emerging discussion and debate is contained in the following pages. These circumstances present a reader who is just coming upon these issues with a few obstacles. First, and foremost, almost nobody has staked out permanent positions. Rather, nearly everyone's thinking and research is evolving (dare we use that word?) fairly quickly. Second, new parties have joined in these debates (e.g. Wilkinson, Feinman and Nicholas, Peregrine) from very different theoretical, disciplinary, and substantive backgrounds and hence with somewhat different vocabularies or, even more troubling, the same vocabularies with different meanings. So far, we have succeeded in talking to, rather than past, each other, but not without a lot of backtracking to define terms and usages. Finally, the attempt to study world-systems comparatively has led many of us into new research areas and new literatures. This has been exhilarating and frightening as we explore new territories, learning who's who, what's what, and which way is up all over again. We hope that this collection will provoke and inspire others to join us.

We would like to thank the members and officers of the International Society for the Comparative Study of Civilizations, especially its President, Michael Palencia-Roth, for graciously encouraging us to organize sessions on world-systems. We also are indebted to Mitchell Weyuker and Joanne

Fennessey at Johns Hopkins and Catherine Day at DePauw for their extraordinary deeds in the preparation of this book. A grant from DePauw's Faculty Development Committee for Completion of Scholarly Work substantially assisted in production of this volume. At Westview Press we are grateful to Dean Birkenkamp and Ellen Williams.

Christopher Chase-Dunn
and Thomas D. Hall

ABOUT THE EDITORS
AND CONTRIBUTORS

Christopher Chase-Dunn is Professor of Sociology at Johns Hopkins University. He is the author of *Transnational Corporations and Underdevelopment* (with Volker Bornschier, Praeger, 1985) and *Global Formation: Structures of the World-Economy* (Basil Blackwell, 1989). He is currently working on the problem of the transformation of modes of production by comparing the modern global political economy to earlier, smaller world-systems.

Gary M. Feinman is Associate Professor of Anthropology at the University of Wisconsin, Madison. A Mesoamerican archaeologist, he has participated in field work in the Valleys of Oaxaca and Ejutla since 1977. He is co-author of three books and has written more than 30 articles on various topics, including craft specialization, demographic change, and regional analysis.

Andre Gunder Frank is Professor of Development Economics and Social Sciences at the University of Amsterdam. He has taught in departments of anthropology, economics, history, and sociology at universities in Europe, North and Latin America. His research has centered primarily on Third World and Latin American dependence (the "development of underdevelopment"), history of the world system, and the contemporary world economic crisis. His work also ranges over international political economy and relations, Marxism, organization theory and management, peace research, socialism, and social movements. His 800-plus publications in 24 languages include 600 versions of articles, chapters in over 100 readers/anthologies, and over 100 different editions of his 30 books, among them *Capitalism and Underdevelopment in Latin America, World Accumulation 1492-1789, Crisis in the World Economy,* and *The European Challenge*.

Barry K. Gills did his postgraduate work at the London School of Economics and Oxford. He teaches in the Department of Politics at the University of Newcastle Upon Tyne. Together with Andre Gunder Frank, he is working on a "World System History" which places world accumulation at the center of the analysis and encompasses five thousand years of world system development. Other research interests are in the international political economy of East Asia, and the political economy of Korea in particular. He is a Fellow of the Transnational Institute, Amsterdam.

Thomas D. Hall is the Lester M. Jones Professor of Sociology at DePauw University. He received his Ph.D. at the University of Washington in 1981. His book on the American Southwest, *Social Change in the Southwest, 1350-1880* (published by University Press of Kansas in its historical sociology series) has been widely acclaimed. He is currently working on the incorporation of ethnic minorities into the world-system in the nineteenth and twentieth centuries, and comparing those processes with processes in precapitalist world-systems.

Linda M. Nicholas is an Honorary Fellow in the Department of Anthropology at the University of Wisconsin, Madison. She has worked as an archaeologist in Oaxaca since 1980. In her research she has taken a regional perspective to the analysis of indigenous systems of land use in both Mexico's Southern Highlands and the southwestern United States.

Peter Peregrine received his Ph.D. in Anthropology from Purdue University in 1990 and is now Assistant Professor of Anthropology at Juniata College. His research is focused on the evolution of complex societies, with particular emphasis on the rise of Mississippian chiefdoms in the American midcontinent. In future research efforts Dr. Peregrine hopes to investigate the utility of world-systems theory in developing a unified theory of cultural evolution in eastern North America.

Stephen K. Sanderson is Professor of Sociology at Indiana University of

Pennsylvania. His main research interests are in the areas of social theory, sociocultural evolution, and comparative macrosociology. He is the author of *Macrosociology: An Introduction to Human Societies* (Harper & Row, 1988; 2nd edition, 1991) and *Social Evolutionism: A Critical History* (Basil Blackwell, 1990). He is currently working on a book that will develop and empirically demonstrate a formal theory of long-term sociocultural evolution.

Jane Schneider is Professor of Anthropology at the City University of New York's Graduate Center. She has conducted anthropological field research in Sicily and is the co-author, with Peter Schneider, of a 1976 book, *Culture and Political Economy in Western Sicily*. A second book, covering the demographic transition in Sicily, is in progress. Other publications relate to a secondary interest -- the comparative history of cloth, clothing, and textile manufacture. An article on the "Anthropology of Cloth" for the 1987 *Annual Review of Anthropology* is one example.

David Wilkinson is Professor of Political Science at the University of California, Los Angeles. He lives in the semiperiphery of Los Angeles but commutes frequently to the core, where he works in the semiperiphery of a discipline whose core (he thinks) is very slowly moving his way.

INTRODUCTION

Christopher Chase-Dunn and Thomas D. Hall

The rise of the world-systems perspective on social change in the modern world has transformed our understanding of how societies develop. Though we may argue about the relative importance of "internal" *versus* "external" factors, almost all social scientists now agree that the larger intersocietal context and hierarchical relations among societies are significant factors in societal development. And it is increasingly agreed that the larger system which is composed of societies is itself an important unit of analysis which can be studied historically and structurally. This volume is dedicated to the project of extending these insights to precapitalist societies and intersocietal systems. We want to determine the extent to which regional world-systems in the past were similar to or different from the contemporary global political economy. And we want to utilize the study of different kinds of world-systems to help us understand how fundamental logics of social reproduction become transformed.

The first task is to examine the concepts which have been developed to describe and analyze the modern world-system to determine their usefulness when applied to earlier systems. Sociologists, historians, political scientists, anthropologists and archaeologists have applied world-system concepts to earlier systems, as reported in the chapters which follow. These efforts to study precapitalist world-systems have led to new, or renewed, disputes over the definitions of capitalism, modes of production, cores, peripheries, and indeed, of world-systems themselves. It is our contention that these disputes

1

should be resolved on the terrain of actual empirical studies of particular intersocietal systems and comparative studies of different types of systems.

Chapter 1 is a prolegomena to the comparative study of world-systems by the editors. As will be obvious, our thinking is still shuttling fairly rapidly between "historical data" and concept formation and theory building. We are exerting efforts to **not** read the present into the past, **nor** read the past into the present, but to use each to learn about the other. We review and critique the literature which addresses conceptualization of world-systems and core/periphery hierarchies and propose synthetic definitions of our own. We outline a preliminary typology of world-systems and propose hypotheses about variation in world-system structures. Most importantly, we argue that world-systems should not be assumed to have core/periphery hierarchies, but rather the existence and nature of intersocietal inequalities should be the focus of research.

Chapter 2 is Jane Schneider's now classic sympathetic critique of Volume 1 of Immanuel Wallerstein's *Modern World-System* which appeared originally in the journal *Peasant Studies* in 1977. Six of the seven other chapters in our collection cite Schneider's article. We feel fortunate to be able to make this valuable contribution more accessible. Schneider takes Wallerstein to task for not pushing world-system analysis far enough (into precapitalist settings) and for defining trade interconnections too narrowly by excluding prestige goods, which she argues are crucial for understanding power relations in precapitalist systems.

Chapter 3 is a joint effort by Barry Gills and Andre Gunder Frank, which argues, contra our position, that there has been only **one** world system (without the hyphen) for the last 5000 years. This system is based on the accumulation of wealth and power by ruling classes at the expense of exploited classes in which the centers of power have shifted over time. Gills and Frank replace the concept of mode of production with "mode of accumulation" and contend that there have not been major transformations in the logic of accumulation such as is implied in the notion of the transition from feudalism to capitalism. Rather they contend that commodity production, private wealth and state-based forms of accumulation have been mixed in different ways during the history of **the** world system.

Chapter 4, by David Wilkinson, comes from the "civilizationist" tradition. He briefly outlines work he has done elsewhere which examines the expansion of "Central Civilization" and its incorporation by force of twelve formerly autonomous regional systems. Contrary to other civilizationists, who define civilizations in terms of institutional and cultural homogeneity, Wilkinson defines his unit of analysis in terms of interconnections--those constituted by sustained political/military conflict or cooperation. This produces a roster of urban-based civilizations beginning with that which emerged in Mesopotamia in the fourth millennium B.C. Wilkinson contends that these are world systems in the sense that they are self-contained entities which do not interact in any sustained or important way with outsiders. In Chapter 4 Wilkinson provides his own definitions of core, periphery and semiperiphery and describes the shifting boundaries of these zones (as he has defined them) for the fourteen civilizations/world systems produced by his approach. This results in a fascinating conclusion: civilizations do not fall; rather they change their centers and expand.

Stephen Sanderson, in Chapter 5, summarizes the intellectual history of evolutionary theory and places world-system theory and its extension to precapitalist systems in the context of debates about social evolution. His major point is that world-system theory is, in fact, a type of evolutionary theory. We do not disagree with this if evolutionary theory is understood to include possibilities for historical open-endedness. We prefer to call our approach "historical development" in order to emphasize this aspect, but we agree with Sanderson that the literature on social evolution is a fertile source of hypotheses for understanding world-system processes. Sanderson also claims that world-systems theory overstates the importance of "external" determinants over "internal" (intrasocietal) determinants of social change. Hopefully systematic comparative research can help resolve this issue.

Chapters 6, 7, and 8 differ from the preceding chapters in their emphasis on specific case materials. In Chapter 6 Peter Peregrine explores the Cahokia-centered world-system located in the North American mid-continent around A.D. 900. This is the mound-building system which Wilkinson calls Mississippian civilization. Peregrine supports Schneider's claim that prestige goods exchanges are a central form of integration, especially in stratified chiefdoms. Following work by Meillassoux, and Friedman and Rowlands, Peregrine argues that a regionally stratified intersocietal system is built on the monopolization and distribution of sumptuary goods. Chapter 6 summarizes the results of his Purdue University archaeology dissertation on Cahokia.

In Chapter 7 Thomas Hall examines the variable roles of nomads in nomad-sedentary relations, and especially their peculiar role in core/periphery hierarchies. The comparison of Central Asian nomads and nomadic Indians in the American Southwest gives a special angle from which to view world-systems comparatively.

Among other things, this comparison suggests that nomadic and sedentary peoples always have problematic relations, but sedentary peoples have steadily gained the upper hand through time and technology. However, because of frequent misunderstandings between these two types of societies, and because most of history has been written by sedentary peoples, future comparative studies must proceed with careful attention to details of nomadic social organization. Clearly, further study of nomad-sedentary relations is vital to informed comparisons of world-systems.

Gary Feinman and Linda Nicholas, in Chapter 8, explicate a model of the Zapotec world-system centered in Monte Albán near modern Oaxaca, Mexico. There are several innovations reported in their research. The most striking is the systematic archaeological survey of a large area to a considerable time depth -- obviously the result of years of work by a large research team. Within that rich source of data they demonstrate how archaeological evidence of a core/periphery hierarchy can, literally, be uncovered. Finally, most germane to this collection, they provide an empirical example of how a local core/periphery hierarchy forms and evolves.

Finally, editorship, like rank, hath its privileges. We exercise ours in a brief Epilogue wherein we assess what has been done, what we have learned, and where we should go next.

1

Conceptualizing Core/Periphery Hierarchies
for Comparative Study

Christopher Chase-Dunn and Thomas D. Hall

The objectives of this chapter are to clarify basic concepts for the comparative study of world-systems and to explicate general propositions about the nature and role of core/periphery hierarchies in historical social change. It is now widely accepted that contemporary social change within national societies is importantly conditioned by the linkages and structural aspects of a global stratified intersocietal network composed of "developed" national societies in core regions, "less developed" peripheral nations, and intermediate semi-peripheral countries. Both historical analysis and formal (quantitative) crossnational research have demonstrated this (Wallerstein, 1974; Meyer and Hannan, 1979; Bornschier and Chase-Dunn, 1985). But in order to understand the basic structural features and system logic of the contemporary global socio-economic system it is desirable to be able to compare it with intersocietal networks[1] which are structurally different. And in order to know how system logic changes (and thus to have insights about how the contemporary system logic might be transformed in the future) it is desirable to study how the logics of world-systems have become transformed in the past. Archaeologists and historians have begun to consider the relevance of core/periphery hierarchies for the evolution of earlier, smaller regional socio-economic systems, but few of these recent studies are explicitly comparative, and

5

confusion about basic concepts undermines the value of even the implicit comparisons which have been made.

We propose to clarify concepts for comparative study and to put forth several hypotheses about core/periphery hierarchies. Concept formation involves both deduction and induction. Since existing concepts about core/periphery hierarchies have been developed primarily from studies of the modern world-system, they need to be modified for comparative use in a study of earlier and very different intersocietal hierarchies. It is important to avoid the mistake of simply imposing vocabularies developed to explain the modern system on earlier systems in ways which distort analysis. Our goal is to formulate concepts and propositions in a way which allows us to understand both similarities and differences among core/periphery hierarchies in stateless, state-based and capitalist world-systems.

This investigation is relevant for macrosociological theories of social change, historical development, and evolution. It has become rather well-accepted that the development of both modern and ancient societies has been importantly conditioned by the existence of larger intersocietal networks of exchange and interaction (e.g., Mann, 1986). There are important controversies over how to conceptualize and bound these larger systems. The strongest world-system position claims that there is usually an explicit boundedness to the larger intersocietal network, and that it is this larger unit which displays system logic and the dynamic processes which affect the historical development of societies. In other words **it is world-systems which develop**, not societies, and these are distinctly bounded units. A looser version simply acknowledges the importance of intersocietal interactions but does not assume that a particular larger unit is the determinant unit which develops or evolves. One of the main goals of future comparative research should be the evaluation of the fruitfulness of various formulations regarding the conceptualization and bounding of world-systems and their general effects on societal development.

What Are World-Systems?

Immanuel Wallerstein (1974, 1979) defines a world-system as an entity with a single division of labor and multiple cultures, and within this category there are two sub-types: world-empires in which the intersocietal division of labor is encompassed by a single overarching imperial polity, and world-economies in which the political system is composed of many states competing with one another within an interstate system. Wallerstein excludes the analysis of stateless societies by characterizing them as "mini-systems" in which, allegedly, production of basic subsistence goods is accomplished within a single cultural entity. The intent of Wallerstein's definition is to encompass those processes which are substantially important for the reproduction and historical development of social structures.

Our definition of world-systems has the same intent, but it is somewhat more general in order to facilitate the comparison of very different intersocietal networks. We define world-systems as **intersocietal networks in which the interaction (trade, warfare, intermarriage, etc.) is an important condition of the reproduction of the internal structures of the composite units and importantly affects changes which occur in these local structures.**

One of the most important structural features of the contemporary global intersocietal system is the stratified set of relations of dominance and dependence between the "developed" and "developing" countries. The study of the mechanisms which reproduce international inequalities is a burgeoning field in cross-national comparative research (see review in Chase-Dunn, 1989: Chapter 11). The concepts of core, periphery and semiperiphery have been developed in studies of the modern world-system. Some scholars have begun the task of studying intersocietal hierarchies in earlier world-systems, but the conceptualizations being used are often confused and confusing. What is needed is an explicit effort to formulate competing notions of coreness and peripherality with an eye to a comparative study of intersocietal inequalities. It is certain that there have been intersocietal hierarchies in the past which operated in ways very different from that of the contemporary global relationship between "developed" and "developing" countries.

In the following we have taken a variation-maximizing approach to the study of intersocietal inequalities in order to explore both the general similarities and the important divergences among different sorts of world-systems. We have been stimulated to search for differences by the very provocative general arguments made by Ekholm (1980) and Ekholm and Friedman (1982). They argue that all state-based world-systems can be characterized as operating according to a logic of "capital imperialism" in which core regions accumulate resources by exploiting peripheral regions. They also contend that conflicts within and between core societies are the primary factors which account for the demise of old cores and the rise of new ones. These general arguments, which are said to apply to both ancient world-systems and the modern world-system, require evaluation by means of systematic comparison of different world-systems. We have developed the hypotheses outlined below in order to elaborate possible differences, but we are also quite interested in the extent to which state-based and capitalist intersocietal systems share certain general features.

It should not be assumed, however, that all intersocietal systems have core/periphery hierarchies. We can certainly imagine hypothetical world-systems without intersocietal inequalities or exploitation. Indeed, most orthodox theories of modern international trade assume equal exchange. The existence of exploitation, domination or equal exchange should not be a matter of assumption, but rather of investigation. We suspect that some stateless intersocietal systems did not have core/periphery hierarchies, while others had only mild and episodic ones. In order to understand the conditions which generate intersocietal inequalities it is necessary to examine cases in which they are absent.

In what follows we will outline our conceptualizations of world-system boundaries, core/periphery hierarchies and a qualitative typology of very different intersocietal systems. Then we will propose several hypotheses regarding the presence, nature and functioning of core/periphery hierarchies in different types of world-systems.

World-System Boundaries

In order to study world-systems comparatively we must conceptualize the spatial boundaries of such systems in a way which allows very different kinds of intersocietal networks to be compared to the modern global political economy. It is commonplace that everything in the universe is in some way connected or related to everything else. But if we are in the business of formulating and testing scientific theories of human historical development, it is desirable to concentrate on those types of interconnection which are most important to the reproduction and transformation of political and socio-economic structures. Lenski and Lenski (1987: 51) refer to a single "world system of societies" as existing "throughout history." The number and sizes of world-systems are, of course, a function of the way in which we define the connections which count. As Lenski and Lenski (1987) say:

Throughout history, human societies have established and maintained relations with one another.... During much of the past direct ties were limited to neighboring societies, since direct relations with distant societies were not possible. But, even then, indirect relations existed. Society A maintained ties with Society B, which in turn, maintained ties with Society C, and so on throughout the system. No society was ever totally cut off from the world system of societies for long, since even the most isolated societies had occasional contacts with others. With advances in transportation and communication during the last five thousand years, relations between societies have increased greatly and direct relations have been established between societies far removed from one another. As a result, the world system of societies has grown more integrated and more complex, and has come to exercise a greater influence on the life of individual societies (1987: 51).

By almost any definition there has been a global world-system since the end of the nineteenth century. Despite what the Lenskis say, before that there were human intersocietal networks which were substantially separate and autonomous with regard to their material and cultural processes of reproduction and development. If we use trade, information flows, political authority, or military competition to define intersocietal system boundaries, the human population of the Earth has, over the last ten thousand years, gone from a situation in which there were thousands of small, substantially separate regional intersocietal networks to the single global network of today.

There are a number of problems which are encountered in all network analyses which need clarification if we want to bound world-systems theoretically and empirically. Differential interaction densities, nested structures, direct and indirect connections, hierarchical *versus* decentralized networks, levels of hierarchy, multicentric hierarchies in which the centers are either directly connected or only indirectly connected through shared peripheries -- these are all possible problems in conceptualizing and empirically bounding intersocietal networks. And, in addition to these complexities, the type of connection and the institutional nature of interactions are important. Thus, even if we decide to focus on material exchanges, it is important to know what is being exchanged, and the institutional nature of the exchange (gift, tribute, commodity trade, etc.).

Before designating an eclectic approach to world-system boundaries we will review the proposals of other scholars. The shift of the unit of analysis from societies to world-systems encourages us to consider interconnections rather than uniformities as the important features of boundedness. Scholars who have debated the best ways to bound "civilizations" (e.g., Melko and Scott, 1987) have divided into those "culturalists" who stress the homogeneity of central values as defining civilizational boundaries, and those other "structuralists" who use criteria of interconnection rather than homogeneity. Within the group of interconnectionists there are several possibilities. Information flows have been used by some archaeologists (e.g., Renfrew, 1977; Schortman and Urban, 1987) to bound regional systems. Most scholars, however, employ either political/military or trade-based interconnections.

Immanuel Wallerstein (1974, 1979) uses two different criteria when he bounds world-systems: 1. mode of production and, 2. trade in bulk goods. Mode of production is the structuralist Marxist terminology for the system logic of social structural reproduction, competition and cooperation. Thus capitalist, tributary, socialist, and kin-based modes of production are understood to be qualitatively different system logics. Wallerstein defines capitalism as a feature of the modern world-system as a whole. By this theoretical maneuver he incorporates peripheral capitalism into the capitalist mode of production, a decided advance over those who see the periphery of the modern world-system as exhibiting precapitalist modes of production. An unfortunate corollary of this "totality assumption" is that each world-system can have only one mode of production, and thus it is not possible for different modes to be articulated within a single world-system. Hence, according to Wallerstein (1989, Chapter 3), the Ottoman Empire was a separate system from the European world-system until it had been entirely peripheralized by the European powers in the nineteenth century, because capitalism was not the dominant mode of production in the Ottoman Empire. This requires defining the obviously important economic and political/military interactions between the Ottomans and the European powers over several centuries as epiphenomenal.

The other criterion used by Wallerstein is the network of exchange of basic goods -- everyday raw materials and foodstuffs. He argues that networks of the production, distribution and consumption of these basic goods unite people across societal boundaries and create the systemic unity of a world-system. In the modern world-system (the "capitalist world-economy") these forward and backward linkages are called "commodity chains," but Wallerstein's usage suggests that non-commodified exchange of material basic goods may also be understood as constituting the interconnections of world-systems in which commodified trade is nonexistent or little developed.

Chase-Dunn (1989: Chapters 1, 16) has argued that Wallerstein's totality assumption is a theoretical mistake which makes the empirical bounding of world-systems in space nearly impossible. This is because we do not have clear conceptualizations of how modes of production are related to the spatial distribution of human activities. Chase-Dunn also argues that the totality assumption makes the study of the ways in which modes of production become dominant within world-systems, and are transformed into qualitatively different system logics, nearly impossible. If, by definition, each world-system has only one mode of production, how can we describe and study instances in which different logics are contending with one another within a world-system? It is much preferable to define world-system boundaries in terms of empirically ascertainable types of network interconnections and then to tackle the difficult question of modes of production and their transformation after this bounding has been done. Wallerstein's second criterion (bulk goods exchange) is more easily operationalized and we will propose its use together with other types of interconnection.

Wallerstein differentiates between basic goods and "preciosities" which are luxury goods with a high ratio of value to weight. He argues that preciosities are not important to the reproduction or transformation of social structures, but only to the rather epiphenomenal aspects of elite life. This argument allows him to focus on the Europe-centered system, and to treat India and China (long linked to Europe by the long distance trade in prestige goods) as "external arenas." But Jane Schneider (Chapter 2 below) convincingly argues that, as most anthropologists have long known, the exchange of prestige goods is not epiphenomenal at all. Prestige goods are often very important to the reproduction of local power structures as elites use them to reward subalterns and to symbolize power. Imported bullion is used to sustain the army of the king and to pay mercenaries, and is thus important to maintaining and changing state structures.[2]

On this basis Schneider argues that there was a larger precapitalist Eurasian world-system long before the emergence of an important core region in Europe. Janet Abu-Lughod's (1989) book on the importance of thirteenth century interactions between Europe and the older core areas of the Near East, India and China adds valuable support to Schneider's contentions.

Other authors have argued that prestige goods economies are not only important to the reproduction of power in some world-systems (e.g., Blanton and Feinman, 1984), but that the process of state-formation in peripheral areas is often facilitated when one lineage monopolizes the import of core preciosities (Webb, 1975). Friedman and Rowlands (1977) and Friedman (1982) have argued that prestige goods economies are important in the processes of the rise and fall of chiefdoms and the emergence of primary states. Even though bulk goods networks typically have much smaller spatial boundaries than networks of prestige good exchange, a comparative study of world-systems needs to examine both of these types of material exchange.

Fernand Braudel (1984), like Wallerstein, developed his terminology in order to make sense of the Europe-centered world-system. Thus he considers commodity exchange and "economic" trade to be the most important type of interconnection. He also thinks that hegemony is best defined in terms of economic domination, which is arguably the case for the modern world-system, but is certainly debateable for earlier world-systems. In world-systems in which the tributary modes of production have been dominant, socially structured inequalities, including those between an imperial core and dominated peripheral regions, were based more completely on political/military power. Braudel (1984: 27) defined the boundaries of world-systems in terms of the scope of economic hegemony of a single city-state. Thus he described world-systems centered on Venice, Malacca, Genoa, Antwerp, etc. Defining a network in terms of a single center precludes the possibility of multicentric networks. It is like treating the British Empire as a separate system from the French Empire. The reality is that these were colonial empires within a larger multicentric intersocietal system. Many, if not most, ancient world-systems were also multicentric in the sense that either the core areas were constituted as an interstate system of several autonomous states, or there were a few large empires interacting with one another. The thirteenth century Eurasian world-system studied by Janet Abu-Lughod (1989) had three separate core areas linked directly by long distance prestige goods trade and indirectly by interactions with shared peripheral regions. The notion of multicentricity should not preclude us from studying the differential extent of centralization within intersocietal systems, but defining these systems in terms of single centers is certainly a mistake.

Two other explicit suggestions for bounding world-systems have been made, both of which focus on political/military interaction rather than trade. Charles Tilly (1984: 62) has suggested the following "rule of thumb for connectedness":

> the actions of powerholders in one region of a network rapidly (say within a year) and visibly (say in changes actually reported by nearby observers) affect the welfare of at least a significant minority (say a tenth) of the population in another region of the network.[3]

Tilly's definition focuses on intentional political authority which is popularly perceived.[4] It addresses the problems of temporal and spatial cutting points which any network approach must confront, and which also needs to be clarified in the trade-based definitions if they are to be operationalized. Not addressed are problems of multicentricity and indirect connections. Are two spatially distant kingdoms contending for domination in an intermediate region part of the same system or are they separate systems?

Another approach is that taken by David Wilkinson (1987). Wilkinson bounds "civilizations/world-systems" by the criterion of interaction through conflict, especially military competition. Thus two empires that regularly engage each other in military confrontations are part of the same system. By this definition Wilkinson creates a spatio-temporal map which depicts the incorporation of fourteen "civilizations" into what he calls "Central Civilization" (Wilkinson, 1987: 32). Citing Simmel and Coser, Wilkinson writes:

> Conflict *always* integrates in a mildly significant way, in that the transaction of conflicting always creates a new social entity, the conflict itself. But durable conflict also integrates more significantly, by creating a new social entity that contains the conflict but is not reducible to it, within which the conflict must be seen as occurring, which is often of a larger scale and longer-lived than the conflict that constituted it. It is therefore legitimate, and it is indeed necessary, to posit the existence of a social system, a single social whole, even where we can find no evidence of that whole existence other than the protracted, recurrent or habitual fighting of a pair of belligerents. Such continuing relations, however hostile, between groups however different,necessarily indicates that both are (were

or have become) parts of some larger group or system. (Wilkinson, 1987: 34; emphasis in the original.)

Because he focuses only on state-based urbanized "civilizations" Wilkinson excludes from consideration those intersocietal networks in which there are no states, but his criterion could also be used to bound them. For example, Raymond Kelly (1985) has studied the ways in which habitual raiding between Nuer and Dinka pastoralists reproduced their kin-based social structures in a fascinating instance of "tribal imperialism." A comparative study of core/periphery hierarchies should include consideration of systems in which there are no states or classes.

Another approach to defining intersocietal linkages has been formulated by Schortman and Urban (1987). Their review of the development of theoretical perspectives in archaeology provides valuable insights into the contributions of diffusionism, studies of acculturation, ecological/evolutionism and world-system approaches to intersocietal interactions. They also review and evaluate the literature of the last two decades on the archaeological study of trade. Their own theoretical formulation of the problem of intersocietal linkages focuses on the concept of information, which is defined broadly as "energy, materials, social institutions, and ideas" (Schortman and Urban, 1987: 68). They point out that the economic aspects of trade are only part of intersocietal interaction, and they emphasize ideological diffusion and, especially, "intersocietal ethnic links" (marriages) among elites involved in prestige goods economies. The relevance of prestige goods economies has already been discussed above, and Schortman and Urban are undoubtedly correct to emphasize the importance of the symbolic and cultural aspects of trade for some intersocietal systems. On the other hand, they completely ignore the systemic aspects of military competition emphasized by Wilkinson.

The problem of world-system boundaries necessarily interacts with the question of the theoretical conceptualization of core/periphery hierarchies because it is necessary to distinguish between peripheral areas which are part of a system and regions which are external. The next section will address this problem. Here we want to propose an eclectic approach to the definition of world-system boundaries.

We propose to combine some of the approaches discussed above. It would be presumptuous to argue that certain forms of interaction are always causally more important for social change, especially when we want to study world-systems with very different sorts of social institutions and developmental logics. It is probable that the most important types of network linkages vary across different kinds of systems, but distinctions of that kind should be the outcome of research rather than the starting point.

We propose to study both economic and political forms of interaction as features of world-system networks. All material exchanges will be considered, although the patterns of different kinds of trade good networks will undoubtedly produce very different networks. It will undoubtedly be necessary to consider how localized networks of basic goods exchange are linked into larger networks of prestige goods exchange.

We will also utilize the criterion of political-military conflict interaction proposed by Wilkinson. Again, this will undoubtedly produce networks with different boundaries, but it is best to use a broad and eclectic approach rather than to exclude elements *a priori*. Simplifications are desirable, but should be made on a basis informed by empirical research.

The Subunit Problem

Another problem which affects the conceptualization and bounding of world-systems for comparative study can be called the subunit problem. What are the subunits of which world-systems are composed? When we use the term "intersocietal systems" this presumes that the subunits are "societies," but much recent analysis has stressed the difficulties of bounding societies even within the modern world-system composed primarily of nation-states (e.g., Tilly, 1984). Within the modern world-system there are a few multinational states, several states which govern only portions of societies, many transnational actors, and societal elements operating at the international or even at the global level. These problems are multiplied when we try to compare world-systems of very different sizes and kinds, especially "precapitalist" systems. Wolf (1982) cautions that group boundaries are inherently fuzzy and permeable. It is important to pay attention to the differing ways in which subunit boundaries are formed and "transsocietal" interactions are constituted across different types of world-systems.

Urban and Schortman (1987) provide an intelligent discussion of the subunit problem, and they propose a solution which works fairly well for some world-systems but not nearly as well for others. They define the subunits as a "spatially delimited body of individuals living within and adapting to a specific physical environment" (1987: 63). This type of subunit, influenced by the ecological/evolutionary framework, works well for some smaller simpler systems, but it ignores important larger subunits, such as states and empires, which combine several types of ecological niches within their boundaries. The way out of this problem is simply to recognize that the sizes and types of organizations which interact within regional world-systems vary, and **larger systems have increasingly nested and overlapping levels of organization.** In the simplest intergroup systems, households are politically organized at the village or intervillage level, and there are no larger overarching political organizations. Households and villages are important subunits in all world-systems, large and small. One important difference between smaller regional world-systems and larger, more complex world-systems is the size of polities and the range of direct economic, military and cultural interactions. It is not necessary to define a single type of subunit which is common to all world-systems, but rather to pay attention to the types and levels of organization within each whole world-system.

The search for bounded world-systems also must address the problem of direct and indirect links. Lenski and Lenski (1987) are correct in saying that all human groups interact fairly regularly and in important ways with immediately neighboring groups. This means that almost all groups are indirectly connected to all other groups. Only impassable physical barriers produce separate networks if we allow **very** indirect connections to count. This still produces a rather large number of substantially separate world-systems before the advent of regularized oceanic transportation. But it would seem advisable to utilize the criterion of the consequences of events and actions to further restrict what we consider to be significant indirect connections. Thus, even though each precontact California tribelet is connected to its neighboring tribelets, and therefore indirect connections extend North, East and South to include the whole of the Americas, there is a rather rapid fall-off in the impact that any action will have on a particular tribelet.

What this means is that, when we are considering down-the-line[5] interactions in which a group interacts primarily with its immediate neighbors, with few long distance direct interactions, we will not find world-system boundaries in the sense of lower density interactions except insofar as these are created by natural barriers to interaction. For these cases it makes sense to choose a group or a connected set of groups as the focus of analysis and to use this "group-centric" focus to determine the boundaries of the relevant interactional network. For example, we can focus on the Pomo and study their world-system in the sense of the relevant intergroup interactions. We could just as easily focus on a different group, and then the "bounds" of the world-system would shift. This kind of "group-centric" approach is unfortunate in some ways because it would be more desirable to allow the bounds of the analysis to be determined by world-system wholes rather than by focal societies.

For the case of down-the-line types of interaction this seems the only solution. Once longer distance direct interactions become important and world-systems networks develop hierarchical and centric patterns, these reduce the difficulty encountered here, but do not eliminate it. What are we to say about the world-system of a village that is on the periphery of two core regions which are not directly connected to one another? We do not want to have as many world-systems as there are possible focal societies, and yet it is empirically the case that each group's insertion into one (or more) world-systems is different. The answer is to use whole world-systems as the unit of analysis in all cases in which this is possible because of longer distance direct interactions and patterns of centralization. In many cases in which interaction is almost completely down-the-line, we will need to employ the group-centric approach, though our choice of which group with which to start may be somewhat arbitrary.[6]

This, in turn, raises another problem: the boundaries and limits of group identities. Wolf (1982: 6) claims that, "by endowing nations, societies, or cultures with the qualities of internally homogeneous and externally distinctive and bounded objects, we create a model of the world as a global pool hall in which the entities spin off each other like so many hard and round billiard balls." Rather, groups are often internally diversified, boundaries are permeable, and memberships fluid. This is especially true of band and horticultural societies.[7] It is important in discussions of ethnicity to not assume that ethnic phenomena are invariant over time and space, but vary with context. The linkages between the variable nature of ethnic identities and the core/periphery hierarchy context remain problematic.[8]

The operationalization of the multi-criteria approach to world-system boundaries will, of course, encounter different problems in different contexts. Archaeological evidence can be used for some kinds of trade networks, although perishable goods such as food tend to leave only indirect traces in the archaeological record. Evidence of authority relations and sustained military interaction is substantially more dependent on written records, although some archaeological evidence, such as the building of defensive walls and the concentration of previously dispersed settlements into larger defensible towns, is also relevant. Ethnographic evidence will certainly be used, especially for nonliterate societies, but ethnographic evidence from stateless societies long influenced by interaction with state-based and market-integrated societies is often a contaminated source for inferences about original stateless world-systems.

Core/Periphery Relations

Considerable controversy still exists about the best way to conceptualize coreness and peripherality in the modern global political economy (e.g., Arrighi and Drangel, 1986; Chase-Dunn, 1989: Chapter 10). This debate has proceeded primarily with the modern global system as its context. The issues are somewhat different when we consider the comparative study of core/periphery hierarchies across different kinds of world-systems. Here we need a more general conceptualization which can accommodate greater variation, and we need to allow for the possibility that some world-systems do not have core/periphery hierarchies.

Applying the notion of a core/periphery hierarchy to other than the modern world-system is itself somewhat controversial. The esteemed economic historian Paul Bairoch (1986) has argued that premodern core/periphery relations are relatively unimportant because there were not, he claims, significant differences in the level of living between the populations of core and peripheral areas, at least compared to the large gap which emerged during the industrialization of the European core. Most historians of the ancient empires would disagree with the statement that core/periphery relations were unimportant, but differential degrees of internal stratification between core and peripheral societies may indeed turn out to be an important difference between the modern world-system and earlier world-systems. While in the modern world-system there is typically less income inequality among households in core societies than in peripheral societies, this relationship was undoubtedly the reverse in many of the ancient world-systems in which the core was an urbanized and class-stratified society while the periphery contained less stratified groups of pastoralists and horticulturalists.

The examination of such patterns and consideration of their role in processes of social change is one of the most interesting aspects of the comparative study of world-systems.

We will define two types of core/periphery relationships for the purposes of comparative study. The first will be called **core/periphery differentiation**, in which societies at different levels of complexity and population density are in interaction with each other within the same world-system as defined above.

The second type is **core/periphery hierarchy**, which will be understood to mean the existence of political, economic or ideological domination between different societies within the same world-system. This includes political domination, extraction of resources through raiding, taxation, tribute, and unequal economic exchange. We are also interested in cultural definitions of superiority/inferiority and how these may interact with more objective forms of exploitation and domination. These ideological aspects will not, however, be employed in our definition of core/periphery hierarchy.

We designate two types of core/periphery relations -- differentiation and hierarchy -- because we think it is mistaken to assume that all relations among "more developed" and "less developed" societies involve exploitation and the processes of the development of underdevelopment which are often found in the modern world-system. We need not assume that the "more developed" society always exploits the "less developed." Indeed there may be cases of the reverse, and cases in which domination exists between societies at virtually the same level of complexity and population density. Thus we seek to analyze how differences in societal size, complexity, technological productivity and internal stratification are related to intersocietal domination. The nature, longevity and consequences for social change in both core and peripheral societies of various kinds of intersocietal relations are the findings which comparative study is intended to produce. Variations in the degree to which core/periphery relations cause the "development of underdevelopment" and the factors which account for such differences are considered below in the section on hypotheses.

We have intentionally left out any consideration of the nature of what is produced and traded between cores and peripheries. The notion that coreness and peripherality in the modern world-system is essentially constituted around a division of labor in which the core produces manufactured goods and the periphery produces raw materials is itself quite controversial (Chase-Dunn, 1989: Chapter 10) and it is known that important reversals of this relationship sometimes occurred within ancient world-systems (e.g., Lamberg-Karlovsky, 1975; Kohl, 1987b). Nevertheless such differences may be important foci of comparative investigation. This can best be pursued by not building these distinctions into our definition of core/periphery relations. Rather we need to investigate in each case the linkages between intersocietal differentiation and core/periphery domination.

The intersection between the problem of world-system boundaries and core/periphery hierarchy mentioned above is especially salient at the edge of the periphery. Wallerstein (1989: Chapter 3) argues that, for the modern world-system, even though an area has been plundered by a core power, it is not yet incorporated and peripheralized until local production has become integrally linked into the "commodity chains" of the larger world-system. It has been often observed that plunder preceded the development of coerced production in both the ancient empires and the Europe-centered world-system. Indeed there may have been systems, such as the Nuer-Dinka case mentioned above, in which plunder was the sole form of core/periphery interaction. It is better to consider the dynamics of such cases rather than defining them out of court at the beginning, and indeed this may provide important insights into the institutional requirements of more stable core/periphery structures. Thus we intend to use Wilkinson's definition, which includes regularized plunder as a form of linkage defining the boundaries of a world-system. By this definition West Africa was incorporated into the Europe-centered world-system when slave raiding became regularized, rather than, as Wallerstein would have it, after the development of colonial agriculture in Africa.[9] Economic exploitation is a more stable form of exploitation than plunder because it does not decimate the peripheral society to the same extent that plunder does. It is not the case, however, that precapitalist cores only extracted tribute and left production processes untouched. The Inkas completely reorganized production in incorporated territories and relocated populations to new regions in which intensified horticulture could be carried out. A general definition should accommodate various forms of exploitation and examine their consequences for social change in both the core and the periphery.

Hall's (1989: Chapter 2) reconceptualization of the incorporation process for the modern world-system expands the outer boundaries of the system to include military alliances and "buffer zone" groups in the "contact periphery." This corresponds to Wilkinson's definition of regularized political/military interaction, and will be very helpful for understanding frontier relations in precapitalist world-systems (e.g., Dyson, 1985).

Clear conceptualization of core/periphery relations allows us to be more specific about the meaning of the semiperiphery concept. As with coreness and peripherality, the definition of the semiperiphery remains controversial even within the modern world-system (see Chase-Dunn, 1989: Chapter 10). At this point we advocate that the semiperiphery concept be defined broadly to encompass all of the following meanings:

1. A semiperipheral region may be one which mixes both core and peripheral forms of organization.
2. A semiperipheral region may be spatially located between core and peripheral regions.
3. Mediating activities between core and peripheral areas may be carried out in semiperipheral regions.
4. A semiperipheral area may be one in which institutional features are in some ways intermediate between those forms found in core and periphery.

Sorting out these different types of semiperipheries remains an empirical as well as theoretical problem. Until more detailed comparisons among different kinds of world-systems are completed, it would be premature to define the semiperiphery concept more narrowly.

A Typology of World-Systems

In order to achieve maximum variation in the nature of world-systems we have developed a preliminary typology based on distinctions found in the literature on social evolution and historical development (see review by Moseley and Wallerstein, 1978). These categories are not conceived as fixed boxes into which a complex set of intersocietal networks must be stuffed, but rather as a set of general signposts for the task of maximizing variation across the diversity of human societies.

The central theoretical distinction we will use in studying system logic is the neo-Marxian notion of mode of production as it has been elaborated in the works of Eric Wolf (1982) and Samir Amin (1980). These scholars outline three major types of societal logic by which social labor is mobilized and resources are distributed: the kin-based mode of production; the tributary (state-based) mode, and the capitalist mode. Building on the work of Marx, and adding insights generated by Karl Polanyi's (1977) theoretical approach, these authors define kin-based relations as normative regulation based on consensual definitions of what exists and what is good. No societies are exclusively structured around this kind of social control, but in some societies, those without classes or states or markets, kin-based mechanisms of control and distribution are the dominant sources of social cohesion.[10]

The tributary modes of production involve the use of physical coercion to mobilize labor. A ruling class establishes control over some essential social resource and then uses this control to extract "surplus product" from direct producers. There are many different institutional forms by which this is accomplished. Most historical societies in which this form of integration is dominant mix a variety of these forms (taxation, tribute, serfdom, slavery, etc.) and also include elements of both kin-based and market forms of integration. However, these latter are usually incorporated in ways which reinforce the fundamentally coercive state-based logic of the tributary mode.

The capitalist mode of production is based on the commodity form, the mediation of human interaction by price-setting[11] markets, and market-like institutions. The commodification of goods, land, wealth and labor are never complete within capitalist systems, but markets play a much greater role than in systems dominated by other modes. Aspects of other modes continue to be found, but they generally are complementary with the reproduction of commodified relations. Thus we want to distinguish between world-systems in which kin-based, state-based and capitalist modes of production are dominant.[12]

By utilizing these distinctions, we are in no way endorsing a unilinear model of evolution. We argue that historical development is open-ended and that important bifurcations and discontinuities of development, rapid transformations, and instances of devolution are normal characteristics of the historical processes of social change (See Sanderson, Chapter 5 below). We wish to evaluate the idea that world-systems, rather than societies, are the relevant units of analysis for understanding these processes, but this does not lead us to ignore the processes which operate within societies.

In order to study the processes and patterns by which modes of production become transformed, we make use of rough set of world-system types based on social structural distinctions. We seek to understand how core/periphery hierarchies may play a role in the reproduction or transformation of modes of production, and so we need to distinguish between types of world-systems in which both core/periphery relations and modes of production vary. We will propose a rough set of categories which will allow us to search for the relevant variation. This approach is not a replacement for the study of long sequences of historical change in particular regions, but is rather only a preliminary step for mapping out the major empirical distinctions between types of core/periphery relations.

We propose the following list of world-system types. The typology indicates the level of structural complexity characteristic of the most complex societies within each whole world-system:

I.   Kin-based mode dominant
     A. Stateless, classless
          1. Semisedentary foragers, horticulturalists, pastoralists
          2. Big man systems
     B. Chiefdoms (classes but not true states)
II. Tributary modes dominant (true states, cities)
     A. Primary state-based world-systems (Lower Mesopotamia, Egypt, Indus Valley, Ganges Valley, China, Mexico, Peru)
     B. Primary empires in which a number of previously autonomous states have been unified by conquest (Akkad, Old Kingdom Egypt, Magahda, Chou, Teotihuacan, Huari)
     C. Multicentered world-systems composed of empires, states, and peripheral regions (Near East, India, China, Mesoamerica, Peru)
     D. Commercializing state-based world-systems in which important aspects of commodification have developed but the system is still dominated by the logic of the tributary modes (Near East, Indian Ocean, China)
III. Capitalist mode dominant
     A. the Europe-centered subsystem since the sixteenth century
     B. the global modern world-system

Under heading I above (kin-based mode dominant) are included all those world-systems in which none of the societies can be said to have true states. A true state is defined following Johnson and Earle (1987: 246) as existing when a regionally organized society has specialized regional institutions -- military and bureaucratic -- which perform the tasks of control and management. This is distinguished from "complex chiefdoms" in the degree to which specialized state organizations have developed. Complex chiefdoms, which are also large and stratified polities, rely on generalized institutions for regional coordination and control. Chiefdoms are distinguished from less stratified stateless societies by the size of the polity, population density, intensification of production, and, obviously, the degree of internal stratification. In true chiefdoms, the chief has institutionalized access to substantial social resources to back up his power which are largely autonomous from the control of other lineage heads. In classless societies, inequalities of power, prestige and wealth are based almost entirely on age and gender criteria, while class formation involves the increasing control over basic societal resources (land, trade, etc.) by a noble class. Such a class can appropriate surplus product based on the labor of direct producers.

The smallest autonomous polities are nomadic foraging bands. We choose to begin our analysis of world-systems with those more sedentary foragers who live most of the year in hamlets.[13] These largely sedentary groups define communal territorial boundaries and engage in regularized intergroup relations which can be analyzed as composing a small world-system of interdependent interaction. As population density per land area increases, foraging strategies become more diversified and intensification of production occurs (horticulture, pastoralism). Big man systems emerge where there are pressures to increase coordination among groups, but these are not sufficient to sustain a more stable leadership hierarchy.

The problem of the causal relationship between primary state formation and class formation has been the focus of a vociferous debate among anthropologists (e.g., Service, 1975; Carneiro, 1970). Most of the work done on this problem has not explicitly taken account of the fact the these processes occurred within the context of core/periphery relations. Exceptions to this are the work of Friedman and Rowlands (1977) and Gailey and Patterson (1987, 1988).

Within category II (tributary modes dominant) there are a number of distinctions which need to be explained. Primary or pristine states are those which develop without contact with existing states. States developing in interaction with existing states are termed secondary. The same distinction can, of course, be applied to empires, and we do so in category IIB.[14] We argue that most primary state-based world-systems were politically structured as interstate systems of competing city-states within a core region. Secondary multicentric empires are distinguished from primary empires by the prior existence of empires and often by the larger size of the constituent empires. The commercializing world-systems are distinguished from most earlier systems by their size, and by the increasing commodification of goods, land, wealth and labor. The use of money spread to the day-to-day lives of common people with the development of smaller standardized denominations of coins, and forms of credit and interest became more developed. Wage labor and other semi-commodified forms of labor became more common. Price-setting markets and commodity production for sale became more widespread within the political economy. Within empires, rulers became somewhat more sophisticated about the way in which they taxed merchants and commodity producers so as not to kill the golden goose; and outside the bounds of empires, in interstitial semiperipheral regions, autonomous city-states controlled by merchant and production capitalists created and sustained market relations between empires and peripheral regions.

The degree of commodification increased, but unevenly and not in the same way in each area. There were spurts ahead and then either devolution to subsistence feudalism or reassertion of imperial control of the economy. The coming to dominance of capitalism in a core region was a tipping point which occurred first in Europe, and then spread with the assistance of the expanding European hegemony.

We do not want the above categories to generate a lot of dispute about which cases go into which categories. Obviously there are many borderline cases for which it is difficult to decide. A different approach would be to analyze very long historical sequences which include the transformations of the social structural characteristics which we are using to distinguish among categories. This would eliminate the problem of "transitional" cases, and would focus attention on those major transformations which ought to be the main focus if we are ultimately trying to understand how fundamental changes could occur in our own time. But we suggest that it makes sense to first focus on the larger patterns of association among different kinds of core/periphery hierarchies and structural features of societies within world-systems. After these matters are mapped out, we can pay more attention to the causal nature of processes of reproduction and transformation.

Hypotheses

In this section we describe our preliminary formulation of theoretical hypotheses about variation in core/periphery hierarchies based on our interpretation of several different literatures: all the recent studies which have explicitly discussed the application of world-system concepts to precapitalist systems;[15] the literature on imperialism and frontiers in the ancient world; the archaeology of diffusion, trade and warfare; and ethnographic studies of intersocietal relations. Elsewhere Chase-Dunn (1989: Chapters 10 ,11) has reviewed the theoretical and empirical studies on the nature and causes of reproduction of the modern core/periphery hierarchy.

The most general questions for a comparative study of core/periphery relations are:
1.   Do all world-systems have stable core/periphery hierarchies?
2.   Do the stability, magnitude and nature of intersocietal inequalities vary systemically with the types of societies which compose world-systems? What is the relationship between core/periphery differentiation and core/periphery domination?
3.   What are the relationships between the dynamics of core/periphery relations and the reproduction/transformation of social structures, institutions and basic system logics?
Here we discuss these broad questions and formulate positive hypotheses from them.

First, the generalizations we make apply to whole world-systems, and thus, whole systems need to be studied to test them. It is known that there is usually considerable variation across peripheral regions within each world-system. This is important and needs to be taken into account. In studies of particular world-systems, differences between regions in the nature of core/periphery relations are an important consideration (e.g., Dyson, 1985). But for the general discussion of cross-system comparisons, we will be talking about "average" or typical core/periphery relations within each system.

Obviously intersocietal networks in which the constituent societies are all at about the same level of complexity do not have core/periphery differentiation as defined above. But of more interest is the matter of core/periphery hierarchies. Do all world-systems have stable core/periphery hierarchies in the sense that some societies exploit or dominate others? This involves consideration of the nature, degree, and longevity of intersocietal exploitation and domination. In addition it is desirable to consider differential rates of development, "co-evolution," the development of underdevelopment, and processes effecting these. Also of interest will be the relative size of core, peripheral and semiperipheral areas, and the nature of relations among core societies and among peripheral societies.

Our first hypothesis is that stable relations of intersocietal domination are difficult to create and reproduce in the absence of hierarchical social institutions within the societies involved. The development of internal stratification and forms of the state are quite important in the stabilization and reproduction of core/periphery exploitation. Thus we predict that kin-based intersocietal systems will have only minimal and short-lived core/periphery hierarchies, and that the least hierarchical of human societies, those of chiefless foragers, will not have any regularized intersocietal domination or exploitation.

We expect that intersocietal exploitation among most semi-sedentary foraging groups is limited to episodic raiding and competition over favorable natural sites. War captive slavery to be found among some of the more hierarchical hunter-gatherers (e.g., the Yurok) and some pastoralists (e.g., the Nuer) is likely to be of a relatively mild kind because slaves must be incorporated into existing kinship networks in order to mobilize their labor, and kinship networks usually bestow rights as well as obligations.

An intermediate case between unstratified and chiefdom-based world-systems is that of the Nuer-Dinka relationships studied by Kelly (1985). The Nuer lacked strong and permanent chiefs, but they did have three levels of hierarchy among villages which enabled them to form larger war bands than the neighboring Dinka, who were similar pastoralists, but had only two levels of intratribal hierarchy. Thus the Nuer systematically raided the Dinka for cattle and women, and expanded into Dinka territory over a 150 year period. Though the Nuer were clearly exploiting the Dinka by appropriating cattle and women, the limited forms of hierarchy within the Nuer society prevented this relationship from stabilizing into a core/periphery hierarchy based on exploitation of coerced labor in the periphery. The Dinka women taken as captives were rapidly assimilated into Nuer kinship structures.

Kristiansen (1987) has studied local and regional hierarchical relations among stateless peoples in Scandinavia. Though he uses the terms core and periphery to describe these relations, he characterizes them as based on the "ritual superiority" of local centers over hinterlands based on the control of prestige goods. Friedman and Rowlands (1977) have argued that core/periphery structures based on prestige goods economies are unstable and subject to rapid spread effects[16] because of the ideological nature of the stratification which is not backed up by military coercion or more stringent dependencies on fundamental goods.

Our second hypothesis is that the stability and exploitativeness of core/periphery hierarchies increases with the degree of stratification within core societies and with the development of certain "technologies of power," (Mann, 1986) which enable centralized empires to extract taxes and tribute from peripheral regions.

We hypothesize that the very first "pristine" states will be found to be more successful at extracting resources from peripheral areas than kin-based cores, but still not as successful as later, more centralized, empires. Also the "co-evolutionary" spread effects of development (Schortman and Urban, 1987; Renfrew and Cherry, 1986) by which new centers emerge as a result of interaction with the original core areas, will be relatively strong compared to "underdeveloping" effects because the techniques for concentrating and sustaining resources in the core are less developed than in later empires.[17]

Thus we are further predicting that core/periphery hierarchies will be relatively more stable, more hierarchical, and more underdevelopmental for peripheral regions once centralized empires have emerged. The decentralizing phase of the process of the rise and fall of empire-centers will reverse this trend somewhat, as increased local autonomy for controllers of land slows the concentration of resources in the center.

The growth of market forms of exchange, monetary systems, local and long-distance market trade, etc. will again increase the "spread" effects relative to the "backwash" effects. More sophisticated empires, in which the state-based mode of production remains dominant, learn to extract surplus from market trade without smothering it. In these instances central empires which provide pacification and guarantee trade routes will strengthen spread effects.[18] Commercialized states also learn to control the disruptive aspects of market relations and to deal effectively with potentially threatening peripheries.

The emerging dominance of capitalism in the Europe-centered sub-system produced a core/periphery hierarchy in which backwash effects strongly outweighed spread effects and the gap between core and periphery rapidly increased. However, technological change is much faster and greater in both core and periphery in the modern world-system because of the historically unique effects of capitalism on incentives for revolutionizing technology. The gap produced is thus a relative one in which peripheral areas do develop, but at much slower rates than the core.

Regarding the matter of core/periphery relations and transformations of the mode of production, Chase-Dunn (1989) has argued that capitalism as a system logic is buffered from its own developmental contradictions by the existence of a necessary and reproduced core/periphery hierarchy. This implies that peripheral capitalism and core exploitation of the periphery should be understood as a necessary and constitutive part of the capitalist mode of production. The modern core/periphery hierarchy acts to sustain the multicentric structure of the core (the interstate system, which is arguably necessary for capitalism) and to disorganize those political forces within core states that would try to transform capitalism into socialism. This last is accomplished by sustaining national class alliances between core labor and core capital, cemented by intracore rivalry and peripheral exploitation.

Ancient core/periphery hierarchies, we suggest research will show, were often central to the reproduction of centralized state apparati. Keith Hopkins (1978) contends that the Roman empire was a system which, like capitalism, needed to expand in order to survive. But, unlike the capitalist world-economy, its expansion was based on conquest, the importation of booty and slaves, and the distribution of land and dependent laborers to a growing class of non-producers. When the empire reached a zero rate of return in terms of spatial expansion it was no longer able to provide the resources necessary to sustain its growing overhead costs. It then began to turn in upon itself, and eventually it crumbled. Hopkins's model, which is similar to the analysis of Anderson (1974), sees the "barbarian invasions" as exogenous shocks which conjuncturally dismembered a state which was already falling of its own contradictions. But though Rome fell, the state-based mode of production and the "Central Civilization" (Wilkinson, 1987; see also Chapter 4) of which Rome was but a part, did not.

In other cases, such as China, the mode of production was "tributary" in the sense that coercive power was used to mobilize labor and accumulation, but this accumulation was primarily accomplished without exploitation of peripheral regions. In many of these cases the periphery did importantly affect the core by threatening border regions or by occasionally conquering the core (e.g Barfield, 1989; Hall, Chapter 7 below). Whether as a source of exploitable resources or military threats, peripheral regions were often important to the reproduction and transformation of social structures within cores.

Many semiperipheral regions have also played important roles in large scale social change. We hypothesize that this is because of the peculiar combination of forces and the organizational opportunities of groups who are "in the middle" of core/periphery hierarchies. Semiperipheral regions, we argue, are unusually fertile zones for social innovation because they can combine peripheral and core elements in new ways, and they are less constrained by core domination than are peripheral areas, and less committed than older core regions to all the institutional baggage which comes along with core status. Of course the particular techniques used by upwardly mobile semiperipheries vary depending on the nature of the world-system in which they are operating. Four types of semiperipheral development are described in Chase-Dunn (1988):

1. conquest by semiperipheral marcher states;
2. extensive and intensive commodification by semiperipheral capitalist city-states;
3. the emerging global domination of the Europe-centered sub-system, which we argue was semiperipheral in the larger Afroeurasian world-system; and
4. the rise and fall of hegemonic core states within the Europe-centered world-system.

A combination of Gerschenkron's (1962) idea of the "advantages of backwardness," Trotsky's (1932) "laws of combined and uneven development" and Service's (1971) "adaptation and adaptivity" can be used to formulate general and specific propositions about semiperipheral development (see Chase-Dunn, 1988).

Measurement Problems

Even though it will undoubtedly be necessary to operationalize the concepts of world-system boundaries and core/periphery relations differently for different cases, especially since we have intentionally chosen to pursue a most-different systems strategy, the goal of testing more general propositions requires us to think about the possibilities of operationalizing concepts in ways that are helpful for formal comparisons across cases. Comparable measures will be especially important for future studies which seek to compare large numbers of world-systems using the methods of formal comparative research.

The problem of comparable measures of system boundaries is important because the way in which cases are bounded could influence the outcome of comparisons among cases. The only way to be sure that one has employed an adequate definition of system boundaries is to compare the results of comparative analyses using competing definitions.

It may be found that it is necessary to use different empirical criteria for bounding world-systems depending on the type of system being analyzed. Though this would be somewhat messy, it would not make the analytic comparison of very different world-systems impossible. For the present we propose to use the multidimensional eclectic conceptualization of boundedness we have described above with attention to the consequences of bounding according to the different criteria.

Testing the hypotheses about the operation of core/periphery hierarchies requires, ideally, that we be able to determine comparatively **degrees of** intersocietal exploitation and of the stability of core/periphery hierarchies. It would also be desirable to be able to compare rates of intersocietal mobility, and the relative balance of "spread" consequences and "backwash" consequences for differential rates of "development" between cores and peripheries. These operational problems have not yet been resolved even for the contemporary global world-system. Nevertheless, we want to clearly designate the desiderata of a more generally comparative research project so that exploratory case studies can be undertaken with these purposes in mind.

The problems of measuring differences in the magnitude of inequalities across social systems are well-known. When the kinds of resources which are socially valued differ and the dimensions of inequality are structured in completely different ways, statements about relative degrees of overall inequality are problematic. This is just as true of intersocietal inequalities as of intrasocietal ones. Though it is often possible to rank objects within a system, such rank orderings do not help with the question of the magnitude of inequalities. For this, interval or ratio scale measurement is required.

Nevertheless, rough estimations of differential magnitudes of intrasocietal inequalities have been convincingly made by Lenski (1966) across very different societal types (e.g., hunter-gatherer, horticultural, agrarian and industrial). We propose to make analogous "guesstimates" of degrees of inequality across very different core/periphery hierarchies.

The problem of indicators of core/periphery inequality has been considered by some archaeologists. Often it is simply assumed that archaeological indicators of core/periphery differentiation can be taken as evidence of core/periphery hierarchy. For example, the existence of a settlement system in which villages and towns are of substantially unequal population sizes may be interpreted as indicating hierarchical interaction between large and small settlements (e.g., Nissen, 1988). But, as many archaeologists have themselves recognized, differentiation can exist without domination (e.g., Renfrew and Cherry, 1986). All exchange is not unequal exchange.

Looking for more direct archaeological evidence for core/periphery domination is challenging. Lamberg-Karlovsky (1975) has argued that the village of Tepe Yahya on the Iranian plateau (where carved soapstone bowls were manufactured and exported to the Sumerian cities) must have been subjected to unequal exchange because burials did not become richer at Tepe Yahya over the long period during which trade occurred. This case contrasts with many others in which involvement in regional exchange networks did lead to increased local stratification as indicated by the emergence of richer burials (e.g., Marfoe, 1987).

Such observations might be used to differentiate between non-exploitative and exploitative intersocietal interactions, and to study the trajectory of interactions within particular world-systems. This usage of mortuary evidence, may, however, encounter grave problems. Wealthier native Californians were cremated, while the remains of poorer villagers were buried. In this case the appearance of more elaborate burials could mean less rather than greater local stratification. And of course there are other causes of changes in burial practices besides the nature of intersocietal interaction.

Though archaeologists have made amazing strides in the use of recoverable results to develop indicators of the spatial structure and the social form of exchange (see review by Schortman and Urban, 1987: 49-55), archaeological evidence alone is often quite problematic for the kind of inferences we want to make. This is why it is important to study cases for which archaeological data can be combined with historical documentary or ethnographic evidence.

Conclusions

We have proposed a set of definitions and hypotheses which allow the world-systems perspective to be extended from its current focus on the Europe-centered system to a consideration of very different sorts of intersocietal networks. In doing this we propose to use the primary analyses of archaeologists, historians and anthropologists as raw materials for constructing a world-system theory of very long-term social change. The comparative strategy we propose will allow us a new purchase on the study of system transformation which may be of use for understanding and transforming our own global political economy.

By defining world-systems and core/periphery hierarchies generally we hope to be able to sort out the important similarities and differences which ought to be the explicit backdrop for understanding future human possibilities. Everything is not different now, and neither is everything the same. In order to know which things are importantly different and which things are importantly the same, it will be helpful to have a systematic theoretical framework for comparing world-systems. This approach does not require that we belittle those who are studying contemporary processes of political, economic and social change. Ultimately the very long run comparisons will need to be combined with more immediate studies in order to produce politically useful insights.

The next order of business is a series of exploratory case studies which explicitly address the problems of concept formation and comparable measurement which we have raised. Ultimately we think that it would be desirable to be able to compare rather large numbers of world-systems in order to have greater certitude regarding the hypotheses we have proposed about core/periphery hierarchies. But we also recognize that the strategy of comparison **across** world-systems needs to be supplemented with studies of single world-systems over very long periods of time. This other strategy is explicit in the approach taken in Gills and Frank (Chapter 3) and Wilkinson (Chapter 4) in this volume. We see comparisons over time as complementary to comparisons over space, and we have made every effort to see that the conceptualizations employed in both approaches find common ground.

NOTES

1. We use the terms world-system and intersocietal system interchangeably. Some readers object to the application of the term world-system to small regional networks of societies, ostensibly because the word "world" implies a large scale or global extent. We prefer the sense of "world" as in the world in which people live and which is important to their lives. In this sense the worlds of people living in stateless societies were relatively small, both with regard to those interactions which were salient in their consciousness and those indirect interactions which influenced the nature of the social structures in which they lived. In larger world-systems the cognitive world is often much smaller than the objective world of indirect economic and political connections.

2. In his most recent discussion of preciosities Wallerstein (1979: Chapter 3) categorizes bullion as a necessary good. The shipments of silver to China from Europe and European colonies long predates the peripheralization of China by Europe in the nineteenth century and supports the notion that these regions were parts of the same larger world-system. One problem with Wallerstein's formulation of the incorporation problem is that it ignores the possibility of equal exchange among regions. In his schema incorporation is followed by peripheralization. This undoubtedly occurred in most areas where the expanding European hegemony was on the rise, but we should not preclude the possibility of equal exchange among co-existing core regions of the sort studied by Janet Abu-Lughod (1989). In his defense, Wallerstein's concepts have been developed mostly for the purpose of comparing the Europe-centered world-system to itself. For the purposes of comparing different world-systems to one another these concepts need to be redefined.

3. And Tilly continues: "Such a criterion indubitably makes our own world a single system; even in the absence of worldwide flows of capital, communications, and manufactured goods, shipments of grain and arms from region to region would suffice to establish the minimum connections. The same criterion, however, implies that human history has seen many world systems, often simultaneously dominating different parts of the globe. Only in the last few hundred years, by the criterion of rapid, visible, and significant influences, could someone plausibly argue for all the world as a single system."

4. The requirement that interconnections should be visible to the connected actors excludes consideration of opaque objective relations. Marx (1967: 71ff) argues that market societies normally operate in terms of a "fetishism of commodities" in which objective relationships between human producers are hidden behind what appear to be relations among things -- commodities and their prices. In the contemporary world-system most actors are only vaguely aware of the extent of the global network of production which materially links them with the labor of distant others.

5. Down-the-line interactions are those in which exchange occurs only among contiguous groups but goods travel long distances from group to group.

6. We can, however, study such groups in settings in which natural boundaries provide the network boundedness, such as isolated islands. Let us remember that the limits of the globe now provide a convenient short-hand for our references to the network boundaries of the modern world-system. The uses of geographical features may be even more convenient for studying older, smaller world-systems for which our data on interactions is much more problematic. We need to be careful however. It might be assumed that high mountains provide effective barriers to trade and thus can be used to designate boundaries between substantially independent networks. This would be a convenient way to designate the Western boundary of precontact central California. But archeological evidence indicates that there were flows of obsidian from sites on the Eastern side of the Sierra Nevada into the Central Valley of California (Ericson,1977;Jackson,1986) and it is ethnographically known that a trade in food stuffs was carried on over the high mountain passes. The linkages between core/periphery processes and geographical features need to be analyzed for precapitalist world-systems in the way that Peter Taylor (1985,1989) has done for the modern world-system.

7. A great deal has been written by anthropologists on boundaries in foraging societies. See Lee and Devore (1968), Leacock and Lee (1982), Lee (1979) and Steward (1955).

8. See Hall (1984) for further analysis of this problem.

9. If we use the criteria of trade in bullion, West Africa has been strongly linked to the Mediterranean and Near Eastern core since at least AD 800. The gold coins minted in Byzantium and Egypt which play such an important part in Janet Abu-Lughod's (1989) study of the Eurasian world-system were predominantly struck from West African gold (see Wolf, 1982:39). If Abu-Lughod's path-breaking work had paid somewhat greater attention to core/periphery relations she would have included much of sub-Saharan Africa in her Eurasian world-system.

10. Recent work by Gailey (1987) and Silverblatt (1987, 1988) supports the hypothesis that the transition from chiefdom to state is part and parcel of both the universal subordination of women in state societies and the tremendous variability in the types and degrees of such subordination. Studies of these especially problematic aspects of core/periphery hierarchies should pay close attention to the role of such changes in the transformation of gender relations.

11. Price-setting markets are those in which the competitive buying and selling of goods by actors operating to maximize their own returns is an important determinant of the rates of exchange (prices) among traded goods. Many forms of exchange which look like markets, are not price-setting markets. In no societies are all social objects commodified, but market societies are those in which the provision of substantial elements of the daily life of the average member is mediated by market forces.

12. While the theoretical perspective behind these distinctions is Marxist, the categories produced are somewhat congruent with those issuing from very different perspectives. Thus societies in which the kin-based mode is dominant correspond roughly to Parsons's (1966) "primitive" societies and Lenski and Lenski's (1987) preagrarian (hunter-gatherer, horticultural) societies. Societies in which the tributary (state-based) modes are dominant are roughly equivalent to Parsons's "ancient" and Lenski and Lenski's "agrarian" categories; and societies dominated by the capitalist mode overlap to some extent with Parsons's "modern" and Lenski and Lenski's "industrial" societies. There are important theoretical differences between these perspectives to be sure, but our point here is that the general categories of comparison are somewhat similar at the operational level.

13. Though we do not try to define the notion of world-systems broadly enough to consider systems composed exclusively of nomads, it is imaginable that nomadic groups did interact with one another sufficiently to constitute fluid and moving world-systems. Such an idea would bring the analysis of interaction spheres composed solely of nomadic bands into consideration as world-systems. Though some might choose to examine such "worlds" and to analyze the larger intergroup interactions of paleolithic groups from a systemic point of view we think that the existence of settled and territorial groups is a basic prerequisite for defining world-systems. We have already pushed the idea of world-systems well beyond what most other scholars consider common sense. By this decision we are not excluding the analysis of nomads who are in interaction with sedentary groups. Indeed these are often important players in core/periphery relations (see Chapter 7).

14. This distinction can also be applied to tribes and chiefdoms. Reactive or secondary social change implies that interactions between various social structures induce changes in some of them toward increased similarity. For example, a state system interacting with a big man system may induce the formation of a tribe with appointed leaders, and may even induce the formation of a chiefdom (Hall, 1989).

15. In the last few years there have been many studies which have applied world-systems concepts to pre-sixteenth century world-systems. We have already mentioned the work of Schneider (see Chapter 2, first published in 1977) and Ekholm and Friedman (1980, 1982) and Ekholm (1980). Other

important works which explicitly discuss the relevance of world-systems concepts are Adams (1977),Kohl (1987a, 1987b), Pailes and Whitecotton (1979, 1986), Blanton and Feinman (1984), Upham (1982), Wilkinson (1988), White and Burton (1987), White and Moore (1988), McGuire (1980), Algaze (1989), Gailey and Patterson (1987,1988), Baugh (1984a,1984b), Dincauze and Hasenstab (1989) and the articles in Mathien and McGuire (1986), Rowlands, Larsen and Kristiansen (1987), and Champion (1989). Kristiansen (1987) is the only scholar who claims to find core/periphery relations in a stateless world-system.

16. We use the terms "spread effects' and "backwash effects" following Myrdal (1971) to differentiate consequences of core/periphery interaction. Under some circumstances such interaction causes peripheral areas to develop in directions which are more core-like (spread effects) whereas other sorts of interaction cause peripheral areas to become underdeveloped (backwash effects).

17. Arguments to this effect have already been put forth by Kohl (1987b) and by Diakonoff (1973) for the Sumerian-centered world-system, but contrary evidence has been found by Lamberg-Karlovsky (1975). Findings based on one or two instances are not sufficient for testing propositions of the kind we are making. Only fairly comprehensive and complete studies which compare whole world-systems can confirm or disprove the hypotheses.

18. Mann (1986: Chapter 5) stresses the beneficial effects on economic development of the "compulsory cooperation" and pacification of large areas organized by the early conquest empires, while other scholars (e.g. Diakonoff, 1973) emphasize the exploitative and destructive effects which these empires had on peripheral regions. It is undoubtedly the case that some empires had greater beneficial effects than others. These matters need to be sorted out by a study which examines all the regions within each relevant world-system and systematically compares world-systems one to another.

REFERENCES

Abu-Lughod, Janet 1989. *Before European Hegemony: The World System A.D. 1250-1350*. New York: Oxford University Press.

Adams, William Y. 1977 *Nubia: Corridor to Africa*. Princeton: Princton University Press.

Algaze, Guillermo 1989. "The Uruk expansion: cross-cultural exchange as a factor in early Mesopotamian civilization," *Current Anthropology* 30:5 (December):571-608.

Amin, Samir 1980. *Class and Nation, Historically and in the Current Crisis*. New York: Monthly Review Press.

Anderson, Perry 1974. *Passages from Antiquity to Feudalism*. London: New Left Books.

Arrighi, Giovanni and Jessica Drangel 1986. "Stratification of the world-economy: an explanation of the semiperipheral zone." *Review* 10: 1:9-74.

Bairoch, Paul 1986. "Historical roots of economic underdevelopment: myths and realities." Pp. 191-216 in Wolfgang J. Mommsen and Jurgen Osterhammerl (eds.) *Imperialism After Empire: Continuities and Discontinuities*. London: Allen and Unwin.

Barfield, Thomas J. 1989. *The Perilous Frontier: Nomadic Empires and China*. Cambridge, MA.: Basil Blackwell.

Baugh, Timothy 1984. "Southern plains societies and eastern frontier Pueblo exchange during the protohistoric period." Pp. 156-67 in *Papers of the Archeological Society of New Mexico*, Volume 9. Albuquerque: Archeological Society Press.

Blanton, Richard and Gary Feinman 1984. "The Mesoamerican world-system." *American Anthropologist* 86(3):673-92.

Champion, Timothy C. 1989. "Introduction." Pp. 1-21 in T.C. Champion (ed.) *Centre and Periphery: Comparative Studies in Archeology*. London: Unwin Hyman.

Braudel, Fernand 1984. *The Perspective of the World*. New York: Harper and Row.

Carneiro, Robert L. 1970. "A theory of the origin of the state." *Science* 169:733-8.

Chase-Dunn, Christopher 1988. "Comparing world-systems: toward a theory of semiperipheral development." *Comparative Civilizations Review* 19:39-66, Fall.

_____ 1989. *Global Formation: Structures of the World-Economy*. Cambridge, MA.: Basil Blackwell.

_____ 1990. "Limits of hegemony: capitalist and global state formation." Pp. 213-40 in David P. Rapkin (ed.) *World Leadership and Hegemony*. Boulder, CO: Lynne Rienner.

Curtin, Phillip 1984. *Cross-cultural Trade in World History*. Cambridge: Cambridge University Press.

Diakonoff, Igor M. 1973. "The rise of the despotic state in ancient Mesopotamia." Pp. 173-203 in I. M. Diakonoff (ed.) *Ancient Mesopotamia*. G. M. Sergheyev (trans.) Walluf bei Weisbaden: Dr. Martin Sandig.

Dincauze, Dena F. and Robert J. Hasenstab 1989. "Explaining the Iroquois: tribalization on a prehistoric periphery." Pp. 67-87 in *Champion* (1989).

Dyson, Stephen L.1985. *The Creation of the Roman Frontier*. Princeton, NJ: Princeton University Press.

Earle, Timothy K. 1977. "A reappraisal of redistribution: complex Hawaiian chiefdoms." Pp. 213-232 in T. K. Earle and J. E. Ericson (eds.) *Exchange Systems in Prehistory*. New York: Academic Press.

Ekholm, Kasja 1980. "On the limitations of civilization: the structure and dynamics of global systems." *Dialectical Anthropology* 5:2(July):155-66.

Ekholm, Kasja and Jonathan Friedman 1980. "Toward a global anthropology." Pp. 61-76 in L. Blusse, H. L. Wesseling and G. D. Winius (eds.) *History and Underdevelopment*. Leyden: Center for the History of European Expansion, Leyden University.

_____ 1982. "'Capital' imperialism and exploitation in the ancient world-systems." *Review* 6:1:87-110.

Frankenstein, Susan 1979. "The Phoenicians in the far West: a function of neo-Assyrian imperialism." Pp. 263-294 in Larsen, Mogens T. (ed.) *Power and Propaganda: Symposium on Ancient Empires*. Copenhagen: Akademisk Forlag.

Fried, Morton 1967. *The Evolution of Political Society: An Essay in Political Anthropology*. New York: Random House.

Friedman, Jonathan 1982. "Catastrophe and continuity in social evolution." Pp. 175-196 in Colin Renfrew, Michael J. Rowlands and Barbara Abbott Segraves (eds.) *Theory and Explanation in Archeology: The Southampton Conference*. New York: Academic Press.

Friedman, Jonathan and Michael Rowlands 1977. "Notes towards an epigenetic model of the evolution of 'civilization'." Pp. 201-278 in J. Friedman and M. J. Rowlands (eds.) *The Evolution of Social Systems*. London: Duckworth.

Gailey, Christine Ward and Thomas C. Patterson 1987. "Power relations and state formation." Pp. 1-26 in Gailey and Patterson (eds.) *Power Relations and State Formation*. Washington, D.C.: American Anthropological Association.

_____ 1988. "State formation and uneven development." Pp. 77-90 in Gledhill, Bender and Larsen (eds.), 1988.

Gershenkron, Alexander 1962. *Economic Backwardness in Historical Perspective*. Cambridge: Harvard University Press.

Gledhill, John, Barbara Bender and Mogens Trolle Larsen (eds.) 1988. *State and Society: The Emergence and Development of Social Hierarchy and Political Centralization*. London: Unwin and Hyman.

Hall, Thomas D. 1984. "Lessons of long-term social change for comparative and historical study of ethnicity." *Current Perspectives in Social Theory* 5: 121-44.

_____ 1989. *Social Change in the Southwest, 1350-1880*. Lawrence: University of Kansas Press.

Hopkins, Keith 1978. *Conquerors and Slaves*. Cambridge: Cambridge University Press.

Jackson, Thomas L. 1986. *Late Prehistoric Obsidian Exchange in Central California*. Ph.D. Dissertation, Anthropology, Stanford University.

Johnson, Allen W. and Timothy Earle 1987. *The Evolution of Human Societies: From Foraging Group to Agrarian State*. Stanford: Stanford University Press.

Kelly, Raymond C. 1985. *The Nuer Conquest: The Structure and Development of an Expansionist System*. Ann Arbor: University of Michigan Press.

Kohl, Phillip 1987a. "The use and abuse of world systems theory: the case of the 'pristine' West Asian state." In *Archaeological Advances in Method and Theory II*. New York: Academic Press, pp. 1-35.

_____ 1987b. "The ancient economy, transferable technologies and the Bronze Age world-system: a view from the northeastern frontier of the Ancient Near East." Pp. 13-24 in Rowlands, Larsen and Kristiansen.

_____ 1988. "The Transcaucasian periphery in the Bronze Age: a preliminary formulation." A paper presented at the Annual Meetings of the International Society for the Comparative Study of Civilizations, Hampton University, May 27. Forthcoming in E. A. Shortman and P. A. Urban (eds.) *Resources, Power and Interregional Interaction*.

Kristiansen, Kristian 1987. "Centre and periphery in Bronze Age Scandinavia." Pp. 74-86 in Rowlands, Larsen and Kristiansen.

Lamberg-Karlovsky, C. C. 1975. "Third millennium modes of exchange and modes of production." Pp. 341-368 in J. A. Sabloff and C. C. Lamberg-Karlovsky (eds.) *Ancient Civilization and Trade*. Albuquerque: University of New Mexico Press.

Lattimore, Owen 1940. *Inner Asian Frontiers of China*. New York: American Geographical Society.

_____ 1980. "The periphery as locus of innovation." Pp. 205-208 in Jean Gottmann (ed.) *Centre and Periphery: Spatial Variation in Politics*. Beverly Hills: Sage.

Leacock, Eleanor and Richard B. Lee (eds.) 1982. *Politics and History in Band Societies*. Cambridge: Cambridge University Press.

Lee, Richard B. 1979. *The !Kung San: Men, Women and Work in a Foraging Society*. Cambridge: Cambridge University Press.

Lee, Richard B. and I. DeVore (eds.) 1968. *Man the Hunter*. Chicago: Aldine.

Lenski, Gerhard 1966. *Power and Privilege*. New York: McGraw-Hill.

Lenski, Gerhard and Jean Lenski 1982. *Human Societies*. 4th Edition. New York: McGraw-Hill.

McNeill, William H. 1964. *Europe's Steppe Frontier, 1500-1800*. Chicago: University of Chicago Press.

Mann, Michael 1986. *The Sources of Social Power: A History of Power from the Beginning to A.D. 1760*. Cambridge: Cambridge University Press.

Marx, Karl 1967. *Capital*, V. 1. New York: International Publishers.

Mathien, Frances and Randall McGuire (eds.) 1986. *Ripples in the Chichimec Sea: New Considerations of Southwestern-Mesoamerican Interactions*. Carbondale: Southern Illinois University Press.

Melko, Matthew and Leighton, R. Scott (eds.) 1987. *The Boundaries of Civilizations in Space and Time*. Lanham, MD: University Press of America.

Moseley, Katherine P. 1990. "Caravel and caravan: West Africa and the world-economies." A paper presented at the annual meetings of the International Studies Association, Washington, D.C. April 11.

Moseley, Katherine P. and Immanuel Wallerstein 1978. "Precapitalist social structures." *Annual Review of Sociology* 4:259-90.

Myrdal, Gunnar 1971. *Economic Theory and Underdeveloped Regions*. New York: Harper and Row.

Nissen, Hans J. 1988. *The Early History of the Ancient Near East, 9000-2000 B.C.* Chicago: University of Chicago Press.

Pailes, Richard A., and Joseph W. Whitecotton 1979. "The greater Southwest and Mesoamerican "world" system: an exploratory model of frontier relationships." Pp. 105-121 in W. W. Savage and S. I. Thompson (eds.) *The Frontier: Comparative Studies*. Norman: University of Oklahoma Press.

_____ 1986. "New world Precolumbian world systems." Pp. 183-204 in Mathien and McGuire.

Parsons, Talcott 1966. *Societies: Evolutionary and Comparative Perspectives*. Englewood Cliffs, NJ: Prentice-Hall.

Polanyi, Karl 1977. *The Livelihood of Man*. Harry W. Pearson (ed.). New York: Academic Press.

Polanyi, Karl, Conrad Arensberg and Harry Pearson (eds.) 1957. *Trade and Market in the Early Empires*. Chicago: Regnery.

Renfrew, Colin R. 1977. "Alternative models for exchange and spatial distribution." Pp. 71-90 in T. K. Earle and J. E. Ericson (eds.) *Exchange Systems in Prehistory*. New York: Academic Press.

Renfrew, Colin R. and John F. Cherry (eds.) 1986. *Peer Polity Interaction and Socio-political Change*. Cambridge: Cambridge University Press.

Rowlands, Michael, Mogens Larsen and Kristian Kristiansen (eds.) 1987. *Centre and Periphery in the Ancient World*. Cambridge: Cambridge University Press.

Sahlins, Marshall 1972. *Stone Age Economics*. Chcago: Aldine.

Schneider, Jane 1977 "Was there a pre-capitalist world-system?" *Peasant Studies* 6:1:20-29.

Schortman, Edward M. and Patricia A. Urban 1987. "Modeling interregional interaction in prehistory." Pp. 37-95 in *Advances in Archeological Method and Theory*, V. 11. New York: Academic Press.

Service, Elman, R. 1971. *Cultural Evolutionism: Theory and Practice*. New York: Holt, Reinhart and Winston.

Service, Elman R. 1975. *Origins of the State and Civilization*. New York: Norton.

Silverblatt, Irene 1987. *Moon, Sun and Witches: Gender Ideologies and Class in Inca and Colonial Peru*. Princeton, NJ: Princeton University Press.

_____ 1988. "Women in states." *Annual Review of Anthropology* 17:427-60.

Steward, Julian 1955. *Theory of Culture Change: The Methodology of Multilinear Evolution*. Urbana, IL: University of Illinois Press.

_____ 1977. *Evolution and Ecology*. Urbana, IL.: University of Illinois Press.

Taagepera, Rein 1978. "Size and duration of empires: growth-decline curves, 3000 to 600 B.C.." *Social Science Research* 7:180-96.

Taylor, Peter 1985. *Political Geography: World-Economy, Nation-State and Locality*. London: Longman.

_____ 1988. "World-systems analysis and regional geography." *Professional Geographer* 40:3:259-65.

Tilly, Charles 1984. *Big Structures, Large Processes, Huge Comparisons*. New York: Russell Sage.

Trotsky, Leon 1932. *History of the Russian Revolution*. V.1, Max Eastman (Trans.) New York: Simon and Schuster.

Upham, Stedman 1982. *Polities and Power: An Economic and Political History of the Western Pueblo*. New York: Academic Press.

Wallerstein, Immanuel 1974. *The Modern World-System, V. 1*. New York: Academic Press.

_____ 1979. *The Capitalist World-Economy*. Cambridge: Cambridge University Press.

_____ 1989. *The Modern World-System, V. 3*. New York: Academic Press.

Webb, Malcolm C. 1975. "The flag follows trade: an essay on the necessary interaction of military and commercial factors in state formation." Pp. 155-210 in J. A. Sabloff and C. C. Lamberg-Karlovsky (eds.) *Ancient Civilization and Trade*. Albuquerque: University of New Mexico Press.

Weigand, Phil C., Garman Harbottle and Edward V. Sayre 1977. "Turquoise sources and source analysis: Mesoamerica and the Southwestern U.S.A." Pp. 15-34 in T. K. Earle and J. E. Ericsons (eds.) *Exchange Systems in Prehistory*. New York: Academic Press.

Wells, Peter S. 1980. *Culture Contact and Culture Change: Early Iron Age Central Europe and the Mediterranean World*. Cambridge: Cambridge University Press.

White, Douglas R. and Michael L. Burton 1987. "World-systems and ethnological theory." Research proposal funded by the National Science Foundation BNS-85-07685 (Anthropology).

White, Douglas and Carmella Moore 1988. "Ethnology in its world historical context: world economic position and warfare." Unpublished ms. Social Sciences, University of California-Irvine.

Wilkinson, David 1987. "Central civilization." *Comparative Civilizations Review* 17:31-59.

_____ 1988. "World-economic theories and problems: Quigley vs. Wallerstein vs. central civilization." A paper presented at the annual meetings of the International Society for the Comparative Study of Civilizations, Hampton, VA. May 26-29.

Wolf, Eric R. 1982. *Europe and the People Without History*. Berkeley: University of California Press.

Zagarell, Allen 1986. "Trade, women, class and society in Ancient Western Asia." *Current Anthropology* 27:5(December):415-30.

2

Was There a Precapitalist World-System?

Jane Schneider*

In his book, *The Modern World-System*, Immanuel Wallerstein applies to Western Europe a theory of social change that other scholars have been developing to analyze the growth patterns of Third World countries (e.g., Amin 1974; Baran 1957; Emmanuel 1972; Frank 1967). This theory, rooted in global political economy, or geo-political economy, contrasts markedly with the unilineal models of social change that dominated social science until recently. Unlike a unilineal model, which posits inexorable and orthogenetic progressions from simple to complex, agrarian to industrial organization, and unlike orthodox Marxism, too, the new theory explains change in terms of forces which originate outside of any particular local region or nation, in the dynamics of world economic organization. The unit of analysis is no longer the evolving regional or national society in transition from a traditional to a modern form but a world economy, in which a few highly centralized core groups mobilize energy resources from a vast peripheral domain.

Wallerstein makes an important contribution to the refinement of global political economy by focusing attention on two interrelated processes that

* Reprinted with permission from *Peasant Studies* Vol. VI, No. 1, January, 1977, pp. 20-29.

derive from core-area energy mobilization and that may be considered critical sources of change. The first process involves the defensive and competitive strategies that interest groups peripheral to a core-area generate when they are directly, or even indirectly, affected by its expansion. Peripheral groups that are not well located from the standpoint of geography and environment may submit to, and even adapt to, external pressure. Groups that are more propitiously located, however, defend against penetration to the point where under some rather special conditions a defensive strategy becomes an offensive one and a new core area evolves. Although, as Wallerstein emphasizes, the enormous gaps in wealth and power between core and peripheral populations remain fixed for long periods of time, the deprivation produced by these gaps and the energy drainage that sustains them inevitably lead to one or another form of resistance. This, and the counter-resistance in which core populations may subsequently invest, have obvious implications for institutional, cultural, and economic change within the regions or nations involved.

The second process that is inherent in world economic organization and underlies social change is the creation and maintenance of interdependent relationships between various national and regional entities. The concept, "regional differentiation," is the key to understanding this process, according to which particular populations come to play particular roles, their economic, political, and cultural institutions changing to meet the demands of specialization. Wallerstein provides a vocabulary with which to describe this process. He suggests that the "initial eligibility" for a particular role is often decided by an "accidental edge" related to past history and current environmental resources and geography. Once the slight edge is established, the operations of the world economy "accentuate the differences, institutionalize them and make them impossible to surmount over the short run" (1974a: 403). In this way, "the slight edge is converted into a large disparity..." (1974: 98). He offers sixteenth-century Poland as an example, relating changes in that country's economic (especially labor) organization, state institutions, and religion to its assumption of the specialized role of breadbasket for North Atlantic Europe.

To summarize, a global theory of social change hinges on two overlapping processes -- one of competition between various geographically localized populations of unequal power; the other of differentiation, division of labor, and interdependence among these same units. Both processes have an ecological dimension since geography and environmental resources influence the assumption of particular specializations, as well as the ability to resist demands posed by external dominants. Both are also historical in that past roles or past resistance leave their imprint on a population's resources and institutional structure, thereby influencing its contemporary ability to repel or adapt to new roles. Wallerstein's comparison of Poland with Russia -- the high point of the book -- shows how the two processes intersect. By virtue of its accidental edge, Russia resisted incorporation into the European-dominated world economy of the sixteenth century. Unlike Poland, it thus remained internally diversified and capable of establishing its own peripheral domain (1974: 303-324).

From the point of view of social science, Wallerstein's most significant contribution is the suggestion that processes of interaction and unequal exchange might explain events not only in Third World areas transformed by European hegemony in the nineteenth and twentieth centuries, but in earlier periods within Europe itself. This establishes a unity of theory between Western and non-Western peoples, the absence of which has long been problematic in unilineal models of change whose ethnocentricisms are consistent with their inability to account for the disparity between Europe's precocious advances and other peoples' "lag." It will be the point of this essay, however, that *The Modern World-System* suffers from too narrow an application of its own theory.[1] For, although Wallerstein admires Owen Lattimore's description of the differentiation process according to which ancient Chinese civilization "gave birth to barbarism," (quoted in Wallerstein, 1974: 98), he does not view the precapitalist world as systematically integrated through the operations of world economic forces. Because most of the book is dedicated to the rise of North Atlantic Europe as the preeminent core area of the world economy -- an event Wallerstein equates with the emergence of the capitalist world-system -- it unfortunately does not benefit from the clarity of argument and coherence of analysis that distinguish his comparison of Poland with Russia.

Wallerstein has assembled a staggering quantity and diversity of data pertinent to the development of modern capitalism. He has analyzed processes of core-area expansion and regional differentiation that unfolded in the wake of this event. His account of differentiation usefully extends to a comparison of state formation in core and peripheral areas, while his discussion of forms of labor mobilization in these respective areas is complex, original, and stimulating. It is when they are measured against such examples of a global theory at work that the lists of factors which he has drawn up to account for various precapitalist events are theoretically unsatisfying, sometimes incomplete, and often confusing. One wants to know why, for example, his analysis of the "rise of England" does not focus attention on that nation's environmental resources, or on its essentially peripheral status in relation to other continental powers, in particular Northern Italy. I will return to these points later on.

This essay attempts to demonstrate that Wallerstein's reluctance to apply the concepts, "core" and "periphery," to precapitalist transformations is a product of the way he views the luxury trade. Before the emergence of the capitalist world-system (which I too will identify, for the sake of convenience, with the rise to core status of England and Holland), most exchanges between distant places involved the movement of luxuries -- of exotic goods or "preciosities" which were very high in value per unit of weight and therefore relatively easy to transport. For many authorities, Wallerstein among them, the difference between luxuries and bulk goods such as food or timber goes beyond their transportability. They are implicitly categorized as opposites: preciosities *versus* essentials or utilities. I suggest that this dichotomy is a false one that obscures the systemic properties of the luxury trade. In the following pages, I will first outline Wallerstein's argument that long distance trade in exotic goods was of little relevance to intra-European change. I will then develop an alternative interpretation according to which Europe as a whole, and England in particular, were reduced to peripheral areas by this trade. I hope that the alternative interpretation will prepare the way for future analyses of precapitalist events within a theoretical framework consistent with Wallerstein's analysis of Russia and Poland.

According to Wallerstein, the capitalist world-system differs from all previous imperiums, which he describes as world-empires. He argues for this distinction on the grounds that before capitalism, the political and economic boundaries of empires coincided, administrative control being extended through tributary relations to the entire area from which energy resources were mobilized. In contrast, the modern world-system is a world-economy in which political integration is intermittent. At its center are strong, well-knit and relatively homogeneous nation states, whose spheres of political control have not been isomorphic with their economic hegemony. Rulers of these states manifest a great deal more respect for mercantile and manufacturing interests than did the despots of precapitalist states. In addition they organize a completely different kind of buffer between the imperial center and the localized populations on whose energy this center draws. Wallerstein's elaboration of the concept "semiperiphery" establishes a mutually exclusive set of dynamics for precapitalist and capitalist empires, in which the former are stabilized through the manipulation of middle sector "cultural" or occupational groups, whereas the latter depend for stability upon independent political entities -- semiperipheral states -- that belong to neither the core nor the periphery (1974: 349-350; 1974a: 403-404).

Consistent with these contrasts between past and present, precapitalist and modern empires, is Wallerstein's acceptance of the view that the ancient empires of Near and Far East were homeostatic and not dynamic (1974: 84-85). For example, although he appreciates that in the thirteenth to sixteenth centuries, China and Europe had roughly comparable populations, and although he shares with Joseph Needham a respect for Chinese technological achievement, he nevertheless emphasizes China's opposition to foreign commerce and the Confucian suppression of early Ming exploration and maritime activity. China's overall commitment, he suggests, was to internal rather than external expansion and to the development of whatever surplus it had into defensive installations against Central Asian "barbarians" on the northern and western frontiers. China blanketed, rather than released, the forces of expansion (1974: 53-63).

Wallerstein's assessment of China and, by implication, of other precapitalist empires suggests why these polities do not enter theoretically into his analysis of the capitalist transformation in Europe. Since, in the Middle Ages, Europe was tributary to none of them, none can be said to have interacted with Europe in ways that were relevant to systemic social change. Chapter one of *The Modern World-System* mentions that precapitalist Europe was a "very marginal area in economic terms," (1974: 17) but marginality is a concept distinct from periphery. In contrast to peripheral areas, marginal ones are disengaged from processes of struggle and competition, differentiation, and specialization in relation to much older and more developed centers of civilization.

Perhaps the most explicit statement of this disengagement is Wallerstein's evaluation of the significance of long distance trade, for although Europeans did not deliver tribute to the metropolises of world empires, they were nevertheless in touch with them through trade. Wallerstein does not argue that this trade was ephemeral. He recognizes that it provided employment for thousands of people, profits for middlemen, and revenues for states. In addition it contributed to the internal stratification of entire populations, since exotic goods imported from afar could be utilized in the demarcation and maintenance of status barriers (1974: 306-307). But he does not think that these effects of long distance trade induced European development, either as stimuli or as obstacles to be overcome. On the contrary, as if to underscore the irrelevance of the luxury trade for change, he applies to Asia, Africa, and the Near East the concept "external arena," because he feels that these areas bore no systemic relationship to Europe until the eighteenth or nineteenth centuries, and then on terms defined by Europeans.

The distinction between periphery and external arena rests upon the conceptual separation of essential from luxury exchanges.

> This is to be sure a distinction rooted in the social perceptions of the actors and hence in both their social organization and their culture. These perceptions can change. But the distinction is crucial if we are not to fall into the trap of identifying *every* exchange-activity as evidence of the existence of a system (1974a: 397-398).

According to Wallerstein, trade in preciosities, unlike trade in essentials, is non-systemic. Each party "exports to the other what is in its system socially defined as worth little, and gets what is socially defined as worth much." Both partners to the exchange reap rewards simultaneously. Distinct from the profits that are made under capitalism, these rewards are mere "windfalls." One partner does not gain at the expense of the other (1974a: 398). Precapitalist Europe traded a number of preciosities with Asia; in particular, it exported precious metals to pay for imported pepper, spices, and silk. Before the rise of capitalism, however, primitive conditions in transportation restricted the movement of bulk goods such as food. Because, by Wallerstein's definition, only the latter type of exchange is systemic, precapitalist trade was a secondary factor, one among many, and not critical to social change (1974: 20-21).

How then does Wallerstein account for the capitalist transformation? In his view this event was propelled by the need to overcome the "crisis of feudalism" -- the wars and plagues, economic collapse, and class conflict that in the fourteenth century reduced the population of Europe by a third to a half. He attributes the crisis to a conjuncture of prior over-expansion, cyclical economic downturns, and (possibly) changing climate. Of these the most important was prior over-expansion. Between 1150 and 1300, demographic and economic growth exceeded environmental capacity, given technologies available at the time. Wallerstein considers but rejects Sweezy's hypothesis that long distance trade stimulated this growth. Perhaps it was one factor, but because it involved primarily luxuries, it was less important than "food and handicraft production," the multiplication of which appears to have been spontaneous:

> ...the scale of this economic activity was slowly expanding, and the various economic nuclei expanded therewith. New frontier lands were cultivated. New towns were founded. Population grew. The Crusades provided some of the advantages of colonial plunder. And then sometime in the fourteenth century, this expansion ceased. The cultivated areas retracted. Population declined (1974: 21).

This statement suggests that an endogenous set of forces was at work, among them spontaneous population growth -- the motor force in many applications of unilineal models of change (see Cowgill 1975).

The crisis of feudalism found its resolution in the creation of the capitalist world-system, two of whose central features we have already encountered: the regional divergence of eastern Europe, which under a regime of highly coerced agricultural labor began to grow wheat for export to the North Atlantic core, and the formation of strong states in this core. The first feature of the system to manifest itself, a pre-condition for other developments, was, however, the "incredible geographical expansion" that began with the Portuguese discovery voyages in the late fifteenth century. Wallerstein has difficulty accounting for these voyages. The textbook explanation that Portuguese navigators and adventurers sought spices and gold satisfies him only in part, for these are preciosities and of secondary importance to an explanation of change. Yet the "motivations" of Portugal are worth puzzling over, for they were motivations of Europe too. Because Portuguese expansion followed the demographic catastrophe of the fourteenth century, it could hardly have resulted from land shortage or over-population. Nevertheless Wallerstein suggests that expansion may have been motivated by a search for food. Europe needed surplus food to support increased development and urbanization (1974: 41-42).

Europe's search for food is well documented in Wallerstein's account of the transformation of eastern Europe into a breadbasket (although except for a footnote on page 218 and a brief reference on page 221 he virtually ignores southern Italy and Sicily, which were functionally specialized to produce surplus wheat as early as Roman times). His documentation of a food quest by Portugal is less convincing. Committed to the proposition that "in the long run, staples account for more of men's economic thrusts than luxuries," (1974: 42) he wants to find staples in the cargoes of Portuguese ships. There was indeed a modest quantity of cereals, imported from the Atlantic islands off the Portuguese coast, but this represented only a minor segment of the total trade and only one component of the island trade as well. Sugar imports were more substantial, but was sugar essential? Wallerstein argues that it provided calories (1974: 43), but so did honey which was widely available in Europe. In the Renaissance courts of Italy the fascination of sugar was such that it was eaten with virtually anything and fashioned into decorative sculptures (Root 1971: 36-40; Tannahill 1973: 223). Sugar went to make rum and later chocolate, which Wallerstein characterizes as "highly appreciated" drinks, but by what criteria were they staple foods? He also mentions dyestuffs and wine which other authorities would similarly classify as luxuries (1974: 43).

It seems to me that dyestuffs and wine, sugar and rum, should not be separated from the textbook explanation for Portuguese (and hence European) geographical expansion. The explorers were searching for luxury goods, especially spices and precious metals, the latter to exchange for more luxuries from the Orient (1974: 39-41). If wine was a useful beverage, then pepper was a useful spice, yet both also indulged the fancies of a status conscious aristocracy.[2] Are we to conclude then that the capitalist transformation began with a caprice? Wallerstein is right to avoid so absurd a position. The way around the dilemma, however, is to discover the relationship between luxuries and essentials, not to make sugar and wine into staple foods.

In a recent article on long distance trade, Robert M. Adams, the archaeologist, argues that even in antiquity trade was a "formidable socio-economic force...in spite of its being confined largely to commodities of very high value in relation to weight and bulk due to the high transport costs, and in spite of its directly involving only a small part of the population" (1974: 247). Rejecting the assumption that change in precapitalist society was an endogenous process that moved populations irreversibly from simple to complex levels of integration, he proposes that we assume for the past as well as the present a model in which more complex societies "dominate weaker neighbors, coalesce, experience predation, develop and break off patterns of symbiosis and all in dizzyingly abrupt shifts." The need to adapt to such shifts is "the most single overwhelming selective pressure to which societies are exposed" (1974: 249; see also Wolf 1967). Marshalling evidence from a number of case studies, some ethnographic and others archaeological, Adams argues that there is a close connection between predation and trade. On the surface benign, the luxury trade could induce massive alterations in technology, leadership, class structure, and ideology within trading populations and in "relay" populations on the transit routes. In addition to promoting symbiosis, trade was also "partly aggressive, and sometimes dangerously competitive" -- a turbulent process (1974: 249).

Adams' argument challenges the idea that luxuries served little purpose other than to satisfy the whims and desires of aristocrats and enable them to maintain distance from status inferiors. This idea is illustrated by Wallerstein's remark that European aristocrats "made (spices) into aphrodisiacs, as though [they] could not make love otherwise," (1974: 41) which implies that the consumption patterns of the very rich were, if not laughable, then harmful only to themselves. Following Malinowski and Mauss on the power of the gift, a case can be made that luxury goods served more fundamental ends. The relationship of trade to social stratification was not just a matter of an elevated group distinguishing itself through the careful application of sumptuary laws and a monopoly on symbols of status; it further involved the direct and self-conscious manipulation of various semiperipheral and middle level groups through patronage, bestowals, and the calculated distribution of exotic and valued goods.

A good analysis of the relationship between gifts and power is Luigi Graziano's comprehensive essay on clientelism (1975). Suggesting that the principle of the gift consists in "the calculated and productive use of generosity," Graziano argues that:

> One gives because in highly stratified societies an effective way to control conflict is to establish a network of personal obligations; one gives, at the same time, in order to crush clients and rivals with onerous obligations sanctioned by the personal submission of the

> defaulting debtor. One gives, in summary, because this is a rational
> means for accumulating power...(1975: 27).

Where there is a clear imbalance of power, but juridical and coercive institutions are absent or weakly articulated, gift-giving performs the function of contract enforcement. As Graziano points out, the subordinate learns that "the only way to continue enjoying the protection and other resources monopolized by the powerful is to loyally return benefits received. The restitution will consist of personal services and, in order to compensate for disparity in resources between patron and client, in compliance to the former's will" (1975: 25).

Patron-client relations, established and maintained through the exchange of gifts and favors, contribute in different ways to the mobilization of energy. By virtue of the obligations created by his bestowals, the patron can often claim a portion of the surplus labor of his dependents. But patrons do not simply lay claim to the energy resources of their clients. Their most significant claims are levied against outsiders to this paternalistic tie. Often, in fact, the intent in constructing a clientele is to defuse organized opposition, class antagonism, and class struggle (e.g., Blok 1969, 1974). Pitting some against others, gift-giving promotes the co-optation of class enemies, making the patron-client relationship a forceful political adjunct to energy capture.[3]

Clientelism also operates at the societal level where it facilitates the mobilization of energy resources through the creation and maintenance of client states whose respective economic contributions may be less significant than their political loyalty. Descriptive accounts of the Chinese tributary system, for example, attribute to such states the same role Wallerstein assigns to semiperipheral states under capitalism. These accounts also portray the fundamental contribution that luxuries made to clientelism on this level. For centuries China wove a vast network of tribute bearing kings and princes across its northern, western, and southern frontiers and garnered their submission through "imperial compassion," including the bestowal of gifts. The emperor or his deputies gave presents to envoys during their visits, upon their departure from the Chinese court, and through ambassadorial missions to tributaries in their own lands. Gifts ranged from silver coins and rolls of silk to Chinese princess brides for rulers (Fairbank and Teng 1941; Wiens 1967).

Many Western historians have commented on the lavishness and generosity of Chinese gifts, which often matched or surpassed the value of the tribute delivered to the emperor by the client state. Indeed, tributary obligations rarely constituted a significant surplus, but were instead a token sampling of unique local wares. Wallerstein utilizes this characteristic of the tribute system to support his distinction between precapitalist and capitalist empires, noting that, under the former, tribute was sometimes a "disguised form of trade disadvantageous to the empire" (1974: 60-61). In a footnote he urges comparison between "this self-defeating political arrangement [and] the frank colonialism Portugal and other European countries practiced on the overseas barbarians" (1974: 61, n. 162).

Yet, gift-bestowal was just an instrument of Chinese foreign policy, the crux of which was expansion. Over the many centuries of its existence, the Chinese Empire, like other empires of the precapitalist world, mobilized energy resources, displaced neolithic cultivators, captured metals and slaves, beyond as well as within its frontiers. The demographic and territorial expansion of the Han Chinese, who pushed back these frontiers, was in fact phenomenal, and, although it was much more gradual than the European expansion of a later period, it may turn out to have been more enduring. For China, as for other great empires of the precapitalist past, the tributary system made expansion possible. Energy was mobilized around as well as through it, often with the blessing and outright assistance of the client states, minimally with the expectation that there would be allies to provide support, including food and other essentials, should the empire or its representatives be attacked. Because the tribute system was maintained through the distribution of luxuries, these goods were also "essential" -- not only in the narrow sense that, through cultural definition of tastes, people became addicted to them, but also in the broader sense that imperialism necessitated "winning distant people with kindness" as well as hitting them over the head. The same principle applies to foreign policy today.

Precapitalist tribute systems at first glance give the impression that reliance upon luxury goods for the creation and maintenance of allies was indiscriminate. Anything a potential ally might consider valuable or, through court ceremonial and ritual, might be influenced to consider valuable, could constitute a gift capable of obligating him to the donor. In fact, however, the various preciosities that circulated in long distance trade differed in the degree to which they could readily be converted into other resources. The greater an object's perceived value over both time and space, the greater was its potential to bind allegiances, and thereby promote energy capture. Goods with high durability, quality control in their production, a widespread reputation for fineness and integrity, and a high degree of natural scarcity were -- with remarkable consistency -- among the most coveted valuables across much of the Old World. Of these, gold and silver, first coined (in alloyed form) in the seventh century B.C., led the list "not so much because they were money as because they were treasured" (Neale 1976: 45, 51).

Those who held gold and silver, whether they ruled states, religious bodies, aristocratic families, or whatever, could feel confident of the stability of their hoards in the future as well as the present, at home as well as abroad. As these magnates, especially the rulers of states, harnessed bureaucrats and soldiers to their service, they found them unwilling to accept as pay anything but precious metals. From a very early time, moreover, the military capability of a state depended not only on numbers and weapons, but on having a storehouse of treasure to bribe allies, ransom prisoners, purchase supplies, pay indemnities, and so on (Grierson 1959). In Neale's words, "one cannot have a pig feast with goat meat, and Charles II and Louis XIV could not conduct a war" without gold and silver (1976: 55).[4]

Wallerstein is aware that bullion provided "a monetary base for circulation within Europe" (1974: 41), but does not fully appreciate its significance for war and diplomacy. His classification of precious metals as preciosities, and the distinction he makes between these and essential goods, cancel out the few passing references to this critical function (e.g., 1974: 197). As a consequence he overlooks an old and fascinating, and perhaps systemic, pattern in long distance trade. Since antiquity, expanding empires have acquired precious metals and other highly valued luxuries, not only by plunder and piracy, but by exporting finished goods, above all cloth. Adams, for example, describes how ancient Mesopotamia acquired lapis-lazuli, pearls, rare woods, ivory, gold, and silver from the "barbarian" interior of Anatolia. The major export to this backward area was woolen cloth, so much that, in addition to the roughly 50,000 sheep it raised, Mesopotamia imported raw wool (1974: 246-47). Similarly, in the early Christian centuries, Indian traders extracted precious metals and spices from the evolving kingdoms of Southeast Asia, whose divine right rulers were ceremonially inducted into the Kshatriya caste by immigrant Brahmin priests. Committed to the intensification of production within their respective territories, these rulers imported status goods, among them beads and cloth (Wheatley 1976).

The theme of precious metals for cloth had its counterpart in ancient China where the imperial court periodically declared that payments of all kinds should be made in silk and porcelain, brocade and lacquerware, rather than in bullion or coin (Fairbank 1969: 75; Servoise 1966; Yang 1952). Like India, China was one of the great civilizations that over the centuries stockpiled precious stones and metals against an impressive outflow of finished textiles. To borrow Braudel's imagery, civilizations like these produced no metals but drained them from the whole world (1973: 338-339).

It should be no surprise, then, that Europeans were historically preoccupied with the outflow of silver and gold, (much of it acquired through trade and plunder, some of it from European mines), and that they too saw a connection between this movement and the movement of cloth. In A.D. 14-37, Tiberius prohibited wearing (imported) silk in Rome, his regulation, according to Needham, closely following a series of Chinese reforms (A.D. 9-23) in which gold coins were called in to be exchanged for bronze causing a "drain on world gold circulation" (1954: 109). Over the next several centuries, rulers throughout Europe similarly passed sumptuary laws in part to stem the export of metals, restricting even the textiles produced by their European neighbors (e.g., Miller 1969: 218-20; Miskimin 1969: 149-150). In addition to providing the coinage these rulers needed to pay loyal dependents and bureaucrats, treasure was the "sinews of war" -- a point well illustrated by the predicament of the late medieval Duke of Burgundy who had difficulty ransoming his son from the Turks because too many gold coins had been drained off to England to purchase English cloth, which this Duke had unsuccessfully tried to ban from his realm (Munro 1972: 53-55).

The familiar mercantilist doctrines of the seventeenth and eighteenth centuries also pointed to a connection between cloth and gold. Belaboring the dangers that were inherent in the export of precious metals, the more farsighted economists proposed that public policy should bolster up textile industries, cheapen labor and other factors of production, and promote the export of manufactures instead of bullion (e.g., Heckscher 1955: 188).

Wallerstein's treatment of the secular, if uneven, export of metals from Europe is contradictory. In addition to citing Andrew Watson's reference to the "strong power of India and China to attract precious metals from other parts of the world" (quoted in 1974: 39-40), he suggests in a footnote that readers consult the "remarkable collaborative article" by Lopez, Miskimin, and Udovitch in which "they argue very convincingly that the years 1350-1500 see a steady outflow of bullion from north-west Europe to Italy to the Levant to India" (1974: 40, n. 85). Yet Wallerstein cannot explain why England and France "complained bitterly" about this outflow, nor why Europeans passionately hoarded bullion at the same time that they exported it extensively to the East (1974: 329-330). At one point he calls attention to the distinction between "bullion as money" and "hoarded bullion" or treasure (1974: 333); but elsewhere simple formulae obscure the complex uses of precious metals: "the bullion flowed east to decorate the temples, palaces, and clothing of Asian aristocratic classes and the jewels and spices flowed west" (1974: 41) -- an innocuous exchange of windfalls, irrelevant to competition for energy among great powers.

To the extent that, contrary to Wallerstein, the flow of precious metals was not benign, but was related, however indirectly, to energy mobilization, it is possible to hypothesize a *precapitalist* world-system, in which core-areas accumulated precious metals while exporting manufactures, whereas peripheral areas gave up these metals (and often slaves) against an inflow of finished goods. As in the modern world-system, most areas fit neither of these categories but constituted either external arenas, or semiperipheral "layers within layers."

Given the hypothesized system, precapitalist Europe was not simply marginal to the older, better established civilizations of the Levant and Asia; it was peripheral to these civilizations whose development it partially supported through the export of metals and, in the early Middle Ages, also of slaves (Verlinden 1955). As such its trajectory of development might fruitfully be compared with that of other bullion-losing, textile-importing areas such as Southeast Asia and West Africa, rather than exclusively with energy-gaining China as is often done. Another parallel to explore is that of the handful of twentieth-century underdeveloped countries which, by accident of geography and environmental resources, are well enough situated to withdraw from external pressure, successfully defend against subsequent penetration, substitute for imported manufactures, and eventually export manufactures in lieu of energy (Seers 1970).

For Europe, the hypothesized conversion from periphery to core took many centuries during which serious reversals and a great deal of internal competition occurred. At various points different regions held the initiative in the conversion process, and as a result, they functioned as minor core areas within Europe itself. Northern Italy, Flanders, and (eventually) England are the prime examples. Yet the complexity which resulted from the simultaneous expansion of several incipient centers of development also had a certain coherence if one accepts the existence of a precapitalist world-system. For that system points to cloth manufacture as the central element in the transition from a dependent to a dominant relationship with the Levant and Far East. It suggests that there were successive, cloth-centered, European strategies to retreat from, then match, and finally to undermine the textile-producing, Oriental areas toward which bullion was moving. The most successful strategies over the long run, if not the short run, appear to have been based on wool -- and for good reason. Until Europeans finally penetrated India, which was not until the eighteenth century, cotton was an Asian specialty and, as Pirenne once wrote, to carry silk to an Oriental monarch was "like carrying water to the river" (1909: 310, n. 2). When Marc Bloch, in *Feudal Society,* referred to the "revolution which saw our Western countries embarking on the economic conquest of the world by way of the East," he had in mind the explosion of export-oriented woolen cloth manufacturing in towns and cities all over the map of Europe (1961: 70).[5]

Textiles figure importantly in Wallerstein's account of numerous precapitalist events. But they figure as factors among other factors, rather than as central elements. As such it is difficult to appreciate the extent to which textile manufacturing, in and of itself, contributed to the fundamental processes of regional differentiation and inter-regional competition prior to the capitalist breakthrough. Wallerstein's treatment of the rise of England illustrates this point. A presumably exhaustive presentation of factors assembled to account for this critical juncture identifies textiles as "the hub of...export trade," but it does not assess the significance of England's abundant and rich pastures for the competitiveness of its cloths in foreign markets (1974: 228-235). In the context of analyzing the failure of Spain to consolidate its empire, Wallerstein many pages earlier alludes to the natural advantage of English pastures (1974: 91); and an unrelated footnote somewhat later quotes Bowden: "It was England's fortune that she possessed a quasi-monopoly of long-staple wool" (1974: 280, n. 268). Yet the only factor of environmental significance to figure as an "accidental edge" in the actual analysis of England's rise is the nation's unusual insularity.

Regarding England's relationship to more developed, continental European powers, Wallerstein is also unfocused. At one point he describes this nation as industrially backward, even in the mid-sixteenth century, and as having been a virtual colony in the Middle Ages (1974: 227). Data pertinent to these characterizations, however, are not brought to bear on the argument, but are scattered throughout the book. A summary in Chapter One of the factors that produced the crisis of feudalism mentions, almost in passing, that "within Europe, there were at least two smaller world-economies, a medium sized one based on the city-states of northern Italy and a smaller one based on the city-states (sic) of Flanders and northern Germany" (1974: 36-37). Although he suggests that "most of Europe was not directly involved in these networks," subsequent footnotes reveal that before the mid-fourteenth century, the principle markets for England's raw wool were the cloth industries of Italy (1974: 150, n. 73) and Flanders (1974: 229, n. 21).

Another footnote quotes Postan, who drew a connection between the early fourteenth-century "collapse of Italian finance...the breeding of the new cloth industry (in England)," and the Hundred Years War (1974: 28, n. 44). Wallerstein, however, does not pursue the implications of this note, using the Hundred Years War only as one of the factors that intensified the crisis of feudalism by forcing states to adopt war economies, and hence to increase taxes (1974: 21, 28-29). Nor does his analysis bring out the subsequent phase of Italian imperialism in England. As the development of the English woolen industry intensified competition for raw wool on the continent, north Italian cities increasingly specialized in the manufacture of silks, brocades, and velvets, and in the transhipment of Oriental luxuries acquired through long distance trade. Wallerstein, borrowing Postan's phrase, refers to the "precocious mercantilism" of the rising English who, in the fifteenth century, squeezed out "alien merchants, the Italians in particular..." But this reference, embedded in the analysis of the rise of England and coming on page 229, is detached from an explanation for anti-Italian sentiment. The explanation is implicit in the footnote on page 40 (mentioned above) which concerns the "steady outflow of bullion from northwest Europe to Italy to the Levant to India," an outflow that moved against Italian and Oriental wares (Holmes 1960).

In other words, *The Modern World-System*, notwithstanding its contribution to elucidating a global economy, contains no sustained discussion of the relationship between the colonial pressure exerted over England by Flanders and northern Italy, and England's *resistance* to this pressure as manifested in the expulsion of Italian financiers and merchants, the development of an indigenous textile industry, the enactment of endless sumptuary laws, and the pursuit of war, just as there is no concentrated assessment of the environmental conditions that permitted this relatively small but fortunate nation to raise both sheep and armies at the same time.

Wallerstein contributes significantly to the refinement of a new theory of change by providing concepts and illustrations that clarify the two fundamental processes upon which applications of the theory depend: the processes of regional differentiation and inter-regional dominance, resistance, competition. In addition, by applying the theory to Europe, his work pushes social science toward an understanding of change in which Western and non-Western, traditional and modern, peoples are subject, if not to similar outcomes, then at least to similar laws. Overall the book is supportive of a position, expressed well by William McNeill, that "surely the assumption of uniformity in the range of human behavior has more to recommend it than any assertion of systematic difference between civilized and uncivilized, rational and non-rational, Western and non-Western modes of conduct" (1974). It appears, however, that Wallerstein's analysis of England's transformation, as of many of the precapitalist events he explores, departs from this position. Leaving out environmental variables of significance to the process of regional differentiation, and failing to examine the full implications of inter-regional dominance, it does not raise the question whether the rise of England can be understood within the same intellectual framework as the fall of Poland.

This essay has suggested that, to discover laws that apply to precapitalist as well as capitalist social change, it is necessary to view the luxury trade not merely as a stimulus to production, or an adjunct to stratification, but also as a series of long distance exchanges of relevance to the capture of energy. Because before the capitalist transformation, primitive means of transportation restricted the flow of bulk goods, we are inclined to think that energy was stagnant too. If, however, some luxuries, and in particular gold and silver, were readily convertible into energy resources across much of the Old World, their movement constituted a disguised transfer of essential goods. The movement of slaves (not discussed here) often paralleled the movement of gold, and was also an energy flow. Slaves ate for ten to twenty years in their homeland before raiders or traders took them off. In effect this eliminated the difficulty of transporting an equivalent amount of food, especially as most of them walked from their neolithic villages to civilization (e.g., McNeill 1964: 28-29; Wilbur 1943).

There is no question that slaves and precious metals conferred status upon their owners and can be classified as luxuries. But, when the concept luxury is opposed to the concept utility, the power and energy dimensions of a rich man's, or a rich institution's, "things" fade from view. Notwithstanding their luxury status -- in fact precisely because they were highly valued -- gold and other preciosities often served a political end, either in war or in the construction of great patron-client chains. As such they were no less critical than food to resource mobilization.

The idea that one should conceptually oppose luxuries to essentials is central to *The Modern World-System*. Difficult to maintain with consistency, I think that it accounts for the book's confusing approach to precapitalist social change. Wallerstein, however, is hardly alone to insist on it. Rather, the implied opposition seems closely related to other dualisms that are profoundly ingrained in Western social thought: between spirit and matter, mind and body, work and play. When placed in such a dichotomous frame of reference, the word "luxury" conjures up the profligate excesses that are suggested by its Latin connotations, lasciviousness and lust.

In conclusion, I would like to propose that thinking about a precapitalist world-system will help clarify the Western intellectual tendency to drive a wedge between necessities and luxuries; the same wedge that separates God from the Devil. The self-confident ideologues of a core-area like Byzantium would not have felt the need to stigmatize luxuries, nor would culture brokers in peripheral areas which over the centuries accommodated to the demands of external dominants. But in Western Europe which, although peripheral, was propitiously located to resist predation, vigilance would have made sense. If so, then Wallerstein's categorical claim that luxuries are non-essential -- read dangerous and corrupting -- originated as the ideological aspect of a secular movement from import restriction and import substitution to eventual industrial development. Such a conclusion puts *The Modern World-System* at a threshold. While not yet giving us culture-free answers to such "big" questions as "Why Europe?" and "Why England?," it nevertheless offers the intellectual tools for a new and much broader understanding of this part of the world than social science has had in the past. One anticipates that it will stimulate undertakings, among historians too, that will push familiar arguments to another level.

NOTES

1. Some of the background for this essay derives from a seminar on Long Distance Trade, sponsored by the Anthropology Program of the Graduate Center of the City University of New York. I am grateful to student and faculty participants for help in formulating ideas about the significance of trade to European development and for specific descriptions of trading networks in other parts of the world. Special thanks go to one of the participants, Peter Schneider, for critically reviewing and mercilessly editing this manuscript, and to Rod Aya, Jo C. Lewis, and Shirley Lindenbaum whose comments also contributed to its final form.

2. In the following reference to pepper, Wallerstein reveals the particular difficulties that surround its classification: "Pepper, it may be argued, was not quite a luxury, nor even spices, for they were essential to the preservation of food and as medicine. Once again, it was a matter of degree. The food that was preserved was largely meat, not quite a luxury but not quite destined either for those on subsistence diets. Likewise the medicines" (1974: 333). Pliny, who could not understand the attraction of pepper to the Roman upper class which imported it "all the way from India!" was more straightforward. Pepper, he wrote, "has nothing in it that can plead as a recommendation to either fruit or berry; its only desirable quality being a certain pungency..." (quoted in Lach 1965: 16).

3. The closest Wallerstein comes to a description of the political significance of luxuries is his suggestion that "elaborate court ceremonial was developed, the better to remove the monarch from contact with banal work (and incidentally the better to provide employment for court aristocrats, keeping them thereby close enough to be supervised and checked)" (1974: 146). He does not pursue the implications of the parenthetical remark.

4. Over the centuries, gold became so universally instrumental to energy mobilization that it served this purpose even where it was abundant, for example in the gold-producing kingdoms of West Africa. In sixteenth-century Bornu, the royal hounds were chained with gold, yet "the Bornuese insisted on paying for the horses (imported from the Barbary coast) with slaves, of which, owing to constant wars with their weaker neighbors, they had far more than they needed. They would give as many as fifteen or twenty slaves for a single horse, but the Barbary merchants would have much preferred gold" (Bolvill 1968: 151).

Terray's analysis of a seventeenth-century kingdom that regularly exported gold indicates that the kings and chiefs stockpiled this metal "either to buy captives or to buy arms which would assist in capturing them" (1974: 333). Rather than being objects of trade, captives in this case mined the gold.

5. Although wool was heavier and warmer than either cotton or silk, this did not detract from its value in tropical and semi-tropical environments where sheep were rare. Even after lighter wools and worsteds began to flood the market in the sixteenth century, heavy fulled broadcloths continued to serve as luxury fabrics in warm climates (Rapp 1975: 520-521).

REFERENCES

Adams, R. M. 1974. "Anthropological Perspectives on Ancient Trade." *Current Anthropology* 15: 211-239.

Amin, S. 1974. *Accumulation on a World Scale*. New York: Monthly Review Press.

Baran, P. A. 1957. *The Political Economy of Growth*. New York: Monthly Review Press.

Bloch, M. 1961. *Feudal Society*, trans. by L. A. Manyon. London: Routledge and Kegan Paul.

Blok, A. 1969. "Mafia and Peasant Rebellion as Contrasting Factors in Sicilian Latifundism." *European Journal of Sociology* 10: 95-116.

_____ 1974. *The Mafia of a Sicilian Village, 1860-1960: A Study of Violent Peasant Entrepreneurs*. New York: Harper and Row.

Bovill, E. W. 1968. *The Golden Trade of the Moors*. second ed. London: Oxford University Press.

Braudel, F. 1973. *Capitalism and Material Life, 1400-1800*, trans. by Mirian Kochan. London: Weidenfeld and Nicolson.

Cowgill, G. L. 1975. "On Causes and Consequences of Ancient and Modern Population Changes." *American Anthropologist* 77: 505-25.

Emmanuel, A. 1972 *Unequal Exchange*. New York: Monthly Review Press.

Fairbank, J. K. 1969. *Trade and Diplomacy on the China Coast: The Opening of the Treaty Ports, 1842-1854*. Stanford: Stanford University Press.

Fairbank, J. K., and S. Y. Teng. 1941. "On the Ch'ing tributary system." *Harvard Journal of Asiatic Studies* 6: 135-246.

Frank, A. G. 1967 *Capitalism and Underdevelopment in Latin America: Historical Studies of Chile and Brazil*. New York: Monthly Review Press.

Graziano, L. 1975. "A Conceptual Framework for the Study of Clientelism." Occasional Papers, Western Societies Program. Cornell University Center for International Studies, Ithaca, New York.

Grierson, P. 1959. "Commerce in the Dark Ages: a Critique of the Evidence." *Royal Historical Society of London*, Series 5, Vol. 9.

Heckscher, E. F. 1955. *Mercantilism*, revised ed., Vol. II. London: George Allen and Unwin Ltd.

Holmes, G. A. 1960. "Florentine Merchants in England, 1346-1436." *Economic History Review*, second series 13: 193-208.

Lach, D. F. 1965 *Asia in the Making of Europe*, Vol. 1, *The Century of Discovery* (Book One). Chicago: The University of Chicago Press.

McNeill, W. H. 1964. *Europe's Steppe Frontier, 1500-1800.* Chicago: The University of Chicago Press.

_____ 1974. "Comment on R. M. Adams, Anthropological Perspectives on Ancient Trade." *Current Anthropology* 15: 251-252.

Miller, J. I. 1969. *The Spice Trade of the Roman Empire, 29 B.C. to A.D. 641.* Oxford: Clarendon Press.

Miskimin, H. A. 1969. *The Economy of Early Renaissance Europe, 1300-1460.* Englewood Cliffs, N.J.: Prentice Hall.

Munro, J. H. A. 1972. *Wool, Cloth, and Gold: The Struggle for Bullion in Anglo-Burgundian Trade, 1340-1478.* Tononto: University of Toronto Press.

Neale, W. C. 1976. *Monies in Societies.* San Francisco: Chandler and Sharp.

Needham, J. 1954. *Science and Civilization in China, Vol. I, Introductory Orientations.* Cambridge: Cambridge University Press.

Pirenne, H. 1909. "Draps de Frise ou draps de Flandre? Un petit problème d'histoire économique à l'époque carolingienne." *Vierteljahrschrift fur Social-und Wirstschaftsgeschichte* 7: 308-315.

Rapp, R. T. 1975. "The Unmaking of the Mediterranean Trade Hegemony: International Trade Rivalry and the Commercial Revolution." *Journal of Economic History* 35: 499-525.

Root W. 1971. *The Food of Italy.* New York: Atheneum.

Seers, D. 1970. "The Stages of Economic Growth of a Primary Producer Country in the Middle of the Twentieth Century," in R. I. Rhodes, ed., *Imperialism and Underdevelopment, a Reader.* New York: Monthly Review Press.

Servoise, R. 1966. "Les relations entre la Chine et l'Afrique au XVme Siècle." *Le Mois en Afrique* 6: 30-45.

Tannahill, R. 1973. *Food in History.* New York: Stein and Day Publishers.

Terray, E. 1974. "Long-distance Exchange and the Formation of the State: the Case of the Abron Kingdom of Gyaman." *Economy and Society*, 3: 315-45.

Verlinden, C. 1955. *L'esclavage dans l'Éurope médiévale, Vol. I, Peninsule Ibérique et France*. Brugge: "Del Tempel."

Wallerstein, I. 1974. *The Modern World-System: Capitalist Agriculture and the Origins of the European World-Economy in the Sixteenth Century*. New York: Academic Press.

_____ 1974a. "The Rise and Future Demise of the World Capitalist System." *Comparative Studies in Society and History* 16: 387-415.

Wheatley, P. 1975. "Satyranta in Suvanadvipa: from Reciprocity to Redistribution in Ancient Southeast Asia." in Sabloff and Lamberg Karlovsky, eds., *Ancient Civilization and Trade*. Albuquerque: University of New Mexico Press.

Wiens, H. J. 1967 *Han Chinese Expansion in South China*. New York: The Shoe String Press.

Wilbur, C. M. 1943. *Slavery in China During the Former Han Dynasty, 206 B.C.-A.D. 25*. Chicago: Field Museum of Natural History.

Wolf, E. R. 1967. "Understanding Civilizations" (A Review Article). *Comparative Studies in Society and History* 9: 446-66.

Yang, L. 1952. *Money and Credit in China; a Short History*. Cambridge, Mass.: Harvard University Press.

3

5000 Years of World System History: The Cumulation of Accumulation

Barry K. Gills and Andre Gunder Frank

INTRODUCTORY SUMMARY

We argue that the main features of the economic and interstate world system already analyzed by Wallerstein (1974) and Modelski (1987) for the "modern" world system, and for earlier ones by Chase-Dunn (1986, 1989) and others, and in this book by Chase-Dunn and Hall (Chapter 1) and Wilkinson (Chapter 4 and also 1987) also characterize the development of this *same* world system in medieval and ancient times, indeed for at least the past five millennia. These features are 1) the historical continuity and development of a single world economy and inter-polity system; 2) capital accumulation, technological progress, and ecological adaptation/degradation as the principal motor forces in the world system; 3) the hierarchical center-periphery political economic structure of the world system; 4) alternate periods of political economic hegemony and rivalry (and war) in the world system; 5) and long political economic cycles of growth/accumulation, center/periphery positions, hegemony/rivalry, etc. Our study of the unequal structure and uneven dynamic of this world system is based, like a three legged stool, on economic, political, and cultural analysis.

This essay covers the following topics and advances the following theses, beginning with the most concrete historical ones and going on to progressively more abstract theoretical ones.

I.   WORLD SYSTEM ORIGINS

•1.   **The origins** of our present world system (WS) can and should be traced back at least 5000 years to the relations between Mesopotamia and Egypt.

•2.   **The ecological basis** of the WS accounts for its origins and much of its subsequent historical development.

•3.   **Economic connections** among various parts of the WS began much earlier and have been much more prevalent and significant than is often realized.

•4.   **World system extension** grew to include most of the Asio-Afro-European ecumenical ("Eastern" hemisphere) landmass and its outlying islands by 600 BC and incorporated much of the "Western" "New World" by 1500 AD, although there is increasing evidence of earlier contacts between them.

II.   WORLD SYSTEM ROUTES AND NEXUSES

•1.   **Maritime routes** furthered economic and other connections among many parts of the WS and contributed to its expansion in important ways.

•2.   **The Silk Roads,** over both land and maritime routes, formed a sort of spinal column and rib cage of the body of this WS for over 2000 years.

•3.   **Central Asia** has been a much neglected focal point of WS history both as a logistic nexus among its regions to the East, South and West and through the recurrent pulse of its own waves of migration and invasion into these regions.

•4.   **The Three Corridors and Logistic Nexuses** in what is now called the "Middle East," "Inner Asia," and some sea straits have always played especially significant bottle-neck choke-point roles in the development of the WS.

III. INFRASTRUCTURAL INVESTMENT, TECHNOLOGY AND ECOLOGY

- •1. **Infrastructural investment** accompanied and supported most parts of the WS from its beginning and throughout its historical development.
- •2. **Technological innovation** also played a similar and related role throughout the historical development of the WS and mediated in the competitive economic and military conflicts among its parts.
- •3. **Ecology**, however, always and still exercises an essential influence and constraint on this WS development.

IV. SURPLUS TRANSFER AND ACCUMULATION RELATIONS

- •1. **Surplus transfer and interpenetrating accumulation** among parts of the WS are its essential defining characteristics. This transfer means that no part of the WS would be as it was and is without its relations with other parts and the whole.
- •2. **Center-Periphery-Hinterland (CPH)** complexes and hierarchies among different peoples, regions and classes have always been an important part of WS structure. However, the occupancy of musical chair places within this structure has frequently changed and contributed to the dynamics of WS historical development.
- •3. **"Barbarian" nomad - sedentary "civilization" relations** have long been and continue to be especially significant and neglected aspects of CPH structure and WS development.

V. POLITICAL ECONOMIC MODES OF ACCUMULATION

- •1. **Modes of accumulation**, more than modes of production, are the essential institutional forms and variations of WS historical development; but they are not only localized or regional.
- •2. **Transitions in modes of accumulation** are not unidirectional in WS history and development.
- •3. **Public/private accumulation** are both collaborative and conflicting institutional forms and mixes of investment and accumulation.
- •4. **Economy/polity contradictions** characterize the WS throughout its history in that economic organization is much wider and WS wide, while

political state and even imperial organization is much more local and regional.

VI. HEGEMONY AND SUPER-HEGEMONY

•1. **Hegemony** is the political *and economic* (and sometimes also cultural) domination of peoples and regions in parts of the WS, which is based on the centralization of accumulation in the same.
•2. **Cycles of accumulation and hegemony** are causally interrelated and characterize the development of the WS throughout its history.
•3. **Super-hegemony** is the extension of hegemony or the hierarchical ordering of primus inter pares hegemonies to centralize accumulation on a WS level. Super-hegemony has been acknowledged for part of the 19th and 20th centuries, but may already have occurred earlier as well.
•4. **Cumulation of Accumulation** is the culminating synthesis of the ecological, economic, technological, political, social, and cultural structures and processes in WS history.

VII. A HISTORICAL MATERIALIST POLITICAL ECONOMY AND RESEARCH AGENDA

•1. **Historical materialist political economic summary conclusions** are drawn from the foregoing arguments.
•2. **Political, economic and cultural three legged stools** characterize the WS through the interrelations and mutual support of all three aspects of social history. Therefore, any historical materialist political economy of the WS must incorporate all three.
•3. **Analytic and research agendas on the structure and dynamics of WS history** over 5000 or more years must search for more system wide characteristics, changes, perhaps even cycles, and development.

I. WORLD SYSTEM ORIGINS

1. The Origins

The designation in time of the origin of the world system depends very much on what concept of system is employed. We may illustrate this problem by analogy with the origins of a major river system. For instance, look at the Missouri-Mississippi river system. In one sense, each major branch has its own origin. Yet the Mississippi River can be said to have a later derivative origin where the two major branches join together, near St. Louis, Missouri. By convention, the river is called "The Mississippi" and it is said to originate in Minnesota. Yet the larger and longer branch is called "the Missouri," which originates in the Rocky Mountains in Montana. Of course, all of these also have other larger and smaller inflows, each with their own point(s) of origin. The problem is how to set a fixed point of origin when in fact no such single point of origin exists for the river system as a whole. In the case of the world system it would be possible to place its origins far up stream in the Neolithic period. However, it may be more appropriate to discuss the origins further down stream, where major branches converge.

By the river system analogy, we may identify the separate origins of Sumer, Egypt, and the Indus as sometime in the fourth to the third millenniums BC. The world system begins with their later confluence. David Wilkinson (1989) dates the birth of "Central Civilization," through the political - conflictual confluence of Mesopotamia and Egypt into one over-arching states system, at around 1500 BC. Wilkinson's work is of very great value to the analysis of world system history. Essentially, the confluence of "Mesopotamia" and "Egypt" gave birth to the world system. However, by the criteria of defining systemic relations, spelled out below, the confluence occurs considerably earlier than 1500 BC. By economic criteria of "inter-penetrating accumulation," the confluence included the Indus valley and the area of Syria and the Levant. Thus, the confluence occurred sometime in the early or mid third millennium BC, that is by about 2700-2400 BC.

2. The Ecological Basis

Historical materialist political economy begins with the recognition that "getting a living" is the ultimate basis of human social organization. The ultimate basis of "getting a living" is ecological however. The invention of agriculture made possible the production of a substantial surplus. Gordon Childe (1951) made famous the term "Neolithic Revolution" to describe the profound effects on human social organization brought about by the production of an agricultural surplus. The subsequent "Urban Revolution" and the states that developed on this basis contributed to the formation of our world system.

From the outset, this social organization had an economic imperative based on a new type of relationship with the environment. The alluvial plains of Egypt, Mesopotamia and Indus are similar in that their rich water supply and fertile soil makes possible the production of a large agricultural surplus when the factors of production are properly organized. However, all three areas were deficient in many natural resources, such as timber, stone, and certain metals. Therefore, they had an ecologically founded economic imperative to acquire certain natural resources from outside their own ecological niches in order to "complete" their own production cycles. Urban civilization and the state required the maintenance of a complex division of labor, a political apparatus, and a much larger trade or economic nexus than that under the direct control of the state. Thus, the ecological origins of the world system point to the inherent instability of the urban civilizations and the states from which it emerged. This instability was both ecological - economic and strategic. Moreover, the two were intertwined from the beginning.

Economic and strategic instability and insecurity led to efforts to provide for the perpetual acquisition of all necessary natural resources, even if the required long distance trade routes were outside the direct political control of the state. This was only possible through manipulated trade and through the assertion of direct political controls over the areas of supply. The internal demographic stability, and/or demographic expansion, of the first urban centers depended upon such secure acquisition of natural resources.

However, in a field of action in which many centers are expanding simultaneously, there must come a point when their spheres of influence become contiguous, and then overlap. As the economic nexus of the first urban civilizations and states expanded and deepened, competition and conflict over control of strategic sources of materials and over the routes by which they were acquired tended to intensify. For example, control over certain metals was crucial to attaining technological and military superiority vis a vis contemporary rivals.   Failure to emulate the most advanced technology constituted, then as now, a strategic default.

The ultimate rationale for the origins of the world system were thus embedded in the economic imperative of the urban based states.   A larger and larger economic nexus was built up.   Specialization within the complex division of labor deepened, while the entire nexus expanded territorially "outward." In the process, more and more ecological niches were assimilated into one interdependent economic system.   Thereby, the world system destroyed and assimilated self-reliant cultures in its wake.

By the third millennium BC, the Asio-Afro-European economic nexus, upon which the world system was based, was already well established. Thereafter, the constant shifts in position among metropoles in the world system cannot be properly understood without analysis of the ecological and technological factors "compelling" certain lines of action.   The rise and decline of urban centers and states can be made more understandable by placing them within the world systemic context.   This also involves paying attention to their role in the economic nexus, particularly with regard to the sources and supply of key commodities and natural resources.   The logic of the political structure of the world system is one in which the security of the member states, and their ability to accumulate surplus, is perpetually vulnerable to disruption.   This situation created a dynamic of perpetual rivalry.   Thus, attempts are made to extend political control over strategic areas of supply in the overall economic nexus.

3.   Economic Connections

New historical evidence suggests that economic connections through trade and migration, as well as through pillage and conquest, have been much more prevalent and much wider in scope than was previously recognized.   They have also gone much farther back through world history than is generally admitted.   By the same token, manufacturing, transport, commercial and other service activities are also older and more widespread than often suggested. The long history and systemic nature of these economic connections have not received nearly as much attention as they merit (Adams 1943).   Even more neglected have been these trade connections' far reaching importance in the social, political, and cultural life of "societies" and their relations with each other in the world system as a whole.   Even those who do study trade connections, as for instance Philip Curtin's (1984) work on cross-cultural trade diasporas, often neglect systematic study of the world systemic complex of these trade connections.

Historical evidence to date indicates that economic contacts in the Middle East ranged over a very large area even several thousand years before the first urban states appeared. The Anatolian settlement Catal Huyuk is often cited as an example of a community with long distance trade connections some seven or eight thousand years ago. Jericho is another often cited example. Trade or economic connections between Egypt and Mesopotamia were apparently somewhat intermittent before 3000 BC, and therefore possibly not systemic. However, both Egypt and Mesopotamia very early on developed economic connections with Syria and the Levant, which formed a connecting corridor between the two major zones. The putative first pharaoh of unified Egypt, Narmer, may have had economic connections to the Levant. Certainly by 2700 BC, Egypt had formal political and economic relations with the city of Byblos on the Levantine coast. Byblos is probably the earliest port of economic contact mentioned in both Egyptian and Mesopotamian historical sources.

For both Egypt and Mesopotamia, war and trade with Syria and the Levant involved the search for access to strategic and other materials, such as timber, metals, oils, and certain luxury consumption goods. The apparent goal of Akkadian imperial expansion was to gain the benefits of putting all of the most strategic routes in one vast corridor from the Mediterranean to the Persian Gulf under its sole control. There is evidence that Akkad maintained maritime economic connections with the Indus, known as "Meluhha," via ports in the Persian Gulf. Thus, Akkad consolidated a privileged position in the overall economic nexus. The city states of Syria and the Levant became the objects of intense rivalry between Egypt and Mesopotamia. Oscillation occurred in the control of these areas: from the first and second dynasties of Egypt, over to Akkad, then to the third dynasty of Ur. By the nineteenth century BC, Egypt again exercised influence over most of the Levant as vassal states. It is clear that throughout a considerable historical period, even to the time of the Assyrian and then the Persian empires, Syria and the Levant played a crucial role as logistical inter-linkage zones and entrepots within the world system. They linked the Mesopotamian, Egyptian, and Indus zones in one world system.

4. World System Extension

Accumulation is a major incentive for, and the ultimate cause of, economic, political, and military expansion by and inter-linkage within the world system. Therefore, the process of accumulation and its expansion is also importantly related to the extension of the boundaries of the world system. Two additional analogies of expansion may be useful to understand the process: the glacier analogy and the ink blot analogy. By analogy to a glacier, the world system expanded along a course of its own making, in part adapting to pre-existing topology and in part itself restructuring this topology. By analogy to an ink blot, the world system also spread outward, beyond its area of early confluence. Probably the most spectacular single instance of this expansion was the "discovery" of the New World and later Oceania. David Wilkinson (1987) also sees Central Civilization as expanding into other areas and societies and incorporating them into itself. In one sense, the process is one of simple incorporation of previously unincorporated areas, on analogy with the expansion of an ink blot.

However, the incorporation of some regions into the world system also involved processes more like merger than mere assimilation, as when two expanding ink blots merge. For instance, the incorporation of India, and especially of China, appear to be more merger than assimilation. Mesopotamian trade with the Indus was apparently well established at the time of the Akkadian empire. Repeated evidence of economic contact with India exists, though with significant periods of intermittent disruption. These disruptions make it difficult to set a firm date for the merger of India with the world system. Chinese urban centers and states appear to have developed essentially autonomously in the archaic Shang period. However, the overland routes to the central world system to the west were already opened by the end of the second millennium BC, particularly as migratory routes for peoples of Central and Inner Asia. The actual historical merger of Chinese complexes into the world system comes only after state formation in China reached a more advanced stage, in the late Zhou period. A series of loose hegemons began with Duke Huan of Qi (685-643 BC) and a process of unification of smaller feudatories into larger territorial states occurred. According to Wolfram Eberhard (1977), the eventual victory of the state of Qin and the creation of the first centralized empire in China was influenced by Qin's strong trade relations with Central Asia. These economic connections allowed Qin to accumulate considerable profit from trade. The Wei and Tao valleys of the Qin state were "the only means of transit from east to west. All traffic from and to Central Asia had to take this route" (Eberhard, 1977 p.60).

The maintenance of maritime and overland trade routes, and the peoples located in the areas between major zones, play key logistical interlinkage roles in the process of merger. In the formation of the world system, the inter-action of high civilization with tribal peoples, especially in Inner and Central Asia, but also in Arabia and Africa, played a crucial but largely neglected role, to which we shall return below.

II. WORLD SYSTEM ROUTES AND NEXUSES

1. Maritime Routes

The advertising blurb of the just published *The Sea-Craft of Prehistory* by Paul Johnstone (1989) reads "the nautical dimension of prehistory has not received the attention it deserves.... Recent research has shown that man travelled and tracked over greater distances and at a much earlier date than has previously been thought possible. Some of these facts can be explained by man's mastery of water transport from earliest times." Generally the sea routes were cheaper and favored over the overland ones. Some particularly important maritime routes are discussed below.

2. The Silk Roads

The Silk Roads formed a sort of spinal column and rib cage - or more analogously perhaps, the circulatory system - of the body of this world system for some 2000 years before 1500 AD. These "roads" extended overland between China, through Inner and Central Asia, to the "Middle East" (West Asia). From there, they extended through the Mediterranean into Africa and Europe. However, this overland complex was also connected by numerous maritime silk "road" stretches through the Mediterranean, Black Sea, Red Sea, Persian Gulf, and along many rivers. Moreover, the predominantly overland Silk Road complex was complemented by a vast maritime Silk Road network centered on the Indian Ocean through the Arabian Sea and Bay of Bengal, and on the South China Sea. These maritime Silk Roads in turn were connected by overland portage across the Kra isthmus on the Malay Peninsula, as well as by ship through the Malaccan Straits between it and Sumatra, etc.

The Silk Roads of course derive their name from China's principal export product to the West. However, the trade of items and peoples extended far beyond silk alone. Indeed, the silk had to be paid for and complemented by a large variety of other staple and luxury goods, money and services, including enslaved and other people who performed them. Thus, the Silk Roads also served as the trade routes, urban and administrative centers, and military, political, and cultural sinews of a vast and complex division of labor and cultural diffusion.

3. Central Asia

If one looks at a map of Eurasia, it becomes clear that Central Asia (in present Afghanistan and Soviet Central Asia) was well positioned to act as the ultimate nodal center. Central Asia was the crossroads of a world system in which China, India, Persia, Mesopotamia, the Levant and the Mediterranean basin all participated. For instance, Central Asia played a key role in the joint participation in the world system of Han China, Gupta India, Parthian Persia and the Roman empire.

However, Central and Inner Asia were also more than the meeting points of others. Inner and Central Asia also originated their own cycles of outward invasory/migratory movements in all directions. These cycles lasted an average of approximately two centuries and occurred in roughly half millennium intervals. For instance, there were waves of invasions from 1700-1500 BC, 1200-1000 BC, around 500 BC, around 0, from 400-600 AD and 1000-1200/1300 AD. Each inner wave pushed out outer waves, except the last one of Chinggis Khan and his successors to Tamerlane after him, who overran all themselves.

Whether or not all these invasions responded to climatic changes, presumably they were both cause and effect of changes in rates of demographic growth and decline, which may in turn have climatic causes. However, they were also caused by - and in turn had effects on - the ecological, socioeconomic and political relations with their civilized neighbors. Thus, Inner and Central Asia and its pulse require special attention in world system history. How central was Central Asia to world system history? To what extent was Central Asia, and not primarily the other civilized areas, something of a motor force of change in the whole system? How was the rise and decline of various cities (Samarkand!) and states in this area related to system wide developments in trade?

The place and role of Central Asia is as important as it is neglected. The entire development of the world system has been profoundly affected by the successive waves of invasion from the Eurasian steppes on the perimeter of the agro-industrial zones. This "system implosion" is such a major phenomenon that it cries out for systemic study and explanation. These system implosions were not *deus ex machina*, but integral to the overall developmental logic of the world system's expansionary trajectory. In particular, the invasions and migrations from Inner and Central Asia were always instrumental in transforming the economic, social, political and cultural life of their neighboring civilizations - and in forming their racial and ethnic complexions. Nor has the enormously important role of Central Asia as an intermediary zone in the world system received the systematic analysis which its functions merit. Other nomadic and tribal peoples, for instance on the Arabian Peninsula before Mohammed and in much of Africa, also participated in world system history and world accumulation in ways which have not been acknowledged except by very few specialists.

4.   The Three Corridors and Logistic Nexuses

Three magnets of attraction for political economic expansion stand out. One is sources of human (labor) and/or material **inputs** (land, water, raw materials, precious metal, etc.) and technological inputs into the process of accumulation. The second is **markets** to dispose of one zone's surplus production to exchange for more inputs, and to capture stored value. The third, and perhaps most significant, are the most privileged **nexuses or logistical corridors** of inter-zonal trade. Bottleneck control over the supply routes of raw materials, especially of metals and other strategic materials, plays a key role in attracting powers to such areas. This may also provide a basis upon which to make a bid for expansion of imperial power. Especially here, economic, political and military conflict and/or cultural, "civilizational," religious and ideological influence all offer special advantages. That is, special advantages for tapping into the accumulation and the system of exploitation of other zones in benefit of one's own accumulation. Therefore, it is not mere historical coincidence that these three nexus areas have recurrently been the fulcra of rivalry, commerce, and of religious and other cultural forms of diffusion.

Certain strategically placed regions and corridors have played such especially important roles in world system development. They have been magnets which attracted the attention of expansionist powers and also of migrants and invaders. Major currents of thought also migrated through them. This attention is based on their role in the transfer of surplus within the world system, without which the world system does not exist. Certain metropoles have become attractive in and of themselves due to their positions along trade corridors, the growth of a market within the metropolitan city, and the accumulated wealth of the metropole itself. The rise and fall of great regional metropolitan centers and their "succession" reflects extra-regional changes in which they participate. For example, the succession of metropoles in Egypt from Memphis to Alexandria to Cairo reflects fundamental underlying shifts in world system structure. So does the succession in Mesopotamia from Babylon to Seleucia to Baghdad.

Three nexus corridors have played a particularly pivotal and central logistical interlinkage role in the development of the world system.

•1. The Nile - Red Sea corridor (with canal or overland connections between them and to the Mediterranean Sea, and open access to the Indian Ocean and beyond).

•2. The Syria - Mesopotamia - Persian Gulf corridor (with overland routes linking the Mediterranean coast through Syria, on via the Orontes, Euphrates and Tigris rivers, to the Persian Gulf, which gives open access to the Indian Ocean and beyond). This nexus also offered connections to overland routes to Central Asia.

•3. The Aegean - Black Sea - Central Asia corridor (connecting the Mediterranean via the Dardanelles and Bosporus to the over-land "Silk Roads" to and from Central Asia, from where connecting routes extended overland to India and China).

The choice between the two primarily sea route corridors mostly fell to the Persian Gulf route. It was both topographically and climatically preferred to the Red Sea route. Moreover, the Persian Gulf corridor had connecting routes overland to Central Asia, which came to serve as a central node in the transfer of surplus among the major zones of the world system.

These three nexus corridors represented not only mere routes of trade. Repeatedly, they were integrated zones of economic and political development and recurrently the locus of attempts to build imperial systems. As the world system expanded and deepened, attempts were made by certain powers to place either two or all three corridors under a single imperial structure. Thus, such a power would control the key logistical interlinkages which have been central to the world system. For instance, the Assyrian empire attempted to control both the Syrian - Mesopotamian corridor and the Nile - Red Sea corridor, but succeeded only briefly and sporadically. The Persian empire likewise controlled both these corridors for a time, and it also had partial control over the Aegean - Black Sea - Central Asian corridor. Thus the Persian empire is the first historical instance of a "three corridor hegemony." Alexander the Great's grand strategic design for a world empire or "world system hegemony" included plans to control all three corridors, plus the Indus complexes and the west Mediterranean basin. His successors split the Macedonian conquests almost precisely into realms parallel to the three corridors. They allowed the Indus to fall out of Seleucid influence to the Mauryan empire and the west Mediterranean basin to control by Carthage and Rome. During the Hellenistic period, the recurrent rivalries between the Ptolomaic and Seleucid dynasties are indicative of continued struggles between the corridors for privileged position in the world system's accumulation processes. Even the Roman imperium did not entirely unify the three corridors however, since Mesopotamia was denied to Rome first by the Parthians, and later by the Sassanian Persians. They used their control of this area to extract considerable profit from the trade between Rome, India, and China.

Of course, each of these three main corridors had competing/complimentary alternative variants and feeder routes of its own. For instance, there were several silk roads between East and West and different feeder routes in East and Central Asia and to/from South Asia. There were also routes connecting Northern and Western Europe through the Baltic Sea via the Dnieper, Don, Volga, and other Ukrainian and Russian routes. There were routes connecting the Adriatic to continental Europe, and the east Mediterranean to the west Mediterranean. Similarly, topological and other factors also favored some locations and routes as magnets of attraction and logistic nexuses in and around Asia. They deserve much more attention than they have received in world history. As the Asio-Afro-European nexus expanded and deepened, the number and role of these routes and choke points increased. At the same time, their relative importance changed vis a vis each other as a result of world system development. Locations such as the Straits of Malacca and of Ceylon had significant logistical roles for very long periods of world system development.

The three overland and sea route corridors and their extensions were the most important nexuses between Europe and Asia for two millennia before the shift to transoceanic routes in the fifteenth and sixteenth centuries. This historic shift from the centrality of the three corridors to that of transoceanic logistical interlinkages was probably the single most important logistical shift in world history and world system development. However, rather than **creating** it *a la* Wallerstein (1974), the shift occurred **within** the already existing world system.

III. INFRASTRUCTURAL INVESTMENT, TECHNOLOGY AND ECOLOGY

1. Infrastructural Investment and Accumulation

Accumulation implies infrastructural investment and technological development. Infrastructural investment takes many forms in many sectors, such as agriculture, transportation, communications, the military, industrial and manufacturing infrastructure, and bureaucratic administration. There is investment even in ideological (symbolic) infrastructure, both of the cult of the state and of religion. In the state form of accumulation, the state seeks to create social wealth in order to extract it. By laying the basis for increases in production and facilitating accumulation, the state increases its own access to surplus and therefore its potential capabilities vis a vis rival states. This in turn helps it to protect "what we've got" and to get more. In the private form, the propertied elites likewise create wealth in order to extract it and invest in infrastructure to facilitate production and thereby accumulation. The ultimate rationale of such investment would in all cases be to preserve, enhance, and expand the basis of accumulation itself. The development of infrastructure and the technology it embodies feed back into the generation of surplus and accumulation. This growth of surplus in turn feeds back into further growth and development of infrastructure and technology in cumulative fashion. The pattern is spiral, whereby the world system itself grows and becomes more firmly "established" via infrastructural investment and accumulation.

2. Technological Innovation

Technological progress in techniques of production, organization and trade, both military and civilian, has long played an important, and often neglected, role in the history of the world system and in the changing relations among its parts. Technological advance and advantage has been crucial throughout history in armaments, shipping and other transportation as well as in construction, agriculture, metalworking and other manufacturing methods and facilities. Progress, leads, and lags in all of these have had significant contributory if not causative effects on (and also some derivative effects from) the regional and other relations of inequality within the world system. Some examples were examined by William McNeill (1982) in *The Pursuit of Power*.

Infrastructural investment is linked to technological change and to organizational innovation. Technological change in archaic and ancient periods, and even in medieval periods, was mostly slower than in modern industrial times. However, the essence of patterned relationships between technological innovation, infrastructural investment cycles, and the cycles of accumulation and hegemony (discussed below) probably have existed throughout history. When and what were the most significant technological innovations in world system history? Which innovations brought about restructuring of accumulation and of hegemony in the world system? Which altered the logistical interlinkages? The diffusion of technology across the world system is another major area for systematic and systemic analysis.

In the general period of the contemporaneous Roman/Byzantine, Parthian/Persian Sassanian, Indian Mauryan/Gupta and Chinese Han empires, cumulative infrastructural investments integrated each of these empires into a single world system. This high level of systemic integration was achieved via the well-developed logistic nexuses and the simultaneity of imperial expansion. At the end of that period, the entire world system experienced a general crisis. Hinterland peoples from Inner and Central Asia invaded Rome, Persia, India and China. They caused (or followed?) a decline in infrastructural investment and (temporary) serious disruption of the world system's logistical interlinkages compared to the previous era.

How is infrastructural investment linked to productivity and increases in productivity to the processes of accumulation in the world system? Techno-logical innovation and technological change has been pervasive in world system development. Gordon Childe (1942) pioneered a materialist analysis of the effects of technology on the ancient economy. Logistic capabilities, for instance those of maritime trade, depend on technological capability. So does the dynamic of military rivalry. Indeed, the expansion of the world system depended from the outset on technological capabilities. Invasions from the "barbarian" perimeter to the civilized centers depended upon the technological and military superiorities of the barbarians. Such invasions did not cease until "civilized" technological developments made the attainment of military superiority by the barbarians virtually impossible. By asserting a new military-technological superiority, the Russian and Manchu empires finally put an end to the strategic threat of Inner Asia in the seventeenth and eighteenth centuries AD.

The industrial revolution gave European powers the military capability to destroy or subordinate contemporary empires in the world system such as the Mughal in India, the Qing in China, and the Ottoman in the three corridors region.

3.   Ecology

Technology has always been intimately associated with the ecological interface of the world system and its natural resource base. For instance, the technologies of farming created a secular trend to place more and more area under agricultural production, thus to increase the sources of agricultural surplus. Particular technological innovations have dramatically affected the ecological interface, particularly those of industrialized production. Since the introduction of these technologies, the trend has been their extension across more and more of the world system, often with devastating ecological consequences.

There have been instances when environmental conditions brought about major changes in world system development. For instance, the salination of soils and silting up of irrigation works affected the relative economic strength of certain zones. For example, already before and even more after the sacking of Baghdad by the Mongols in 1258, Mesopotamia experienced relative decline. This was partly due to such environmental factors, and partly to shifts in logistical interlinkages in the world system.

Certain areas have been extremely difficult to incorporate into the world system for primarily ecological and/or topographical reasons.   These difficulties (still) characterize, for instance, the Tibetan plateau, the Amazonian basin, the Great Northern Arctic of Canada and the Soviet Union, and Antarctica. The social ecology of the peoples of Inner Asia, which Owen Lattimore (1940) contrasted to that of sedentary agricultural peoples, was a major factor in the world system's development for most of world history. The present ecological crises of industrial civilization remind us that ultimately ecology and the natural environment set limits on the expansion of the world system and on sustaining production and accumulation. If there have been any ecological cycles, rhythms, or trends, we should investigate what they are and how they have affected world system development.

IV.   SURPLUS TRANSFER AND ACCUMULATION RELATIONS

1.   Surplus Transfer and Interpenetrating Accumulation

The capture by elite A here (with or without its redistribution here) of part of the economic surplus extracted by elite B there means that there is "interpenetrating accumulation" between A and B. This transfer or exchange of surplus connects not only the two elites, but also their "societies'" economic, social, political, and ideological organization. That is, the transfer, exchange or "sharing" of surplus connects the elite A here not only to the elite B there. Surplus transfer also links the "societies'" respective processes of surplus management, their structures of exploitation and oppression by class and gender, and their institutions of the state and the economy. Thus, the transfer or exchange of surplus is not a socially "neutral" relationship, but rather a profoundly systemic one. Through sharing sources of surplus, the elite A here and the classes it exploits are systemically interlinked to the "mode of production," and even more important, to the **mode of accumulation in B** there. By extension, if part of the surplus of elite B here is also traded, whether through equal or more usually unequal exchange, for part of the surplus accumulated by elite C there, then not only B and C but also A and

C are systemically linked through the intermediary B. Then A, B and C are systemically connected in the same over-arching system of accumulation.

This means that surplus extraction and accumulation are "shared" or "interpenetrating" across otherwise discrete political boundaries. Thus, their elites participate in each others' system of exploitation vis a vis the producing classes. This participation may be through economic exchange relations via the market or through political relations (e.g., tribute), or through combinations of both. All of these relations characterize the millenarian relationship, for instance, between the peoples of China and Inner Asia. This inter-penetrating accumulation thus creates a causal interdependence between structures of accumulation and between political entities. Therefore the structure of each component entity of the world system is saliently affected by this interpenetration. Thus, empirical evidence of such interpenetrating accumulation through the transfer or exchange of surplus is the minimum indicator of a systemic relationship. Concomitantly, we should seek evidence that this interlinkage causes at least some element of economic and/or political restructuring in the respective zones. For instance, historical evidence of a fiscal crisis in one state or a zone of the world system (e.g., in third century Rome) as a consequence of an exchange of surplus with another zone would be a clear indicator of a relationship at a high level of systemic integration. Evidence of change in the mode of accumulation and the system of exploitation in one zone as a function of the transfer of surplus to another zone would also constitute evidence of systemic relations. Evidence of political alliances and/or conflict related to participation in a system of transfer of surplus would also be considered evidence of a systemic relation-ship. According to these criteria, if different "societies," empires, and civilizations, as well as other "peoples," regularly exchanged surplus, then they also participated in the same world system. That is "society" A here could and would not be the same as it was in the absence of its contact with B there, and *vice versa*.

Trade in high value luxury items, not to mention precious metals in particular, may, *contra* Wallerstein (1974, 1989), be even more important than lower value staple trade in defining systemic relations. This is because the high value "luxury" trade is essentially an inter-elite exchange. These commodities, besides serving elite consumption or accumulation, are typically also stores of value. They embody aspects of social relations of production, which reproduce the division of labor, the class structure, and the mode of accumulation. Precious metals are only the most obvious example, but many "luxury" commodities have played a similar role, as is admirably argued by Jane Schneider in chapter 2 above. Thus, trade in both high value "luxury" items and staple commodities are indicators of interpenetrating accumulation.

2.   Center-Periphery-Hinterland (CPH)

Center-periphery-hinterland (CPH) complexes and hierarchies among different peoples, regions and classes have always been an important part of world system structure. However, the occupancy of musical chair places within this structure has frequently changed and contributed to the dynamics of world system historical development. To what extent (and why?) have the world system and its parts been characterized by center-periphery and other structural inequalities? Wallerstein (1974 and other works) and Frank (1978 a,b, 1981) among others, have posed questions and offered answers about the center-periphery structure of the world system since 1500. Ekholm and Friedman (1982), Chase-Dunn and Hall (Chapter 1) and others are trying to apply similar analyses to world systems before 1500. The "necessity" of a division between center and periphery and the "function" of semiperipheries in between are increasingly familiar, not the least thanks to the widespread critiques of these ideas. Chase-Dunn and Hall (Chapter 1) survey the propositions and debates. Wilkinson (Chapter 4) examines center-periphery structures all over the world for 5,000 years. Rowlands, Larsen, and Kristiansen (1987) analyze center and periphery in the ancient world. Indeed, now this entire book is dedicated to examining precapitalist center-periphery relations. We argue, however, that these relations also characterize *this same world system* for several millennia back.

Chase Dunn and Hall (Chapter 1) and Wilkinson (Chapter 4) have already made the argument that center-periphery hierarchies characterize systemic development much further back in world historical development than 1500 AD. In fact, center-periphery relations characterize development since the origins of the state and systems of states. However, we agree with Thomas Hall (1986 and chapter 7 below) that we need a more comprehensive "center-periphery-hinterland" (CPH) concept than most other scholars have used. Hall (1986) refers to "contact peripheries." This hinterland is not directly penetrated by the extracting classes of the center, but nevertheless it has systemic links with the center-periphery zone and its processes of accumulation. Wallerstein's use of the term hinterland to mean external to the world system is insufficient because it neglects the structural and systemic significance of zones which are "outside" of, but nonetheless related to, the center-periphery complex. We, of course, wish to stress the contribution to accumulation among all participants, especially through the transfer of surplus, made by these hinterland-periphery-center "contacts." These CPH relationships have been insufficiently analyzed.

The CPH complex does not refer to mere geographical position, nor only to unequal levels of development. CPH also refers to the relations among the classes, peoples and "societies" that constitute the mode of accumulation. The CPH complex is the basic social complex upon which hegemony, as discussed below, is constructed in a larger systemic context. More research is necessary on how "geographical" position in a hegemonic structure affects class position in the CPH complex. We could expect to find that the class structure of a hegemonic state may be significantly altered by the surplus that this state accumulates from its subordinates in the CPH complex. For example, the subsidy to the plebeian class of Rome may be taken as an example of such systemic effects. Conversely, we might expect a CPH complex to give rise to increased exploitation of producers in subordinate positions.

The "hinterland" contains natural resources, including human labor, which are tapped by the center-periphery. However, what distinguishes the hinterland from the periphery is that the peoples of the hinterland are not fully, institutionally, subordinate to the center in terms of surplus extraction. That is, they retain some degree of social autonomy. If a hinterland people come under political means of extraction by the center, then the process of "peripheralization" begins. Nevertheless, despite a degree of social autonomy from the center, the hinterland is in systemic relations with the center. The frequency of center-hinterland conflict is one indicator of such systemic relations. The hinterland may also have functional roles in logistical interlinkage. In this sense, the hinterland may facilitate the transfer of surplus between zones of the world system. These roles of hinterlands merit as much theoretical attention in determining positional shifts and systems change as those of semiperipheries.

The center (or core) - periphery - hinterland concept is not intended to replace, but to extend, Wallerstein's (1974 and elsewhere, Arrighi and Drangel 1986) core - semiperiphery - periphery formulation. However, the semiperiphery has always been a weak and confusing link in the argument. The hinterland "extension" may confuse it still further and may counsel reformulation of the whole complex. For instance at a recent conference (with Wallerstein, Arrighi and Frank among others), Samir Amin suggested that the semiperiphery has functionally become the real periphery, because it is exploited by the center; while the "periphery" has been marginalized out of the system, because it no longer has anything (or anybody) for the center to exploit for its own accumulation. As argued above however, historically the hinterland has also contributed to core accumulation in the CPH complex.

Thus, CPH complexes are integral to the structure of the world system in all periods. They must be studied, not only comparatively, but also in their combination and interaction in the world system. It is important to examine how center - periphery zones expanded into the hinterland in order to understand the way in which accumulation processes were involved. The rationales of expansion and assimilation in the hinterland appear to be related to the "profitability" of such expansion, in terms of tapping new sources of surplus. They also help resolve internal contradictions in the center-periphery complex brought about as a result of exploitation and demographic pressure. Class conflict in the center-periphery complex is affected by the expansion of accumulation into the hinterland. Demographic trends are an important factor; the hinterland provides new resources to sustain the growing population of the center-periphery zone. The physical geographical limits of hinterland peripheralization by the center seem to be set by both logistical capabilities and by a cost-benefit calculus. Areas are occupied primarily if they can be made to pay for the cost of their own occupation or are deemed to be strategically necessary to protect another profitable area. Conversely, such areas are again abandoned if, or when, their occupation proves to be too costly. Fortification at such systemic boundaries has a dual function of keeping the barbarians out and keeping the producers in. That is, such fortification impedes military disruption of the zone of extraction and also impedes the escape of dependent-subordinate producers into the "free" zone.

3.   "Barbarian" Nomad - Sedentary "Civilization" Relations

It is important to examine how systemic links between center and hinterland are formed. How does the hinterland interact over time with the center-periphery complex and thereby affect changes in the structure of that complex itself, and vice versa? A particularly important aspect of this question is the nature of the historical relations between the so-called tribal "barbarians" and the so-called "civilized" "societies." How are the barbarians "assimilated" into civilization and yet also transform civilization? Throughout most of world history, this barbarian-civilization relationship has been crucial to the territorial expansion of the state, imperialism, and "civilization."

The work of Arnold Toynbee (1973), Thomas Hall (1986, 1989), Eric Wolf (1982), William McNeill (1964) and Owen Lattimore (1940, 1962) illuminate many aspects of how these center-periphery-hinterland hierarchies are created, deepened, and systemically transformed. Toynbee's "system implosion" is of particular interest. Robert Gilpin (1981) follows Toynbee to show how an older center is eventually encircled and engulfed by new states on the periphery, which implode into the center. Thus, a "center-shift" takes place by way of an implosion from the former periphery to the center of the system. For instance, this occurred with the creation of the Qin empire at the end of the Warring States period in China. It also happened with the creation of the Macedonian empire at the end of the classical period in Greece. In even earlier examples of such hinterland impact, the "tribal" Guti, the Amorites, the Kassites, and the Akkadians were intimately involved in the political cycles of archaic Mesopotamia. Each of these peoples made a transition from hinterland roles to that of ruling class in the center. Moreover, these invasions of the center by the hinterland took place for systemic reasons, not just gratuitously. Eberhard (1977) and Gernet (1985) analyze how Inner Asian nomads repeatedly invaded China to appropriate its productive structure and economic surplus. Frederick Teggart's (1939) study of correlations of historical events in Rome and China analyzes the systemic causal connections across the whole Asio-Afro-European economic nexus, which caused hinterland-center conflict in one zone to affect relations in another zone. The sequencing of conflicts follows a logic that corresponds to both logistical elements in the nexus, struggles over shares of accumulation, and social tensions due to the expansionary pressure of the center-periphery complex into the hinterland.

V. POLITICAL ECONOMIC MODES OF ACCUMULATION

1.   Modes of Accumulation

If we are to study any "modes" at all, we might better study the modes of
accumulation, instead of the "mode of production." In the world system,
production is the means to an end. That end is consumption and accumulation.   It may be useful to study the differences, the mutual relations,
combinations or the "articulations" of "public" (state) and "private" and
"redistributive" and "market" modes of accumulation. It is doubtful that any
of these modes, or other modes, have ever existed alone in any pure form
anywhere. However, we should study not only how modes of accumulation
differ and combine with each other "locally," but also how they interconnect
with each other throughout the world system as a whole. Thus, world system
history should both differentiate and combine modes of accumulation:
horizontally through space as well as vertically through time. The "articul-
ation" of modes is a way of analyzing how the mode(s) of accumulation in
one zone of the world system is(are) affected by systemic links with other
zones' mode(s) of accumulation.   Can the overall world system be
characterized by a single mode of accumulation? If not, why not?

Shifting the focus of analysis from production to accumulation need not
abandon analysis of the class structure. In fact, a focus on the relations of
accumulation should sharpen the analysis of class relations. Geoffrey de Ste
Croix (1981) argues that the key to every social formation is how the
"propertied classes" extract the surplus from the working classes and ensure
themselves a leisured existence. He defines a mode of production based on
the means by which the propertied classes obtain **most** of their surplus. This
approach is an alternative to trying to determine what form of relations of
production characterize the **entire** social formation. That is, he focuses on the
dominant mode of accumulation. Ste Croix delineates several means of
extracting surplus: wages, coerced labor (in many variants), rent, and through
the state (via taxes, corvee labor, and through "imperialism"). Interestingly,
Ste Croix explains the fall of the late Roman empire as due primarily to gross
over-extraction of surplus, over-concentration of wealth in the hands of the
upper classes, and the over-expansion of the bureaucratic and military
apparatus (1981 pp 502-503). The latter is similar to Paul Kennedy's (1987)
argument about military-economic overextension in *The Rise and Fall of the*

Great Powers. This analysis implies a link between cycles of accumulation and cycles of hegemony, to which we will return below.

Equal, or perhaps even greater, analytical emphasis is necessary on horizontal inter-elite conflicts over apportioning "shares" of the available social surplus. This struggle has its focus in the ultimate political determination of the mode of accumulation. To say that the elites of different zones of the world system share in each others' system of exploitation and surplus extraction through interpenetrating accumulation, is not to deny possible differences between these zones in terms of the mode of accumulation. The exchange or transfer of social surplus both affects and is affected by class structure. However, interpenetrating accumulation affects both the producing strata and the extracting-accumulating strata, though in different ways.

2. Transitions in Modes of Accumulation

Perhaps the single greatest weakness in historical materialism to date has been the failure to theorize transitions between modes in a world systemic context. Traditional Marxist interpretations of world historical development relied heavily on a schema of transitions between modes of production in a predetermined unilinear progression. This overly simplistic framework of analysis has long since been abandoned and revised by most historical materialists. We propose instead to study transitions between modes of accumulation. However, they did not occur merely within each "separate" zone of the world system. Rather they were the key determinants of transition in both the "parts" and especially the whole of the world system. Therefore, the research task is not to search solely or even primarily for indigenously generated determinants of transition between modes, but rather to analyze the overall interactions of each zone of the world system with the dynamic of the entire world system. This is true of both the economic and the political aspects of modes of accumulation.

It would also be a mistake to attempt too strict an analytical separation between "agrarian" and "industrial" modes of accumulation in the world system. Even in very archaic phases of the world system, the economic nexus included non-agricultural sources of production and accumulation. The role of industry and commerce before the onset of "industrialization" in the modern world system require much more study than they have received. The associated social and political relations of accumulation have changed very significantly across world historical time, but not in any predetermined or unilinear progression of modes of accumulation. The precise nature and timing of such transitions is still an open empirical question.

3. Public/Private Accumulation

In principle, there are four possible permutations of private and public accumulation:

- 1. Dominant Private Accumulation (the state "facilitates" private accumulation).
- 2. Dominant State Accumulation (private accumulation "facilitates" state accumulation).
- 3. All Private Accumulation.
- 4. All State Accumulation.

Type 1, dominant private accumulation, may correspond to mercantile states and to modern democratic states. Type 2, dominant state accumulation, may characterize a number of bureaucratic states and empires as well as certain modern authoritarian regimes. Type 4, all state accumulation, might be characterized by states such as ancient Sparta, the Inca empire, and some modern (state) "socialist" states. Type 3, all private accumulation, raises the theoretical question of whether private accumulation is in fact possible at all without the state, or at least without the presence of the state somewhere in the overall economic nexus. There may be niches in the world system's economic nexus where all private accumulation may occur, but it has been difficult to identify instances of this.

State accumulation is typically characterized by a much larger scale and much greater potential capabilities to extract surplus than any sole private accumulator is capable of organizing. That is why "imperialism" is such an attractive means of accumulation. State accumulation centralizes accumulation more than private accumulation. For this reason, these two modes of accumulation and their respective elites are locked into a perpetual conflict over apportioning the shares of the surplus. Both private accumulating classes and the state elite, as a "state-class," struggle to form a coalition of class fractions. Such a "hegemonic bloc" of class fractions allows them to cooperate to utilize the political apparatus to establish the dominant mode of accumulation. The oscillation between predominance by the private accumulators and the state class in a social formation is a key dimension of the cycles of accumulation, discussed below.

4. Economy/Polity Contradictions

There is a contradiction between a relatively unbounded economic nexus and a relatively bounded political organization of this economic nexus in world system development. The total economy of the major states and centers of the world system is not under their sole political control. This tension is universally recognized today as affecting the structure of modern capital accumulation. However, this phenomenon is not new. This economy-polity contradiction is characteristic not only of the so-called contemporary age of "interdependence," but has in fact **always** been a factor in world system development.

Even though since its origin the world system has developed logistical interlinkages that create a single overarching economic system, the political organization of the world system has not developed a parallel unity. Why is that? For the modern world system, Wallerstein (1974 and other works) argues that the capitalist mode of production structurally inhibits the creation of a single "world-empire." That is, in this view the resolution of the economy/polity contradiction in the modern world system by a single overarching political entity is inhibited by its **capitalist** mode of production. However, it appears that even in other modes of accumulation, it has not been possible to create a single political structure for the entire world system. Attempts to do so have been failures. The Mongol attempt in the 13th century perhaps came closest to success. The question of why the world system has never successfully been converted into one political entity should be seriously posed. The answer may be structural, or simply a matter of logistical and organizational limitations. Whatever the answer to this question about politics in the world system, it need not deny and may even strengthen the thesis of its essential economic unity.

VI. HEGEMONY AND SUPER-HEGEMONY

1. Hegemony

Hegemony is a hierarchical structure of the accumulation of surplus among political entities, and their constituent classes, mediated by force. A hierarchy of centers of accumulation and polities is established that apportions a privileged share of surplus, and the political economic power to this end, to the hegemonic center/state and its ruling/propertied classes. Such a hegemonic structure thus consists schematically of a hierarchy of CPH complexes in which the primary hegemonic center of accumulation and political power subordinates secondary centers and their respective zones of production and accumulation.

The rise and decline of hegemonic powers and cycles of hegemony and war are lately receiving increasing attention, e.g., by Modelski (1987), Thompson (1989), Wallerstein (1974, 1988), Wight (1978), Goldstein (1988) and others, and even best seller status (Kennedy 1987). Most of these studies confine themselves to the world system since 1500. However, (we argue that) the world system began earlier and was previously centered outside Europe. Therefore, the same, and even more questions, about hegemonic rise, decline, cycles, and shifts apply - and even more interestingly - to the larger and older world system, prior to Europe's rise to super-hegemonial economic and political power within it. Where and when were there hegemonic centers in the world system before 1500, and in what sense or how did they exercise their hegemony? David Wilkinson (1989) has made a systematic study of world states and hegemonies that could serve as the starting point for an answer.

The following are some other important questions. As one hegemonic center declined, was it replaced by another and which and why? Were there periods with various hegemonic centers? Did they "coexist" side by side, or with how much systemic interconnection? In that case, did they complement each other, or did they compete with each other, economically, militarily, or otherwise until one (new?) center achieved hegemony over the others? Rather than continuing to look merely comparatively at contemporary hegemonic structures in different zones of the world system or to investigate the dynamic of each region separately, we must look at systemic links among all the constituent political organizations of the world system. Of course, these especially include contemporaneous hegemonic structures.

Hegemony takes a variety of historical forms. They vary from highly centralized integrated bureaucratic empires, to very loosely structured commercial or maritime hegemonies. In the latter, much of the surplus is captured not via direct political coercion, but via commodity exchange, albeit via unequal exchange. How and why do these various forms of hegemony occur at particular times and places? How do they reflect the interests of the actors which choose them and the prevailing conditions in the world system at the time?

Given the absence in the historical record of any single "world system hegemony," we must look to the rise and decline of hegemonies in each of the major zones of the world system in order to construct an overall picture of the hegemonial cycles, rhythms and trends in the various regions and their possible relations. For instance, the oscillation between unitary hegemonies and multi-actor states systems has already been recognized as a key pattern of world historical development (Mann 1986, Wilkinson 1989). These oscillations and the succession of hegemonies in each part of the world system should not be analyzed only on a comparative basis, but from a world systemic perspective. Only in this way can the dynamics of the world system's economy/polity contradiction be more fully understood.

All this suggests that the primary object and principal economic incentive of a bid for hegemony is to restructure the overarching system of accumulation in a way that privileges the hegemon for capital/surplus accumulation. Simply put, hegemony is a means to wealth, not merely to "power" or "order." That is, "power" in the world system is both economic and political at all times. In fact, economic power is political power, and vice versa. Turning Michael Mann (1986) on his head, the ends of power are above all control over accumulation processes and the determination of the dominant mode of accumulation. The processes of accumulation are more fundamental to world system history than Mann's forms of social power *per se*. The political and economic processes in the world system are so integral as to constitute a **single process** rather than two separate ones. Success in accumulation plays a critical role in success in a bid for hegemony. This is true not only of modern states, but even of archaic ones. For instance, the victory of the state of Qin in the Warring States period in Chinese history depended greatly on its innovations in tax structure, infrastructural investments, bureaucratic administration, and trade links to the world system. All of these gave the Qin very real advantages in accumulation and in military capabilities over its more traditional "feudal" rivals.

2. Cycles of Accumulation and Hegemony

The perpetual "symbiotic conflict" between private accumulating classes and state accumulating classes is indicative of cycles of accumulation. The oscillation between unitary hegemonies and multi-actor states systems is indicative of cycles of hegemony in the world system. Cycles of accumulation and cycles of hegemony are probably causally interrelated. This causal inter-relationship appears to date from very early in world system history in various parts of the world system.

These cycles and their interrelationship are the central phenomena of the world system's longest cumulative patterns. These cycles have partly been analyzed by Gills' (1989) analysis of synchronization, conjuncture, and center-shift in the cycles of East Asian history. Briefly, prior to the in-dustrialization of production, the phase of accumulation in which private accumulating classes become dominant seems to be closely associated with the decline of hegemonies and their political fragmentation. That is, decentraliza-tion of accumulation affects the decentralization of political organization. These processes may be called "entropic." Phases of accumulation in which the bureaucratic state elite is dominant seem to be associated with the consolidation of hegemonies. That is, the centralization of accumulation affects the centralization of political organization and vice versa. However, rising and declining hegemonies also call forth opposing (and also temporarily supporting) alliances to thwart existing and threatening hegemonial powers. Shifting alliances seem to promote some kind of "balance of power." All this may seem obvious, but the cyclical dynamic of hegemony (also through political conflict and shifting alliances) in relation to the process of accumula-tion has not previously been given the attention it deserves.

Implosion from the hinterland upon the center appears to be most likely to occur in entropic phases of the system. The hinterland, and perhaps the periphery, take advantage of weakness or entropy in the center to restructure the structure of accumulation. This may occur by usurping political power at the center, or by "secession" from the center altogether.

Too much attention has been given only to the political and strategic aspects of long cycles of war and leadership to the exclusion of the underlying dynamics of accumulation. General war, as Modelski (1987) argues, does indeed produce new sets of victors who go on to establish a new order. However, one should not merely examine the political and military aspects of these cycles. The new victors, without exception, also proceed to restructure the structure of world accumulation. This, and not mere political realignments or "order" alone, is the ultimate end of such general conflict. The intense military rivalry that precedes hegemony may stimulate production, but much of the economic benefit is consumed in the process of rivalry and war. Typically, a new hegemony is followed by a period of infrastructural investment and economic expansion, which is "the hegemonic prosperity phase" of accumulation. A unified hegemony usually reduces or even eliminates previous political obstructions to the greater integration of the economic nexus. This has a tremendous impact on the process of accumulation.

We must contemplate the existence, and study the development of a wider world system farther back in world history to find answers to a host of questions about the dynamics of states systems and cycles of accumulation and hegemony. Particularly important are questions about the existence of world system wide accumulation processes and shifts in the centralization of accumulation from one zone of the world system to another. How do such shifts affect cycles of hegemony? What are the real patterns and "laws" of the world system's overall expansion, transformation, and decay?

3. Super-Hegemony

The historical process of economic surplus management and capital accumulation is so interregional and inter-"societal" as to lead to the conclusion that it constituted a process of **world accumulation** in the world system over the millennia. A privileged position therein, in which one zone of the world system and its constituent ruling-propertied classes is able to accumulate surplus more effectively and concentrate accumulation at the expense of other zones, could be called "super-hegemony." Thus, super-hegemony is also a class position in the overarching world accumulation processes of the world system. Thus, while there may at one time be different hegemonic powers in the regional subsystems, only one of them would be "super-hegemonic" if and when it is "more equal than the others" some of whose accumulation it manages to channel to itself and to centralize in its own super-hegemonic "super-accumulation." A research agenda is to examine the causes of possible super-hegemony, positional shifts from one zone to another, and the degree to which super-hegemony is transformed into further economic and political power within the world system. While hegemony is built up of CPH complexes, super-hegemony occurs in the largest field possible, that of the entire world system and all of its constituent hegemonic structures.

Thus, super-hegemony links all the constituent hegemonies into one overarching systemic whole. Of course, the degree of institutional integration among distinct hegemonies is not as great as the degree of integration within each hegemony. Nevertheless, contemporary and/or contiguous hegemonies are not autonomous if inter-penetrating accumulation exists. In the entire class structure of the world system, in whatever mode of accumulation, the super-hegemonial class position is the most privileged and the ultimate "center of centers" in the world accumulation process.

To what extent did this overarching super-hegemony rest or operate on more than the mere outward exercise of political power and the radiation of cultural diffusion? In particular, to what extent and through what mechanisms did such overarching super-hegemony include centralized (super-hegemonial) capital accumulation? Was accumulation fed through the inward flow and absorption of economic surplus generated in and/or transferred through other (sub)-hegemonial centers? The answers to both questions are in general affirmative, and we can find ample confirmative historical evidence if we only look for it. For instance, William McNeill (in conversation with Frank) suggests that China itself accumulated capital by absorbing surplus and capital from the West in the several centuries before 1500 AD. Was China therefore super-hegemonial? Prior to China, India was possibly super-hegemonial in the world system. In the period of the eighth and ninth centuries AD, the Abbassid Caliphate, with its great metropole at Baghdad, may have been super-hegemonial. The development of European domination over the Mughal, Qing and Ottoman empires should, however, also be understood in terms of the conjuncture of European expansion and these regions' entropic phases of accumulation and hegemony. In the nineteenth century, Great Britain is a candidate for super-hegemonial status, followed by the United States in the mid-twentieth century, and possibly Japan in the very late twentieth and early twenty-first century.

Thus, super-hegemony need not be limited only to the capitalist world economy, but may have existed at other times in the history of world system development. Super-hegemony is more flexible than empire, or imperialism. Super-hegemony operates not only through political and inter-state level(s) of diplomacy, alliance, and war, but also and maybe more importantly, through super-accumulation.

If super-hegemony existed before recent times, how, when and why did the super-hegemonial center of the world system, the most favored locus of accumulation, shift around the world system? What effects did such shifts in super-hegemonial centers have upon and what "functional" role, if any, did they play in the world system's development? For instance, the super-hegemony of the Abbassids in the eighth century was reflected in their ability to defeat Tang China at Talas in 751, their treaty of alliance with the Tang in 798 AD, and their continued ability to control Central Asia. Perhaps the super-hegemony of Britain contributed to its ability to arbitrate the balance of power on the continent of Europe and to defeat bids to impose a unitary hegemony, such as that by Napoleon? The super-hegemony of the United States after 1945 allowed it to restructure the international order and greatly expand its economic and military influence in the world system. It remains to be seen whether or how Japan might translate super-hegemonial status in world accumulation processes into further political and economic power in the world system in the twenty-first century.

4. Cumulation of Accumulation

How long, then, has there been an overarching and interpenetrating world system process of capital accumulation, which affected the structure of the structures of which it is composed? In other words, how long has there been a cumulative process of capital accumulation on a world system scale? The (occasional and temporary) existence of super-hegemony also implies super accumulation at those times, as noted above. Even in the absence of super-hegemony, however, the process of accumulation in one zone of the world system would not have been the same without the linkages to the process of accumulation in another zone or zones of the world system. Therefore, even competing hegemonies and linked structures and processes of accumulation could have contributed to the world system wide cumulation of accumulation. Indeed, such an overarching structure of accumulation and the resulting process of cumulation of accumulation implies that there may be a unitary "logic" of systemic development.

The cumulation of accumulation in the world system thus implies not only a continuous, but also a cumulative, historical process of ecological, economic, technological, social, political, and cultural change. Cumulation of accumulation involves or requires **no uniformity** among these processes throughout the system or its parts, **no unison** among its parts, **no unidirectionality** of change in either the parts or the whole, and certainly **no uniformity of speed of change**.

On the contrary, both the historical evidence and our analysis suggest **unity through diversity** (to use the phrase Mikhail Gorbachev used at the United Nations). The unity of the world system and its cumulative process of accumulation is based on the diversity of center-periphery-hinterland, mode of accumulation, and hegemonic differences we have emphasized. Of course they also rest on the variety of social, gender, racial, ethnic, cultural, religious, ideological and other differences, which characterize wo/mankind. Historical change in both the whole (system) and its parts takes place in many "progressive" and "retrogressive" directions, and not unidirectionally or even in unison between here and there.

For this reason among others, historical change also takes place and even cumulates, not uniformly, but at changing rates, sometimes fast, sometimes slowly, sometimes (degenerating) in reverse. Indeed, as in physical transformations and in biological evolution, historical change suddenly accelerates and/or bifurcates at critical junctures. More than likely, contemporaries are rarely aware that they are living and acting in such "special" periods -- and many who think so at other times, are not. Hindsight seems to throw more light on history than foresight or even contemporary side-sight or introspection. Yet even historical hindsight has a long way to go, especially in grasping the dynamics and variability of historical change. We briefly return to these problems below under the title of "dynamics."

VII. A HISTORICAL MATERIALIST POLITICAL ECONOMY AND RESEARCH AGENDA

1. Historical Materialist Political Economic Summary and Conclusions

In this paper we made three key arguments. The first is that the world system pre-dates the development of modern capitalism, perhaps by several thousand years. The second is that accumulation processes are the most important and fundamental processes of the world system throughout its development. The third argument is that, though the mode of accumulation underwent many historical transformations, there has been a continuous and cumulative process of accumulation in the world system. Therefore, we argue that a new research agenda is needed to focus more analysis on these cumulative processes of accumulation over the entire historical development of the world system - of some five thousand years at least. The secular trends, cycles, and rhythms of the modern capitalist world system thus become more contextually understandable within the much longer cycles, trends, and rhythms of the historical world system, and particularly of its process and cycles of accumulation.

We based our argument upon a new set of criteria for defining what constitutes a "systemic" interaction. The transfer or exchange of economic surplus is the fundamental criterion of a world systemic relationship. Diplomacy, alliances and conflict are additional, and perhaps derivative, criteria of systemic interaction. Thus, we introduced the criterion of "interpenetrating accumulation" into the definition of the world system. By applying these criteria we saw the origins of the world system recede by several millennia. The world system had its ultimate origins in the development of an archaic Asio-Afro-European economic and political nexus, which first developed in the area now known as West Asia, the Middle East and the Eastern Mediterranean about 2500 BC. Once in existence, this world system continued to develop, expand, and deepen. It eventually either assimilated and/or merged with all other center-periphery-hinterland zones to form our modern world system. Its relatively unbounded economic nexus is perpetually in contradiction with a more bounded political organization of the economic nexus. Cycles of accumulation and cycles of hegemony, like center-periphery-hinterland relations, have characterized the world system and its subsystems from its inception.

World system history forms a genuine continuum within which cycles of accumulation and cycles of hegemony are the two most fundamental phenomena. These two cyclical phenomena are intercausally systemically interrelated to one another. They are the basis of our assertion that there are cumulative accumulation processes in the world system over such an extended time frame.

Significant aspects of our argument were anticipated - alas, without our taking due note thereof - by Kajsa Ekholm and Jonathan Friedman (E & F) under the title '"Capital Imperialism and Exploitation in Ancient World Systems" a decade ago (1982, original 1979). It may be useful briefly to review some major points of agreement and disagreement with them.

1. Emergence and development of the World system. E & F argue that

> Our point of departure is that the forerunner of the present kind of world system first emerged in the period following 3000 B.C. in Southern Mesopotamia. Here we can describe the first example of the rise of a center of accumulation within a larger economic system and the development of an imperialist structure....the expansion of the E.D. [Early Dynastic] system eventually incorporates the entire region from the Indus to the Mediterranean in a regular trade network....(89, 97).

> Our argument is that the general properties of imperialist-mercantilist expansion are common to ancient and modern worlds irrespective of specific local forms of accumulation (92).

We agree that the world system began long before "the modern world system," and we also see its emergence in Mesopotamia. However, in our view the formation of the world system was more the result of interregional relations between Mesopotamia and other regions in the "Middle East" and the Indus Valley. We also agree that the world system then expanded and took on certain "general properties," which still define it today (see below).

2. Capital Accumulation. E & F and we agree on the centrality of capital accumulation in this long historical process and system(s) and that "capital" exists not only under "capitalism."

The accumulation of capital as a form of abstract wealth is a truly ancient phenomenon.... "Capital" is not tied to a specific form of exploitation. It is, rather, the forerunner, or perhaps identical to, merchant capital in its functioning....(pp. 88, 100).

However, E & F define capital as:

...the form of abstract wealth represented in the concrete form of metal or even money that can be accumulated in itself and converted into other forms of wealth, land, labor, and products (p. 100).

Our concepts of capital and its accumulation are broader than theirs. We stress the existence and combination of both state and private capital, and we include non-monetary forms of the production, extraction, transfer, and accumulation of surplus. We also pay more attention than they do to the interregional dimensions of accumulation and supra regional super accumulation. Moreover, we stress the cumulative, albeit cyclical, process of capital accumulation -- which also contributes to continuity in the world system.

3. Center-periphery Structure(s). E & F, like we, argue that

The system to which we refer is characterized, not only by an accumulation of capital, but by the emergence of an imperialist pattern: center/periphery structures are unstable over time; centers expand, contract, and collapse as regular manifestations of the shift of points of accumulation. These phenomena are, we think, more general than modern capitalism....(88).

We agree, but our CPH complex extends this center-periphery structure to include the hinterland, when it also contributes to accumulation in the center and to transformation in the system as a whole. Moreover again, we stress the systemic relations among various CPH complexes, which make up the world system as a whole.

4. Economy/Polity Contradictions, Hegemony and System Transformation.
E & F and we agree that systemic economic relations tend to be more
extensive than political ones.

> The existence of a production/resource area wider than that of a
> political unit which must be maintained is the fundamental weakness
> of such systems (93).

This contradiction gives rise to instability in and transformation of the system:

> Center/periphery structures are drastically unstable because of the
> vulnerability of the centers in the external (supply/market) realm
> which is so difficult to control....Evolution is, as a result, a
> necessarily discontinuous process in space. Centers collapse and
> are replaced by other areas of high civilization. The development
> of total systems is not equivalent to the development of individual
> societies. On the contrary, the evolution tends to imply the shift of
> centers of accumulation over time....(93).

Again, we agree; but we discuss these relations and transformations as
cycles of hegemony. We also relate hegemony to the center-periphery
complex and to accumulation within it. However, we also urge the study of
possible overarching system-wide super-accumulation and super-hegemony.

5. World systems or World system? E & F seem to be unsure about which
it is. Elsewhere, they definitely say systems, (eg Ekholm 1980). Here E & F
say:

> Our point has been to stress the fundamental continuity between
> ancient and modern world- systems.... We are, perhaps talking about
> the same world system. The forms of accumulation have not
> changed so significantly. The forms of exploitation and oppression
> have all been around from the earliest civilization although, of
> course, they have existed in different proportions and varying
> combinations....There are, to be sure, a great many differences, but
> the similarities are, perhaps, a more serious and practical problem
> (105, 106).

That is our point as well. However, we now wish to stress the fundamental similarity and continuity not so much **between** ancient and modern world systems. We are definitely talking about **common** characteristics and **continuity** within the *same* **world system.**

Therefore, there is good reason, justification, and merit to do an historical materialist political economy of world system history. Almost all historical and (other) social scientific analysis of the world and its parts before 1500 AD (and most of them for the time since then also) have neglected these systemic aspects of world historical political economic processes and relations. Some scholars (e.g., Tilly 1984) have considered doing such a world system history and have rejected the task as inadvisable or impossible. Others, like Farmer (1977, 1985), Chase-Dunn (1986), Ekholm (1980), and Ekholm and Friedman (1982) have started down this road, but have apparently taken fright and stopped or even turned back. A few scholars, especially Childe (1942), McNeill (1964, 1990), Stavarianos (1970), and most recently Wilkinson (1987, 1989) have made pioneering advances toward writing a world system history. Frank (1990) examines their and many other theoretical and historical considerations and rejects their reservations as unfounded. He then proposes why and how these and other pioneering works should be extended and combined to do a history of the world and its world systemic historical materialist political economy along the present lines.

2.   Political, Economic and Cultural Three Legged Stools

A historical materialist political economy of cumulation of accumulation in world system history does not exclude or even downgrade social, political, cultural, ideological, and other factors. On the contrary, it relates and integrates them with each other. Nor need such a study be "economic determinist." On the contrary, this study would recognize the interaction and support of at least three legs of the social stool, without which it could not stand, let alone develop. These three legs are: the organization of political power; the identity and legitimation through culture and ideology; and the management of economic surplus and capital accumulation through a complex division of labor. Each of these is related to the other and all of them to the system as a whole and its transformation.

A historical materialist political economic analysis of the historical development of this world system should incorporate ecological, biological, cultural, ideological, and of course political factors and relations. Thus, there is justification and merit in also seeking to explain many political institutions and events and their ideological manifestations through the ecological and economic incentives and limitations that accompany if not determine them. In particular, we should pay much more attention to how the generation and capture of economic surplus helps shape social and political institutions, military campaigns, and ideological legitimation. Economic institutions, such as Polanyi's (1957) famous reciprocity, redistribution and market, appear mixed up with each other and always with some political organization. Many political institutions and processes also have economic aspects or "functions."

The three component aspects, the three legs of the stool, are embedded in the mode of accumulation. No mode of accumulation can function without a concomitant **ideology of accumulation**; an **economic nexus** founded on a complex division of labor in which class relations facilitate extraction of surplus; and finally a **political apparatus**, which enforces the rules and relations of accumulation through the ultimate sanction of "legitimate" coercion. The ideology and political apparatus are integral aspects of the mode of accumulation. They are not super - structurally "autonomous" from each other or from the characteristics of the economic nexus. However, ideology and political competition and emulation sometimes appear to take on at least a semi-autonomous character. Even if we grant this, it does not invalidate the alternative assertion that overall they are not autonomous from the economic nexus.

We reject any vulgar unidirectional schema of causality whereby the economic nexus must necessarily determine the ideology and political apparatus of a mode of accumulation because they are not in fact separate. We suggest an alternative concept of the mutual inter-causality among the three aspects of a mode of accumulation which is historically specific to each case. Indeed, particularly in periods of transition between one mode of accumulation and another, ideological and political forces can play an extremely significant role in determining the structure of the economic nexus that emerges from the transition. It is in these periods especially that broad based social movements intercede in world (and local) history. These social movements are often neglected altogether, or they are considered but not sufficiently analyzed in their structural and temporal world systemic context.

We can well depart from vulgar economism, but not necessarily from a form of "economic" determinism, if by economic we mean giving the political economic processes of accumulation their due.

3. Analytic and Research Agendas on the Structure and Dynamics of World System History.

Most important perhaps are the dynamics of the world system, that is how the world system itself operates, behaves/functions, and transforms (itself?). Are there trends, cycles, internal mechanisms of transformation in the pre-(and post-) 1500 world system? When and why does historical change accelerate and decelerate? What are the historical junctures at which quantitative turns into qualitative change? What are the bifurcations at which historical change takes one direction rather than another. And why? Perhaps general systems theory offers some answers or at least better questions also for this (world) system. For instance, Prigogine and Sanglier(1988) analyze how order is formed out of chaos, and how at critical times and places small changes can spark large alterations and transformations in physical, biological, ecological and social systems.

Recent studies by, for instance, Ekholm and Friedman (1982), Chase-Dunn (1986), and others are looking into both structural and dynamic properties of partial "world" systems before 1500. However, it may be possible to trace long (and within them shorter) cycles of accumulation, infrastructural investment, technological change, and hegemony much farther back in world system history. Not only may they have existed, but they may often have had considerable relative independent autonomy from policy and politics *per se*. Indeed as in more recent times also, much of this policy was, and is, instead more the effect of and response to largely uncontrolled cyclical changes. Moreover, policy tends to reinforce more than to counteract these cycles and trends. This cyclical process and policy response may be seen in the decline of various empires, including the present American one.

In particular, to what extent has the process of capital accumulation and associated other developments been cyclical? That is, were there identifiable subsystemic and system-wide acceleration/deceleration, up/down, swings in structure and process? And were any such swings cyclical, that is endogenous to the system, in the sense that up generated down and down occasioned up again? This kind of question has been posed, and some answers have been offered for the world system (or its different economic and political interpretations) since 1500. For instance, Wallerstein (1974) and Frank (1978) find long cycles in economic growth and technology. Modelski (1987) and Goldstein (1988) find long cycles in political hegemony and war. Wallerstein also posits a life cycle of expansion and foreseen decay of the system. Toynbee (1973), Quigley (1961), Eisenstadt (1963), and others have made comparative studies of the life cycles of individual civilizations before 1500. So have archaeologists like Robert M. Adams (1966). But to what extent were there also world system wide fluctuations and cycles, and what role have they played in the transformation and development of the world system?

Infrastructural investment apparently occurs in cyclical or phased patterns, and in direct correspondence with the cycle/phase of accumulation and of hegemony. Newly formed hegemonic orders are usually associated with a subsequent intense phase of infrastructural investment, followed by general economic expansion and a concomitant increase in accumulation. Therefore, it could also be fruitful to search for a long lasting continuous up and down cycle of super-hegemony.

Thus, infrastructural investment cycles would be related to cycles of accumulation and cycles of hegemony in the world system. Are there also cumulative aspects of infrastructural investment that affect subsequent world system development? We incline to an affirmative answer. However, we do not believe that this cumulation necessarily takes place in or through a single "capital-imperialist" mode of production, and still less one based on the primary use of a political apparatus to exercise imperial political power for this accumulation, as apparently posited by Ekholm and Friedman (1982). Other competitive "economic" mechanisms operating within the very CPH and hegemonic structure of the world system can also further the process of cumulation in the world system. How did private and state investment interact in world system development? For instance, what is the role of private infrastructural investment in creating and sustaining the complex logistical interlinkages of the world system? To what extent does state infrastructural investment create and sustain the logistical interlinkages of the world system? How does the conjuncture and synchronization of phases among contemporary hegemonies affect the respective cycles of infrastructural investment?

If we view the entire five or six millennia development of the world system as a unified cumulative continuum and seek to explain its most significant trends, cycles, and rhythms, based on an historical materialist political economy, then a "world system history" should follow. Such a world system history should not merely be a comparative history of the world or even a comparative history of world systems. An historical materialist world system history would regard class formation, capital accumulation, state formation, and hegemonic construction throughout the world system as being integral aspects of the one, cumulative, process of world historical world system accumulation and development. This history would not be Euro-centric, and should avoid any other form of centricism. A comprehensive world system history would be humanocentric.

We mean humanocentric in two senses. One is that world history must encompass the structure and development of the system, which importantly determines the lives of all humanity, and not just a (self)selected part of it. Second, world (system) history should leave room for how people shape their own and world history. Most history is written top down by and/or for the victors in historical struggles. Of course, the hierarchical and center-periphery structure and mechanisms of social transformation in the system merit attention, as we have emphasized. However, human history and the world system itself also emerges out of multiple bottom up social movements and other struggles. Some were successful in their time and place. Many were defeated. Both intervened in forming and transforming world system history. More specifically, popular dissatisfaction and its socio-political expression helped shape and transform societies and empires from reform movements in ancient Sumer and peasant uprisings in "dynastic cycle" China to today. The scholarly difficulty of incorporating these social movements into a world system history is only exceeded by the political importance of doing so. Yet we must try; since it is the very structure and development of the world system, which (cyclically?) generates and continually regenerates the social (movement) and other struggles -- and vice versa. A Luta Continua!

REFERENCES

Adams, Brooks 1943. *The Law of Civilization and Decay: An Essay on History.* New York: Alfred A. Knopf.

Adams, Robert Mc 1966. *The Evolution of Urban Society: Early Mesopotamia and Prehistoric Mexico.* Chicago: Aldine Co.

Amin, Samir 1989. "Le System Mondial Contemporain Et Les Systemes Anterieurs," Unpublished Manuscript.

Arrighi, Giovanni and Jessica Drangel 1986. "The Stratification of the World-Economy: An Exploration of the Semiperipheral Zone." *Review* X:1(Summer):9-74.

Chase-Dunn, Christopher 1986. "Rise and Demise: World-Systems and Modes of Production," Unpublished Manuscript.

Childe, Gordon 1942. *What Happened in History?* Harmondsworth, Middlesex: Pelican.

_____ 1951. *Man Makes Himself.* New York: Mentor. de Ste Croix, G.E.M. 1981. *The Class Struggle in the Ancient Greek World.* London: Duckworth.

Curtin, Philip 1984. *Cross-cultural Trade in World History.* Cambridge: Cambridge University Press.

Eberhard, Wolfram 1977. *A History of China.* Fourth revised Edition. London: Routledge Keagan Paul.

Eisenstadt, S.N. 1963. *The Political Systems of Empires.* Glencoe, Illinois: The Free Press.

Ekholm, Kasja 1980. "On the Limitations of Civilization: The Structure and Dynamics of Global Systems." *Dialectical Anthropology.* 5:2(July):155-166.

Ekholm, Kasja and Jonathan Friedman 1982. "'Capital' Imperialism and Exploitation in Ancient World-Systems". *Review* IV:1(Summer):87-109.

Farmer, Edward L. 1985. "Civilization as a Unit of World History: Eurasia and Eurasia's Place in it." *The History Teacher.* Vol 18, No. 3, May.

_____ et al 1977. *Comparative History of Civilization in Asia.* Reading, Mass: Addison-Wesley.

Frank, Andre Gunder 1978 a. *World Accumulation 1492-1789.* New York: Monthly Review Press and London: Macmillan Press.

_____ 1978 b. *Dependent Accumulation and Underdevelopment.* New York: Monthly Review Press and London: Macmillan Press.

_____ 1981. *Crisis: In the Third World.* New York: Holmes and Meier, and London: Heinemann.

_____ 1990. "A Theoretical Introduction to Five Thousand Years of World system History." *Review* 13:2(Spring):155-250.

Gernet, Jacques 1985. *A History of Chinese Civilization.* Cambridge: Cambridge University Press.

Gills, Barry K. 1989. "Synchronization, Conjuncture and Center-Shift in East
    Asian International History", paper presented at the joint International
    Studies Association, British International Studies Association Conference,
    London, 1 April 1989.

Gilpin, Robert 1981. *War and Change in World Politics*. Cambridge: Cam-
    bridge University Press.

Goldstein, Joshua 1988. *Long Cycles: Prosperity and War in the Modern Age*.
    New Haven: Yale University Press.

Hall, Thomas D. 1986. "Incorporation in the World-system: Toward a
    Critique" *American Sociological Review* 51:3(June):390-402.

_____ 1989. *Social Change in the Southwest, 1350-1880*. Lawrence, KS:
    University Press of Kansas

Johnstone, Paul 1989. *The Seacraft of Prehistory*. London: Routledge.

Kennedy, Paul 1987. *The Rise and Fall of the Great Powers*. New York:
    Random House.

Lattimore, Owen 1940. *Inner Asian Frontiers of China*. Boston: Beacon Press.

_____ 1962. *Studies in Frontier History: Collected Papers 1928-1958*. Oxford:
    Oxford University Press.

Mann, Michael 1986. *The Sources of Social Power, Volume 1: A History of
    Power from the beginning to AD 1760*. Cambridge: Cambridge University
    Press.

McNeill, William H. 1964. *The Rise of the West. A History of the Human
    Community*. Chicago: University of Chicago Press.

_____ 1982. *The Pursuit of Power: Technology, Armed Force and Society since
    AD 1000*. Chicago: University of Chicago Press.

_____ 1990. "The Rise of the West After Twenty Five Years", *Journal of
    World History*. 1:1(Spring):1-21.

Modelski, George 1987. *Long Cycles in World Politics*. London: Macmillan
    Press.

Prigogine, Ilya and Michele Sanglier eds. 1988. *Laws of Nature and Human
    Conduct: Specificities and Unifying themes*. Bruxelles:

Polanyi, Karl 1957. *The Great Transformation - The Political and Economic
    Origins of Our Time*. Boston: The Beacon Press.

Quigley, Carroll 1961. *The Evolution of Civilizations. An Introduction to
    Historical Analysis*. New York: Macmillan Co.

Rowlands, Michael, Mogens Larsen and Kristian Kristiansen, eds. 1987. *Centre and Periphery in the Ancient World.* Cambridge: Cambridge University Press.

Schneider, Jane 1977. "Was there a pre-capitalist world-system?" *Peasant Studies* VI:1(January):20-29.

Stavrianos, L.S. 1970. *The World to 1500: A Global History.* Englewood Cliffs: Prentice Hall.

Teggart, Frederick J. 1939. *Rome and China: A Study of Correlations in Historical Events.* Berkeley: University of California Press.

Thompson, William 1989. *On Global War: Historical-Structural Approaches to World Politics.* Columbia: University of South Carolina Press.

Tilly, Charles 1984. *Big Structures, Large Processes, Huge Comparisons.* New York: Russell Sage Foundation.

Toynbee, Arnold 1973. *A Study of History.* Oxford: Oxford University Press.

Wallerstein, Immanuel 1974. *The Modern World-System. Vol 1.* New York: Academic Books.

_____ 1988. *The Modern World-system III.* New York: Academic Books.

_____ 1989. "The West, Capitalism, and the Modern World-System," Prepared as a chapter of Joseph Needham, *Science and Civilization in China*, Vol. VII: *The Social Background,* Part 2, Sect. 48. *Social and Economic Considerations.*

Wight, Martin 1978. *Power Politics.* New York: Holmes/Meier.

Wilkinson, David 1987. "Central Civilization." *Comparative Civilizations Review* 17(Fall):31-59.

_____ 1989. "The Future of the World State: From Civilization Theory to World Politics", Paper presented at the Annual Meeting of the International Studies Association, London, March 28-April 1, 1989.

Wolf, Eric 1982. *Europe and the People Without History. Berkeley:University of California Press.*

4

Cores, Peripheries, and Civilizations

David Wilkinson

The terminology of "core" and "periphery" allows us to address substantive issues of interest to the study of world politics, of world systems,[1] and of civilizations: issues of geographic differentiation, inequality, and uneven change. Power, pelf, prestige, progress, population and piety are significantly **centric**: spatially located, concentrated, radiating outwards, radially diminishing. To some degree, but not completely, their spatial distributions overlap, creating the sense of historic "cores" for macrosocieties; at some timescales, cores seem stable, at some longer scales they move in apparently nonrandom ways.

Reprise. This is one in a series of papers exploring the relationship of civilizations theory to world politics. In this series (e.g., Wilkinson, 1987) I have defined "a civilization" using criteria of level-and-politicomilitary-connectedness[2] rather than the more customary criteria of level-and-cultural-uniformity. Screening a list of some seventy candidates yielded a list of fourteen entities which appeared to be societies at a civilized level (criteria: cities, record-keeping, economic surplus, non-producing classes, etc.) which were also connected **world-systems** -- militarily closed, geotechnologically isolated social-transactional networks with an autonomous political history during which they did not take or need not have taken much account of the possibility of conquest, invasion, attack -- or alliance and cooperation -- from any outsiders, although the members of each such system did recurrently conquer, invade, attack, ally with, command, rule, legislate, cooperate with, and conflict significantly and effectively with (and only with) one another.

Table 1 gives the resulting roster of civilizations/world systems.

Table 1. A Roster of Fourteen Civilizations
(listed in their approximate order of incorporation into Central Civilization)

Civilization	Duration	Terminus
1. Mesopotamian	before 3000 B.C. - c. 1500 B.C.	Coupled with Egyptian to form Central
2. Egyptian	before 3100 B.C. - c. 1500 B.C.	Coupled with Mesopotamian to form Central
3. Aegean	c. 2700 B.C. - c. 560 B.C.	Engulfed by Central
4. Indic	c. 2300 B.C. - after c. A.D. 1000	Engulfed by Central
5. Irish	c. A.D. 450 - c. 1050	Engulfed by Central
6. Mexican	before 1100 B.C. - c. A.D. 1520	Engulfed by Central
7. Peruvian	before c. 200 B.C. - c. A.D. 1530	Engulfed by Central
8. Chibchan	? - c. A.D. 1530	Engulfed by Central
9. Indonesian	before A.D. 700 - c. 1700	Engulfed by Central
10. West African	c. A.D. 350 - c. 1590	Engulfed by Central
11. Mississippian	c. A.D. 700 - c. 1700	Destroyed (Pestilence?)
12. Far Eastern	before 1500 B.C. - after c. A.D. 1850	Engulfed by Central
13. Japanese	c. A.D. 650 - after c. 1850	Engulfed by Central
14. Central	c. 1500 B.C. - present	?

Figure 1 is a chronogram showing the lifespans and relative (Mercator) locations of the civilizations in the roster.

FIGURE 1.

THE INCORPORATION OF TWELVE CIVILIZATIONS INTO ONE "CENTRAL CIVILIZATION."

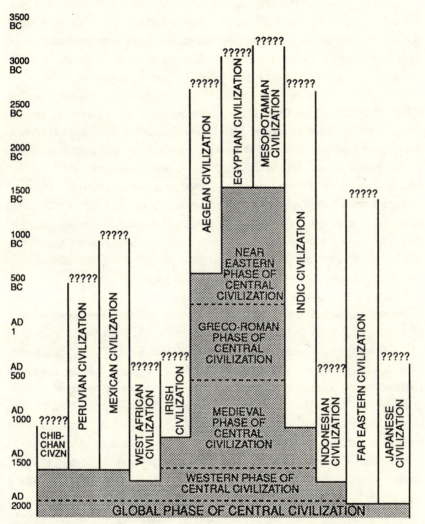

This figure illustrates the successive incorporation of autonomous civilizations into a larger, composite "Central civilization" (in grey).

The most striking effect of the new definition on accustomed lists of civilizations is that such accustomed entities as Classical-Hellenic/Greco-Roman civilization, Hittite civilization, Arabian/Magian/Syriac/Iranic/Islamic civilization(s), Orthodox Christian civilization, Russian civilization, and even our own familiar Western civilization, must be reclassified either as **episodes** of or as **regions** within a previously unrecognized social-network entity, by my definition both a civilized society and a world system, hence a single civilization. This civilization I have labeled Central civilization.

Central civilization was created in the Middle East during the 2nd millennium B.C. by an atypical encounter between two pre-existing civilizations. Civilizations may coexist, collide, break apart or fuse; when they have fused, they have typically done so by an asymmetric, inegalitarian engulfment of one by the other. But the linking of the previously separate Egyptian and Mesopotamian civilizations through Syria was an atypical, relatively symmetric and egalitarian "coupling" which created a new joint network-entity rather than annexing one network as a part of the other entrained to its process time. The new Central network, in an unbroken existence and process since then, has been atypical in another way: it has expanded, slowly by the reckoning of national and state turnover times, but quite rapidly by comparison to other civilizations, and in that expansion has engulfed all the other civilizational networks with which it once coexisted and later collided. Now expanded to global scale, Central civilization constitutes the single contemporary instance of the species "civilization." Figure 1 shows "Greco-Roman" and "Western" as epochs of regional **dominance** within Central civilization; these dominant regions in fact constituted long-lived, but impermanent, **cores** of Central civilization. The Near Eastern, Medieval and global phases of Central civilization also possessed cores, but they were larger and less culturally homogeneous than the Greco-Roman and Western cores.

Civilizations considered in their political aspect (and as world systems, in their world-political aspect) ordinarily have one or the other of two political structures: the **states system** (= state system = multi-state system = system of many independent states) and the **universal empire** (= universal state = world state = one-state system). Figure 2 is the chronogram from Figure 1, complicated by symbolization of the states-system periods, the epochs of universal empire, and the currently unclassifiable eras of each civilization.

FIGURE 2.

ALTERNATIONS BETWEEN STATES SYSTEMS AND UNIVERSAL EMPIRES

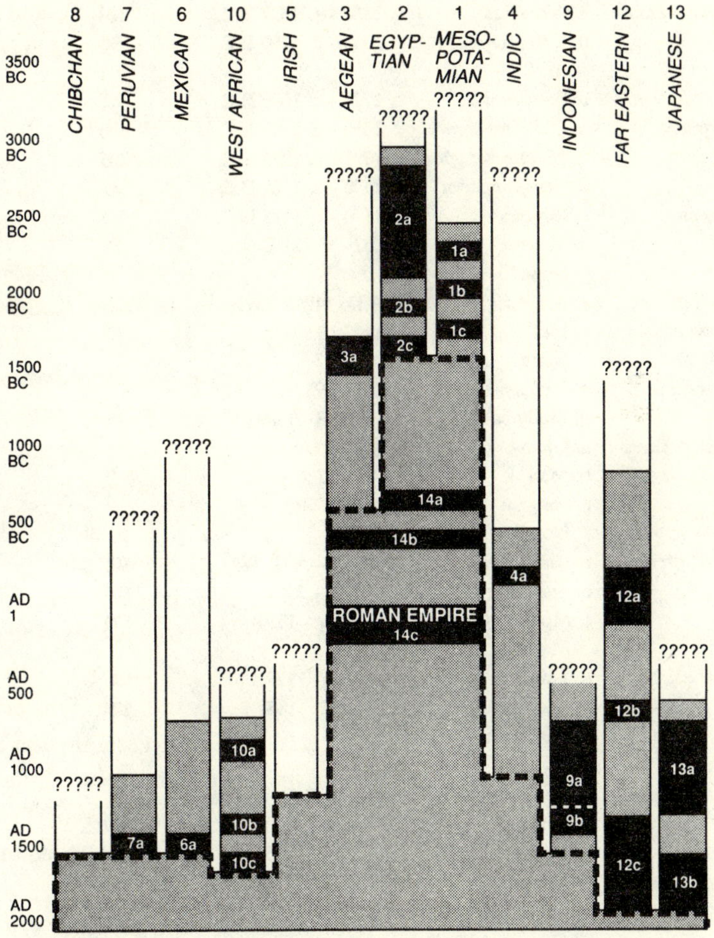

Each vertical bar in this chronogram represents a civilization: See Figure 1.
Central civilization is set off by a dashed line ▬ ▬ ▬ ▬ ▬ ▬ ▬ ▬ ▬ ▬

■ WORLD-STATE PERIODS: See Table 2

▨ STATES-SYSTEM PERIODS: See Table 3

□ POLITICAL STRUCTURE NOT YET CLASSIFIABLE

About twenty-three universal empires and about twenty-eight states systems may be identified. The universal empires of the fourteen civilizations are listed in Table 2 (see also Wilkinson, 1988), the states systems in Table 3.

Table 2. The World States of the Fourteen Civilizations

Civilization	State	Span	Duration
1. Mesopotamian	a. Akkadian	c. 2350 - c. 2230 B.C.	120
	b. Third Dynasty of Ur	c. 2050 - c. 1960 B.C.	90
	c. Babylonian	c. 1728 - c. 1686 B.C.	42
2. Egyptian	a. Old Kingdom	c. 2850 - c. 2180 B.C.	670
	b. Middle Kingdom	c. 1991 - c. 1786 B.C.	205
	c. New Kingdom	c. 1570 - c. 1525 B.C.	45
3. Aegean	a. Minoan	c. 1570 - c. 1425 B.C.	145
4. Indic	a. Maurya	c. 262 - c. 231 B.C.	31
5. Irish	None?		
6. Mexican	a. Aztec	c. A.D. 1496 - 1519	23
7. Peruvian	a. Inca	c. 1470 - 1533	63
8. Chibchan	None?		
9. Indonesian	a. Srivijaya	c. A.D. 695 - late 13th C.	600
	b. Madjapahit	A.D. 1293 - 1389	96
10. West African	a. Ghana	c. A.D. 950	?
	b. Mali	c. A.D. 1330	?
	c. Songhai	c. A.D. 1500	?
11. Mississippian	None?		
12. Far Eastern	a. Ch'in-Han	221 B.C. - A.D. 184	405
	b. Sui-Tang	A.D. 589 - 750	161
	c. Mongol-Ming-Manchu	A.D. 1279 - 1850	571
13. Japanese	a. Taiho	A.D. 702 - 1336	634
	b. Hideyoshi-Tokugawa	A.D. 1590 - 1868	278
14. Central			
Near Eastern Phase	a. Neo-Assyrian	663 - 652 B.C.	11
	b. Persian-Macedonian	525 - 316 B.C.	209
Greco-Roman Phase	c. Roman	20 B.C. - A.D. 235	255

Table 3. The States Systems of the Fourteen Civilizations

Civilization	States Systems	Notable States	Duration
1. Mesopotamian	A. Pre-Sargonid to c. 2350 B.C.	Uruk, Kish, Nippur, Ur, Lagash, Umma, Elam, Mari, Agade	?
	B. Pre-Urnammu c. 2230 - c. 2050 B.C.	Agade, Guti, Erech, Ur, Lagash, Uruk, Elam, Assyria	180

Table 3. Continued

Civilization	States Systems	Notable States	Duration
1. Mesopotamian (continued)	C. Pre-Hammurabic c. 1960 - c. 1728 B.C.	Ur, Uruk, Isin, Elam, Lagash, Eshnunna, Larsa, Babylon, Mari, Kassites, Assyria	232
	D. Post-Hammurabic c. 1686 - c. 1500 B.C. (becomes 14A)	Babylon, Sea Lands, Kassites, Hittites	—
2. Egyptian	A. Pre-Narmer to c. 2850 B.C.	Upper Egypt, Lower Egypt	?
	B. First Intermediate c. 2180 - c. 1991 B.C.	Heracleopolis, Thebes	189
	C. Second Intermediate c. 1786 - c. 1570 B.C.	Thebes, Xois, Avaris	216
3. Aegean	(A. Pre- Thalassocracy to c. 1570 B.C.?)	(Knossos, Phaistos, Mallia?)	—
	B. Post-Thalassocracy c. 1425 - c. 560 B.C. (merging into 14A)	Mycenae, Knossos, Pylos, Troy, Athens, Thebes, Tiryns, Miletus, Samos, Sparta, Corinth, Phrygia, Lydia	—
4. Indic	A. Pre-Asoka to c. 262 B.C.	Maghada, Kosala, Ujjain, Vamsas, Kalinga	?
	B. Pre-Engulfment c. 231 B.C. - c. A.D. 1000	Maghada, Bactria, Sakas, Kushana, Andhra, Kanauj, Palas, Gurjara-Prathiharas, Pallavas, Chalukyas, Pandyas, Rashtrakutas, Cholas, Ghaznavids	1231
5. Irish	(A. Pre-Engulfment to c. A.D. 1050?)	(Tara, Dublin, Munster, Ulster, Connaught?)	?
6. Mexican	A. Pre-Montezuma to c. 1496	Tenochtitlan, Texcoco, Tlacopan, Azcapotzalco, Mixtecs, Zapotecs, Tarascans, Tlaxcala	?
7. Peruvian	A. Pre-Huayna Capac to c. 1470	Cuzco, Charcas, Chimu, Quito	?
8. Chibchan	(A. Pre-Engulfment to c. 1530?)	(Tunja, Bacata?)	?
9. Indonesian	A. Pre-Srivijayan to c. A.D. 695	Srivijaya, Malayu, Kalah	?
	B. Pre-Madjapahit (late 13th C. A.D.)	Srivijaya, Singosari, Madjapahit	?
	C. Pre-Engulfment c. 1389 - c. 1550	Madjapahit, numerous Malay States	—

Table 3. Continued

Civilization	States Systems	Notable States	Duration
10. West African	A. Pre-Ghana to 10th C. A.D.?	Ghana, Songhai	?
	B. Pre-Mali 11th C. A.D. - 1325	Diara, Soso, Mossi, Manding, Songhai	?
	C. Pre-Songhai A.D. 1433 - 1493	Manding, Songhai, Tuaregs	60?
11. Mississippian	(A. Pre-Natchez?)		?
	(B. Post-Natchez?)		?
12. Far Eastern	A. Pre-Ch'in 771 - 221 B.C.	Ch'in, Chin, Han, Chao, Wei, Ch'u, Ch'i, Lu, Sung, Yen	550
	B. Pre-Sui A.D. 184 - 589	3 Kingdoms, W. Chin, 6 Dynasties, 16 Kingdoms, N. Wei, E. Wei, W. Wei, N. Ch'i, N. Chou, S. Ch'en, Sui, Annam, Champa, Nan-Chao, Tu-yu-hun	174
	C. Pre-Mongol A.D. 750 - 1279	Uighurs, Tufan, Nan-chao, 5 Dynasties, 10 Kingdoms, Khitans, (Liao), Hsi-Hsia, N. Sung, Jurchen, (Ch'in), Ch'i, S. Sung, Annam, Khmer, Champa, Wu Yueh, Mongols, Koryo	529
13. Japanese	A. Pre-Taiho c. A.D. 300 - 702	Koguryo, Paekche, Silla, Imna, Yamato	402
	B. Pre-Hideyoshi c. A.D. 1336 - 1590	Ashikaga, Yoshino, Enryakuji, Ikko, Various daimyo	254
14. Central	A. Pre-Assurbanapal c. 1500 - 663 B.C.	Egypt, Mitanni, Hittites, Elam, Babylon, Assyria, Urartu, Damascus, Israel, Tyre, Judah, Ethiopia, Media, Nubia	837
	B. Pre-Darius 652-525 B.C.	Assyria, Armenia, Elam, Babylonia, Media, Anshan, Persia, Lydia, Egypt, Libya, Ionia, Judah, Tyre, Meroe	127
	C. Pre-Augustan 316 - 20 B.C.	Syracuse, Carthage, Macedonia, Rome, Seleucids, Egypt, Pontus, Armenia, Parthia	296
	D. Post-Roman A.D. 235 - present	Rome, Persia, Byzantium, Arab Caliphate, Frankish Empire, Holy Roman Empire, Mongol Khanate, Ottoman Sultanate, Spain, Austria, France, Britain, Germany, Japan, Russia, America	1750+

Both universal empires and states systems ordinarily have **cores**. The core in a universal empire will usually be the metropolitan territory and people which conquered, united and governed the world system; the core in a states system will ordinarily include its great-power oligarchy.

Terminology and assumptions. At this point, it seems useful to stipulate some definitions, which will in due course become issues, since definitions contain the bones of revered but unnamed ancestral theories, and disturb the spirits rendered thereby non-ancestral. In this case the terminology offered will contain and embody explicit theoretical assumptions, which (being assumptions) will be expounded, but not defended.

An ideal-type civilization / world-system / macrosociety, because its characteristics are unequally distributed over space; and, because they are distributed centrically; and, because their unequal distributions overlap; and, because the inequalities are connected intrinsically to its past history of expansion (for civilizations tend strongly to expand, Central civilization being an extreme rather than an exceptional case) characteristically possesses:

(1)   a **core** (central, older, advanced, wealthy, powerful)

(2)   a **semiperiphery** strongly connected to the core (younger, fringeward, remote, more recently attached, weaker, poorer, more backward), and

(3)   a weakly connected **periphery** (nomads; peasant subsistence producers not yet attached to a city; **and** other civilizations that trade but do not habitually fight or ally with the subject civilization).

Civilizations usually begin in a geographically restricted area composed of cities and the hinterlands their fighters can control; this is surrounded by an area to which the new cities are politically irrelevant. We may call these zones the (initial) urban **core**, controlled **semiperiphery**, and uncontrolled **periphery** of the civilization.[3]

Civilizations usually expand over time by raiding, invading and conquering adjacent areas; and by sending out colony-cities and military settlements and trading forts; and by fascinating and addicting previously indifferent peripheral people to their products (gods, drugs, laws, weapons, music, ornaments, commodities, etc.). The territories affected by this civic expansion -- whether the expansion be colonialist, imperialist, cultic, developmental -- may be considered to have been incorporated by the civilization when their occupants -- settlers or settlees -- undergo urbanization and begin to interact politically on a regular basis -- as subjects, allies, tributaries, enemies -- with the civilizational core. This area of later expansion and control is the (enlarged) semiperiphery of the civilization.

Once a semiperiphery exists, and it comes to exist quickly, it also persists. Thus one of the main continuing patterns that reveals itself in the history of civilizations and world systems is that they tend -- not by definition, but empirically -- to be markedly geographically tripartite. In the **core**, military force, political power, economic wealth, technological progress, cultural prestige, and theogony are concentrated. The **periphery** is far from the core in all senses, containing peoples and territories known but scarcely noted. The **semiperiphery**, more or less recently penetrated or engulfed, is a zone characterized by military subjection, powerlessness, relative poverty, technological backwardness, and low cultural prestige.

But while the tripartition of a civilization is very durable, no area has permanent tenure in any role, and tenure of coredom is rather precarious. The global civilization of today, which expanded from a Mesopotamian-Egyptian core, is not ruled from Uruk, nor from Egyptian Thebes; the lobbyists of the world do not seek favors in Agade, nor do its engineers and physicians study in an Imhotep institute of Gizeh; there are no great powers based in the Fertile Crescent; Babylon is not the world's Hollywood; Amon's devotees are few. Cores are not eternal; civilizations can outlast their original cores. A history of cores must therefore be kinematic, describing their rises, shifts and falls; a theory of cores must ultimately be dynamic, accounting for their motion and change.

A theory of **peripheries** must largely account for their secular decline. Civilization as such -- the sum of the territories and peoples of the various civilizations -- has expanded continually since its origins, despite some regional setbacks and a single holocivilizational collapse (that of Mississippian civilization), by conquering and colonizing and assimilating its non-civilized peripheral peoples and territories. This contradicts the idea that civilizations rise and fall, rise and fall: they almost never fall. It also contradicts the image of peaceful sedentary civilized peoples always threatened and occasionally overwhelmed by neighboring barbarians: most of the "overwhelming" has been inflicted by the civilized societies on their peripheral neighbors. When noncivilized peripheral peoples -- usually nomads -- attack and conquer civilized territory, the result has ordinarily been that they settle down, take over, enjoy ruling the civilization, and continue expanding it; on the whole, peripheral peoples have not developed a sense of peripheral identity and pride sufficient to impel them to destroy the civilizations they have sporadically conquered. Civilizations, on the contrary, strongly tend to destroy their peripheries, through incorporation.

Tenure in the semiperiphery is more secure than core tenure (cores decline) or peripheral tenure (peripheries are devoured). But there is some upward mobility. A semiperipheral area remains semiperipheral as long as it is politically annexed to, urbanologically subordinate to, militarily dominated by, culturally provincialized by, economically outaccumulated by, technologically outcompeted by, and cultically devoted to, the old core. When and where the semiperiphery acquires states as influential, forces as dangerous, cities as populous and wealthy, culture as attractive, technique as progressive, gods as efficacious as those of the core, that part of the semiperiphery **becomes** core; the core area expands to encompass it. And if the old core should peak and decline, be overtaken and passed in its military and political, demographic and economic, cultural and technical and theological development by its semi-periphery (or a part of it), so that the old core becomes a historic backwater, becomes marginal to the affairs of the civilization, while the former semi-periphery becomes the new core, we may properly say that the core of the civilization has shifted. And cores do shift: witness Karnak, witness Babylon.

The ideas of core-periphery distinctions and inequalities are important to theories of civilizations (especially Carroll Quigley's evolutionary theory, 1961) and of world systems (especially Immanuel Wallerstein's world-systems analysis -- Hopkins, Wallerstein, *et al.*, 1972; Wallerstein, 1974, 1975, 1979, 1982, 1983, 1984). I would like to make a stab at roughly locating cores for the civilizations/world systems I recognize, discuss the empirics of their gross movement patterns, and juxtapose these "facts" to the theories of Quigley and Wallerstein -- which differ terminologically and substantively from each other, and from the exposition just given -- so as to judge which, or what combination, or what alternative theory, seems most helpful in describing, explaining, and projecting core-periphery behavior.[4]

Empirics: Cores and Core Shifts in Thirteen Civilizations

The most direct approach to sketching the general locations and movements of civilizational cores, as defined above, would be to assume that in a universal empire, the capital city and metropolitan district have politico-military core status by definition, and probably contain the cultic core, extract and consume economic surplus, maintain the cosmopolis with the largest urban population, support the cultural elite, and contain the loci of invention: hence their location coincides with the core, and shifts of capital/metropole are core shifts. This assumption is a useful ideal-type fiction rather than a universally true empirical generalization; we shall see that exceptions soon emerge. A desirable future project would be to measure rather than assume these consistencies, and observe the order in which preeminences are gained and lost by cores. Correspondingly, in a states system the great powers, the rich states, the religious centers, the **megalopoleis**, the cultural producers and critics, the great engineers, should be assumed to correspond closely enough that one of these measures will ordinarily suffice to demark a core state, absent contrary data. Where there are contradictions, power will take precedence over wealth in our narrative. In the civilizational game, diamonds may be forever; but clubs are always trumps.

1. Egyptian. Egyptian civilization was frequently united under a world state; core shifts are indicated by movements of the capital. After a predynastic period which may have been all-core/no-core[5] (primacy dispersed among nomes), an Upper Egyptian state conquered the country c. 2850 B.C., but then moved its capital to Lower Egypt (Memphis), where power remained in Dynasties I-IV, to c. 2440 B.C. The kings were war-leaders, and gods, gods'-sons, or high-priests, as well; the pyramids display the compresence of technique (architecture) and wealth (manpower mobilization, funeral offerings) with art and power.

The Vth dynasty (2440-2315) sees a small expansion of the core to nearby Heliopolis (Lower Egypt), and power-sharing with the priesthood of the sun-cult of Re.

Dynasty VI (c.2315-2175), witnessing the loss of a universal state and the rise of a states system under the local "nomarchs," also seems to reflect the evaporation of the Lower Egyptian core without any clear replacement. This then seems to be an all-core/no-core period.

A new core, more dispersed or perhaps faster-shifting, seems to have emerged gradually, with prominent states appearing at Memphis (Dynasty VII) in Lower Egypt, Coptos-Abydos (VIII) in Upper Egypt, Heracleopolis (IX-X) in Middle Egypt, and Thebes (XI) in Upper Egypt. (These dynastic capitals are partly simultaneous, partly sequential.) In due course the emerging core shrank, receding southwards, until it stopped at Thebes (Middle Kingdom, under Mentuhotep II, c. 2050).

A Theban dynasty (XII, c. 1991-1786) returned the capital northward, to Lisht (Lower Egypt), near Memphis, while maintaining the imperial god Amon at Karnak (Upper Egypt), near Thebes. This is a notable instance of core partition and specialization, an exception to the general practice of concentrated function.

Circa 1785-1570 Egyptian civilization was politically fragmented under dynasties XIII-XVII, partly simultaneous regional dynasties: XIII at Thebes, XIV at Xois (Lower Egypt), XV -- Hyksos invaders -- at Avaris (Lower Egypt), XVI Hyksos, XVII Thebes. This may be another all-core period, or one of a rapidly-shifting core.

Egypt was reunited under dynasty XVII (Thebes), during whose tenure Egyptian civilization couples with Mesopotamian to form Central civilization; until then, the military, political, religious and economic structure of Egyptian civilization was Theban-core.

This capsule history may be read as follows, in core terms. (1) There was usually, but not always (predynastic, dynasty VI, and perhaps XIII-XVII), a semiperiphery in Egyptian civilization. (2) Its core shifted frequently, from the time-perspective of the civilization. (3) The duration of core stability, or speed of core shift, fluctuated, with no core enduring more than 4 centuries. (4) Core preeminences -- military, political, economic, religious, technical, cultural -- were usually, but not always (dynasty XII's divided core) collocated in space. (5) Ex-core areas (Memphis in XII, Thebes in XVII) sometimes regained core status; but core shifts more often recruited new areas (Heliopolis in V, Coptos-Abydos in VIII, Heracleopolis in IX, Thebes in XI, Xois in XIV, Avaris in XV).

The Egyptian core history shows directional movement combined with expansive-contractive pulsation, in the following sequence: all-core/no-core - a Southern core - a Northern core - all-core/no-core - Middle - Southern - Northern - all-core/no-core - Southern. Two different rhythms may underlie this sequence. The core shuttles between south and north, implying the fall of an old core to semiperipheral status simultaneous with the rise of a semiperipheral area to core status; whatever conditions rendered aged cores incapable of continuing seem to have been eliminated by a term in the semiperipheral purgatory. Behind this shuttle pulses the longer rhythm of states system -- universal empire, in which decentralization and core-enlargement alternate with centralization and core-contraction, implying an alternation of equalization processes -- limited semiperipheral rise or limited core decline -- with polarization processes. The core process is clearly related to, but not reducible to, the states system -- universal empire political process.

2. **Mesopotamian.** The Uruk-core period of the second half of the 4th millennium B.C. appears to have been succeeded by an all-core period. (Cf. Algaze, 1989.) The Early Dynastic 1st dynasty of Uruk may be legendary, but the legend suggests another period in which Sumer, and within it Uruk, had core status. Later core evolutions include:

c. 2600-2500 Akkad (Kish)
c. 2500-2360 Sumer (Ur, Lagash, Umma)
c. 2360-2180 Akkad (Agade)[6]
c. 2180-2060 dispersed -- Akkad (Guti of Agade) and Sumer
    (Uruk, Lagash) -- hence all-core/no-core
c. 2060-1950 Sumer (Ur)
c. 1950-1700 dispersed -- Ur, Isin, Larsa, Elam, Nippur,
    Babylon, Mari, Assyria, Qatna, Aleppo, Eshnunna
c. 1700-1530 Akkad (Babylon)
c. 1530-1500 dispersed -- Hittites, Kassite Babylon, Sea-Land.
    (Beyond about 1500 BC Mesopotamian and Egyptian civilizations are,
    as noted previously, understood as parts a larger, Central civilization,
    whose core history is capsulized **infra**.)

Most generalizations applied above to Egyptian core history appear largely applicable to Mesopotamian as well. There was usually, but not always, a semiperiphery. The core shifted "frequently" -- from the civilization's duration-perspective! Core preeminences were usually combined -- but Nippur was a specialized religious center. Cores lasted a century or two. Old cores
occasionally, exceptionally, resurged. There was a north-south core alternation or "shuttle," and a separate concentration/dispersal rhythm associated with a

states system -- universal empire oscillation. Mesopotamia was, however, longer and more frequently in a "dispersed" or "all-core" condition.

The latter difference may have been consequential. Wesson has argued in general (1978:1-18) and specifically with respect to Sumer and Egypt (1978:42-44, 90-91) that "pluralism" of several sorts been causally connected to creativity in civilizations. A similar point is made by Ekholm and Friedman (1982:96). Core dispersion would seem to be yet another sort of "pluralism," likely to be similarly connected.

3. **Aegean.** An historical "gross anatomy" reveals a Cretan core (c. 2600-1425), with palaces on Crete (Knossos, Mallia, Phaistos, Hagia Triada) and dispersed trade-raid-taxing centers ("Minoa" seaports). This is succeeded by a Greek-mainland core (c. 1425-1100, with centers at Mycenae, Pylos, Tiryns, Athens, Thebes), and a semiperiphery including Miletus, Melos, Knossos, Troy. This structure is in turn replaced, after an all-core epoch of many *poleis*, by a rather dispersed largely Anatolian and insular core (c. 750-560) including Miletus, Phocaea, Chalcis, Eretria, Rhodes, Lesbos, Thera, Corinth, Megara, Achaea, as centers of colonialism around much of the Mediterranean; plus non-Greek Phrygia and then Lydia, which eventually provided the link that brought Aegean civilization into Central civilization during this period. The Cretan core fell as the Mainland semiperiphery rose; the Anatolian semi-periphery rose only after much of the Mainland core fell.

There was usually, but not always, an Aegean semiperiphery. The Aegean core did shift. The Cretan core was however quite durable, lasting perhaps 800 years; "occasional" rather than "frequent" core shifts seem to characterize Aegean civilization (one per millennium, vs. 8 per millennium in Mesopotamian, and a similar frequency for Egyptian). There was no "shuttle" with a clear renascence of a former core region.

4. **Indic.** In the Indus valley epoch (c. 2500-1500), a dual core emerged, upstream at Harappa (Punjab), downstream at Mohenjo-Daro (Sind). The Aryan conquest and city-breaking destroyed this core, an all-core/no-core epoch ensuing (inhabited ruined cities), until a new core arose in the Ganges Valley, where Hastinapur was a major center to the flood in c. 900 BC. Though the sixteen great states of Indic civilization around 600 BC stretched from the Punjab (Gandhara, Kamboja) to the Deccan (Asmaka), most cities (Sravasti, Kapilavastu, Rummindei, Kusinagara, Sarnath, Varanasi/Benares, Rajagriha, Bodhgaya/Sambodhi) lay among six states (Kosala, Malla, Vrijji,

Kasi, Anga, Magadha) of the middle and lower Gangetic basin; this represents the emergence, perhaps even the re-emergence, of a Ganges core.[7]

The Maurya conquest and empire contracted the core to the metropolitan state, Magadha, and its capital and religious center Pataliputra/Patna c. 260 B.C.   With the fall of Maurya after c. 230, the core as expanded as semiperipheries rose to core status -- Ionians (Yavanas) in Bactria and the Punjab; Chera, Pandya and Chola in the far south in the 2nd century BC; Saka-Pahlava and Yue-chi Kushana in the 1st century BC and Andhra-Pallava from the 1st century AD. The epoch seems no-core/all-core.

A brief Kushana empire was established in the north (upper Ganges and Indus basins) by Kanishka at Peshawar c. A.D. 78-100. incidentally re-forming an Indic core.   Another dispersal and all-core period followed, with Satavahana/Satakani in the Deccan, Ujjain/Malwa, Pallava, Ceylon, all noteworthy centers.

The Gupta empire, once more with Magadha as metropole and Patna as capital c. 330-c. 500, restored a Gangetic civilizational core, though not quite qualifying as a universal state. Following the Guptas, there was a dispersal again: Huns (Ephthalites), Malwa, Magadha, Ujjain, Pallava, Chalukya, Chola, Pandya all notable.

A Gangetic empire was founded by Harsha at Kanauj 606-647, reconstituting a core.   Then once more a dispersal: Kanauj, Gurjara-Pratihara, Pala, Rashtrakuta, Rajputs, Sind, Chola, Pallava, Chalukya, Vengi, Pandya, Ceylon, Chandella, Paramara, Yaminis of Ghazni.

If we consider (as I prefer to) the engulfment of Indic by Central civilization to have been accomplished by the Muslim invasions in the 11th century, India next became a semiperiphery of Central civilization, and remains so. If we do not consider Indic civilization to have been integrated into Central civilization till the 18th century, the period from the 11th to the 18th centuries continued the alternation of north Indian core empires with states-system chaos, hence of semiperipheralization with core expansion.

In either case, after an initial core shift, the pattern of a core empire/semiperiphery alternating with a states system/expanded core is well established. However, the dispersed-core or all-core pattern predominates, and contracted cores are short-lived. Cores are preferentially located in the north, with some alternation between Ganges-valley and Indus-valley metropoles, but a stronger inclination to the Ganges. Magadha was twice a metropole.

5. **Irish**. Turgesius (Turgeis) the Viking, after intensive looting from A.D. 837 on, set up a "longport" or naval camp at Dublin in 842 for greater convenience in plundering Irish states, churches and monasteries. The many Irish kings and occasional hegemonic high kings resisted. The Norse pressed, the Irish pressed back, each nation fought within itself; Dublin sacked Armagh and was itself sacked. By 842 Irish-Norse alliances are recorded in the *Annals of Ulster*, by 856 the "Gallogoidel" Norse-Irish mixed bands were a distinct fighting group. No core was evident.

Periodically an Irish dynasty or king did achieve hegemonic high-kingship, first the northern Ui Neill of Ulster (from Malachy I, 846-862, to Malachy II, 980-1002 and 1014-1022), then upstart kings of Munster (Brian Boru, 1002-1014, Turlock O Brien 1064-1086, Muircertach O Brien 1086-1119), of Connacht (Turlock O Connor 1121-1156, Rory O Connor 1166-2286), or of Ulster (Muircertach Mac Lochlainn 1156-1166). Some of the eleventh-and twelfth-century high kings achieved hegemony over the Norse cities -- raided, took hostages, imposed tribute (Malachy II and Brian Boru and Muircertach Mac Lochlainn on Dublin) or actually reigned from them (Turlock O Brien from Limerick) or named their kings (Turlock and Muircertach O Brien, and Turlock O Connor, for Dublin). One could defend the proposition that there was an Ulster core around 1000, a Munster core around 1100, a fast-moving unstable core in the 12th century (prior to the Norman invasions which attached Irish to Central civilization). However, power seems to have been so dispersed, personal, resisted, and rapidly displaced that, at time scales comparable to those at which cores persisted in other civilizations, there was no clearly definable core to Irish civilization. All the kingdoms seem to have had rough equality, roughly upheld.

6. **Mexican**. About 1200-600 B.C. the "Olmec" area appears to be core, with Gulf coast sites (San Lorenzo, La Venta, Tres Zapotes) and Basin of Mexico sites (Tlatilco).

By 600 B.C., the valley of Oaxaca (Zapotec Monte Alban, with the Temple of the Danzantes showing slaughtered "Olmecs," and Mitla) had become the core. Semiperipheries rose: Teotihuacan in the Basin, Mayan Kaminaljuyu (Guatemala City) in the Guatemalan Highlands in the Late Preclassic (300 BC-AD 250), perhaps qualifying this as an all-core/no-core period.

From about A.D. 200-700 ("Classic" period) the core was the Basin of Mexico, centered on Teotihuacan; semiperipheries seem to have included the

Gulf Coast (El Tajin; Teotihuacan pottery), Oaxaca (Monte Alban; pottery; Zapotec quarter of Teotihuacan), and the Maya region (probable colonization of Kaminaljuyu as a subimperial center; Teotihuacan figures on Tikal stelae, Teotihuacan-style pottery at Copan and Escuintla). Teotihuacan influence waned and was not replaced among the Maya in the 6th century, and the Late Classic Lowland Maya rose to core status in the 7th and 8th centuries.

There was a collapse at Teotihuacan around 700-750, apparently under the impact of northern-peripheral "Chichimec" invaders (including Toltecs). After the destruction and abandonment of Teotihuacan there seems to have been an all-core/no-core period: Cholula, Tula and Xochicalco in Central Mexico, El Tajin on the Gulf Coast, and Late Classic Maya Lowland Palenque, Piedras Negras, Tikal, Uaxactun, Copan, were all of importance.

The rise of Toltec Tula more or less coincides with the fall of the Southern Lowlands Classic Maya cities in the "Epiclassic" 9th-10th centuries (Copan abandoned after 800, Palenque after 810, Tikal abandoned end of 10th century), and of Monte Alban (abandoned c.900) in the 10th, suggesting that the Basin of Mexico was once again moving to core status. During this Basin-core epoch (11th-12th centuries), West and Northwest Mexico rose to be an important semiperiphery, and the Maya lands declined to semiperipheral status: Chichen Itza was occupied by Toltecs c. 1000-1180 and dominated the Northern Maya Lowlands; the Southern Lowlands remained depopulated; the Highlands showed Toltec influence.

Tula and the Toltec empire collapsed in the 13th century, perhaps again under the impact of northern-peripheral "Chichimec" invaders. The 14th century was again all-core/no-core: the Tarascans at Tzintuntzan in West Mexico, the Mixtec in Oaxaca (Monte Alban and Mitla), the Totonac at Cempoala on the Gulf Coast, Quiche in the Guatemalan Highlands, Mayapan dominating the Northern Yucatan Lowlands, the Tepanecs at Azcapotzalco in the Basin, mercantile Putun sea-traders at Cozumel and along the Gulf coast.

The 15th century saw the rise of the Aztecs of Tenochtitlan, hence the return of a Mexico-Basin core.

In shorter compass: a Gulf-and-Basin dual core; a shift of the core to Oaxaca; an all-core/no-core epoch; a Basin core; an all-core/no-core epoch; a Basin core; an all-core/no-core epoch; a Basin core. There was a semiperiphery about as often as not. Core lifetimes ranged from two to six centuries. The Basin of Mexico was usually, but not always, the core; no "shuttle" appears, but the equalization/polarization rhythm is distinct, though a universal empire emerged only from the final polarization.

7. **Peruvian.** Six phases seem distinguishable:

(1) Initial Ceramic, 1900-1200 B.C.: in monumental communally constructed ceremonial complexes -- highland Kotosh before 1800, coastal El Paraiso and central-coast Cerro Sechin (c. 1200). Probably all-core/no-core.

(2) Early Horizon, 1200-300. Widespread cultural unity in Chavin style, after N. Highland Chavin de Huantar, perhaps a Kotosh offshoot, spread through most of Peru, with a north coast manifestation (Cupisnique) and a south coast region (Paracas). Chavin seems to be the civilizational core on grounds of cultural domination; no universal state or core empire is apparent.

(3) Early Intermediate, 300 B.C.-A.D. 700: Cultural diversity, nationalism, interregional warfare. Coastal sites: Vicus, Moche (militaristic-expansionist), Lima (Maranga, Pachacamac, Cerro de Trinidad sites), Nazca (Cahuachi, Tambo Viejo), Atacameno. Highland sites: Cajamarca, Recuay, Huarpa (Huari; expansionist), Waru, Tiahuanaco (expansionist). Regional cultural variety and political polycentricity suggest this was an all-core/no-core period.

(4) Middle Horizon, A.D. 700-1100. Cultural unity under Tiahuanaco (southern) and Huari (northern) cultures and empires, with the Huari style derivative and the Huari center and empire shorter-lived (though greater in extent, with sites at Cajamarca, Cajamarquilla, Pachacamac, Chakipampa, Pacheco, Piquillacta). Probably best classified therefore as a twin-core period but (as with Harappa/Mohenjo Daro), arguably either Huari-core or Tiahuanaco-core.

(5) Late Intermediate 1100-1438/78. Cultural diversity. Peruvian coastal cultures, states and styles: Chimu (Chanchan), Chancay, Pachacamac, Chincha (La Centinela), Ica. Highlands: Cajamarca, Chanca, Killke (Cuzco), Lucre, Colla, Lupaca. Constant fighting, several empires: all core/no-core.

(6) Late Horizon 1438-1532. Cultural unity or unification imposed via Inca expansion from Cuzco, with notable sites at Machu Picchu, Cajamarca, Huanuco Viejo, Cushichaca, Tambo Colorado, Ollantaytambo.

The sequence seems then to be: all core/no-core; Chavin core; all-core/no-core; Huari-Tiahuanaco core; all-core/no-core; Cuzco core. The move from Chavin to Huari-Tiahuanaco was southward, that to Cuzco northward again. Core and all-core periods were very long, especially earlier, e.g., the 9-century Chavin core and 1000-year all-core Early Intermediate period. All-core seems the norm. Core epochs were too few to display a shuttle. Old cores did not resurge.

8. **Chibchan.** At the Spanish conquest, Chibchan civilization was politically bipolar, with some indication that the more sparsely populated, economically advanced, militarily aggressive state of the Zipa in Cundirramarca (Cundinamarca) was a semiperipheral upstart attacking the smaller, denser, more traditional, older religious-center core states allied with the Zaque in Boyaca, and that the Spanish conquest anticipated a core shift (and implemented it when the Zipa's capital of Bacata became the Spanish administrative center Santa Fe de Bogota). But there is not a long enough archaeological record for the Chibchan case to contribute much to our inquiry into core-periphery kinematics.

9. **Indonesian.** The locations of the key states are not all certain. A tentative sequence would be: Sumatran core (Ko-ying) 2nd century A.D.; all core/no-core 3rd-4th centuries; Javan core (Ho-lo-tan) 5th century; Sumatran core (Kan-to-li) 6th century; all-core/no-core 7th century; Sumatran core (Srivijaya) 8th-12th centuries; all-core/no-core 13th century (rise of Singosari in Java and Ligor in Malaya); Javan core 14th century (Madjapahit); Malayan core 15th century (Malacca); engulfed by Central civilization in 16th century, perhaps with the capture of Malacca.

This sequence shows an oscillation between core and no-core/all-core phases (4 core, 3 all-core periods) and a core shuttle among Sumatra (3 times), Java (twice) and Malaya (once). The all-core phase prevails earlier, the core phase later. When the core shifted, it returned to a former core area somewhat more often than it moved to a never-core location.

10. **West African.** A case could be made that the core of West African civilization was, and remained throughout its autonomous history, the general area of the great bend of the Niger river. However, given that the shift of power over the centuries was from Ghana's universal empire (Kumbi Saleh), to the Soso hegemony, to Malian empire (Timbuktu), to Songhai empire (Gao, Timbuktu), to the Hausa confederation (Zaria, Kano, Katsina), and that this sequence shows a general tendency (the Soso ascendancy and Songhai return to Timbuktu excepted) eastward and downriver, it makes somewhat more sense to speak of a slow and fairly steady eastward drift, with Kumbi out of the core in the 13th century after its sack by Sumanguru of Soso (1203) and its destruction by Sun Diata of Mali (1240). The overall drift is rather more like the Aegean than the Egyptian pattern.

11. **Mississippian.** The Adena core is in the Ohio Valley; Hopewell has an Ohio and an Illinois twin-core; the Temple Mound core seems to lie in Illinois, around Cahokia. This may be treated as a single very slow shift, or an expansion to and contraction around a new, formerly semiperipheral site. It is not clear whether all-core epochs were interpolated.

12. **Far Eastern.** Macroscopically, northern China was the core area of Far Eastern civilization from Shang times (late 2nd millennium B.C.) through the Later Han (3rd century A.D.). When one looks more closely the picture becomes at once more blurred, more shifting, and more complex: there are cores within the core. While the economic-demographic-cultural core seems to remain in the Yellow River plain, political-military power (imperial capitals; great powers) oscillates. Shang capitals (e.g., the last, An-yang/Yin) seem to lie within the economic core. The Chou, formerly a semiperipheral client people, first establish a metropole on their home territory in the Wei Valley (capital Sian), then move east (to Lo-yang), nearer the economic-demographic core.

With the breakup of the Eastern Chou core empire, the civilizational core remains in North China, but again partitions: small populous rich central states, politically and militarily weak but culturally progressive, are surrounded by large young states which become politico-militarily dominant. This period is therefore a split-core taxonomic puzzle.

The Ch'in and Former Han universal empires continue the core split: the political and communications center is again in the Wei valley (Ch'ang-an), the economic-demographic center downriver in the Yellow River plain. The Later Han ends the division by again moving the capital eastward, to the westerly fringe of the demographic core (Lo-yang).

The Three Kingdoms symbolize the expansion of the core area from North China to Szechwan and the Yangtze basins, and seem to reflect an all-core epoch. This continues during the Southern and Northern Dynasties, accompanied by a shift of population from the Yellow River to the Yangtze basin due to steppe-nomad invasions, destruction and depopulation, which push the core southward.

A new politico-military power emerges in the northwest under Sino-nomad elites and states, and under the Sui and T'ang states creates first a core empire and then a universal state encompassing the bulk of the semiperiphery as well as the core.

From late T'ang onward, the expansion of the civilized area without full acculturation of Koreans, Khitans, Uighurs, Tibertans, Tai, Annamese, Tanguts, etc. makes it appropriate to refer to "China" as such as the core area of the Far Eastern civilization -- meaning by "China" approximately the territories united by the Northern Sung, i.e. excluding 20th-century Korea, Manchuria, Mongolia, Sinkiang, Tibet, Yunnan, Vietnam. The enlarged core was divided by Chin and Southern Sung, reunited by the Mongols, and may be considered to have remained the Far Eastern core under Ming and Manchus, down to the absorption of Far Eastern by Central civilization in the 19th-20th centuries.

Far Eastern civilization has normally had a core. Core preeminences have however often been partitioned in space: politico-military and demographic-economic-cultural cores split apart, then drift together. The Far Eastern core has tended to expand more than to shift, even more markedly than will be seen in the core history of Central civilization. The Far Eastern core has been very durable indeed. On the other hand, the cultural hegemony of the core states (ability to Sinicize peripheral peoples as or after they are semiperipheralized) diminished noticeably in the Later Han, and again diminished with the later T'ang.

13. Japanese. The Nara period (710-784) sees what is probably the first core along with the first fixed capital. The move to nearby Heian (Kyoto), in 794, leaving the Nara monasteries behind, is a local shift of this rather tiny core. The division of function between administrative-religious Kyoto and politico-military Kamakura (1185-1333) expands the core, with both capitals serving as cultural-artistic centers.

Decentralization in the Ashikaga period (1336-1568) sees the growth of economic centers -- Sakai (Osaka), Hyogo (Kobe), Hakata (Fukuoka) -- while the politico-cultural capital returns to Kyoto after the divided dynasties of the Yoshino period (1336-1391); this seems an all-core/no-core period.

Further commercial decentralization (Nagasaki 1570-1638, Hirada 1609-1641) is reversed by the Azuchi-Momoyama national unification period (1568-1600), during which the functioning core contracts, perhaps as narrowly as to the Oda castle at Azuchi (1578-1582), the Hideyoshi castle at Osaka (1538-1598) and finally in the Tokugawa period (1600-1868) to the Tokugawa military base of Edo-Tokyo, which becomes the political-economic and cultural center. Kyoto remains the formal capital and enjoys a brief renaissance in the last decades of the Tokugawa period, which marks the beginning of the 19th-20th century incorporation of Japanese into Central civilization.

The reckoning would seem to be: an all-core/no-core period; core at Nara; core shift to Heian; core expansion Kyoto-Kamakura, and later Kyoto-Yoshino; an all-core period; core at Edo-Tokyo. The core epochs seem the norm, lasting longer than the all-core periods. A functionally split core prevails.

Empirics: Expansion and Core History of Central Civilization

Writing an approximate history of core areas and core shifts in Central civilization will be a considerably more complex undertaking than doing the same for even Indic and Far Eastern civilizations, the next most taxing candidates. The task is complicated by Central civilization's 3 1/2-millennium expansion, which has converted periphery into semiperiphery and allowed semiperipheral areas to enter an expanding core. Before locating the motion and change of the Central core over time and space, we need to estimate the expansion of Central civilization as a whole. That expansion can be usefully examined, and the issues that must arise in its study exposed, by searching for the frontiers of Central civilization over time.

It is convenient to use eight compass directions in this examination. Central civilization, starting from a core in the Nile Valley + the Fertile Crescent, has expanded **southeastward** into Arabia; **eastward** into Iran, India, Southeast and East Asia; **northeastward** into Central Asia and Siberia; **northward** into the Caucasus, the Ukraine, Russia; **northwestward** into Anatolia, the Balkans, northwest Europe; **westward** through the Mediterranean basin, then to the New World; **southwestward** into West Africa; and **southward** into the Sudan, the Horn, East, Central and Southern Africa. What follows is a sketch, again hypothetical and preliminary, of what should became a fertile field of civilization research: suggested answers (or subquestions) to the question, When did Central civilization arrive where, how, and what did it encounter there?

The "arrival" of an extant civilization in a new territory is represented by its establishment of strong and durable political links, conflictual or cooperative -- conquest, imperial integration, recurrent war, alliance, etc. Its imputed pace of expansion will depend upon the intensity and duration of the political connections established by threat, attack, invasion, conquest, occupation etc. Brief or weak linkings will pose problems: an urban area that perceives a continuing threat from another is linked to it in a single political system precisely by the threat; yet an intercivilizational interaction, much stronger than a mere threat -- invasion and conquest -- may, if the invaders go home and never return, or the conquerors lose all political linkage with their home civilization, produce no lasting or significant transactional linkage at all between the "source" and "target" civilizations.

When some picture of the local "arrivals" of Central civilization is developed, the question of when (if at all) the Central **core** arrived in the same territories can then be addressed. Core status has surely arrived when and where, in a states system, one of the independent semiperipheral states (e.g., the United States) becomes a Great Power;[8] or, in a universal state, when a new capital city is built in a semiperipheral area (e.g., Constantinople). A semiperipheral state, or a nonmetropolitan province of a world state, may or may not have attained core status -- the circumstances of each particular case would have to be examined -- if, in a peaceful epoch of its world system, it happened to become the system's center of wealth, culture, invention, or piety.

Central civilization, and its core, have on occasion contracted or shifted. We must be able to say when a territory is lost to a civilization, or to its core, in general.

A territory is lost to a civilization when it is de-urbanized, or when its cities' ongoing politico-military connection thereto is cut, by voluntary mutual isolation or by the de-urbanization or depopulation of an intervening and connecting area. A territory is thrust out of the core when conquered and occupied. It slips out of the core peacefully when, declining in power, wealth and prestige, its provinces/states and peoples come to be patronized, taken for granted, treated as backward, uplifted, advised, educated, helped, used, abused, proselytized, enlightened, snubbed, etc., when previously they had been accustomed to patronize, help, enlighten and abuse. Measurement of peaceful loss of core status is more difficult, or requires inspection of longer historical durations, than measurement of loss through conquest.

The southeastward expansion of Central civilization. I would provisionally treat the trade settlements in Bahrein (Dilmun) and Qatar from the late 2nd millennium B.C., and the Yemenite kingdoms of Minya, Sheba, Qataban and Hadramaut from the early to middle first millennium B.C., as southeastward extensions of the Central semiperiphery to incorporate coastal Arabia.

The dating for the incorporation of the Persian Gulf coast will remain provisional until political-archeological data are recovered. The Red Sea coast dating involves a centralist/pluralist controversy. It could be argued, though I would not do so, that an autonomous Yemenite civilization existed from at least c. 750 B.C. ("Saba" known to the Assyrians) to some later date when it was incorporated into Central civilization: c. 500 B.C. (consolidation of Sheba in response to Persian conquests in N. Arabia); or the 1st Century B.C. (Roman invasion of Yemen); or the 1st Century A.D. (formation of Axum as a "bridge" state between Central and "Yemenite" civilizations?); or the 4th Century A.D. (first Axumite conquest of Yemen); or the 6th century A.D. (second Axumite conquest of Yemen; Persian conquest of Yemen); or even the 7th century (Muslim conquest of Yemen and Syria). But I prefer the interpretation that the Persian Gulf and Red Sea settlements represent southeastward extensions of the Central semiperiphery, rather than autonomous civilizations, in which case they have remained outside the Central core until today.

The eastward expansion of Central civilization. Elamite Susa seems to represent the initial eastward outpost of Central civilization's core, Susa's hinterland the initial semiperipheral *Ostmark*. The Medean-Persian-Macedonian eastmarch is the Indus, while Persepolis/Istakhr, Ecbatana/Hamadan, and Rayy join Susa as the easterly core cities in that age. Central civilization's frontier retreats westward with the Seleucid evacuation before the Mauryas. Menander's kingdom advances it eastward again, to the upper Indus. The Roman universal state drives Mesopotamia out of the core into semiperipheral status; it returns to the core with the Sassanids and Abbasids. The Surens and Sakas probably succeed the Greek principalities as easterly marchers. The Kushans, White Huns and Turks probably jitter between peripheral and semiperipheral status, and the eastern frontier jitters with them.

The eastern frontier of Central civilization is pushed into the Punjab again by Mahmud of Ghazni's raids around 1000 A.D. and deeper into India by the Delhi dynasties. The Mongol invasion destroys some of the eastern urban extensions of Central civilization, especially in Afghanistan. Timur's invasions of India re-establish the (hostile) connections, and the Mughals complete the linkage of the Indic to the Central civilizational network, thereby pushing the eastern frontier of Central civilization to the delta of the Ganges.[9]

As regards the easterly progress of the Central core: Semiperipheral Anatolia begins a long tenure as core territory with Constantine, and returns to the semiperiphery with the 19th-century Ottoman decline. Mesopotamia enjoys core status until Timur's wars drive it down and out of the core of Central Civilization. While the Nile Valley jitters between core and semi-periphery during the Turco-Islamic dynasties, India, semiperipheralized by the Muslim conquest, makes a bid for core status under the Mughals; both Egypt and India re-enter the semiperiphery during the Western empires, and remain there today after the Western retrenchment -- as do Mesopotamia and Anatolia.

To return to the eastward march of Central civilization: European military-economic-political penetration and rivalries bring southeast Asia (both the continental portion, which is prised from Far Eastern civilization, and the autonomous Indonesian civilization) into the Central semiperiphery in the 16th-18th centuries; there it still remains.[10] The Manchu empire, Japan and Korea -- the rest of Far Eastern, and all of Japanese, civilizations -- enter Central civilization's semiperiphery in the 19th and/or 20th centuries, some-where between the Opium Wars and World War I, and immediately begin to struggle for core status. Japan attains core status in a military sense 1905-1918, loses it in 1945, regains it economically from the 1970's, militarily sometime in the 1980's. China probably achieved core status in the 1970's, and has probably not yet lost it. (In the last map, I have however excluded the non-Han, poor and near-empty west of "China" from core status on the ground that contemporary "China" is a multinational empire.)

The northeastward expansion of Central civilization. The expansion of Central civilization along a "northeastward" axis begins from Ecbatana/Hama-dan and Rayy. Next come Hecatompylus/Damghan, Merv and Bactra/Balkh; Bactria (the state) may even have been a core state, but the Yue-Chi, Kushans, White Huns and Turks in Bactria (the territory) were certainly at best semiperipheral.

A debate exists over whether Central Asia ever had civilizational autonomy; I incline to see it as always an extension of Central civilization, but one whose records of linkage have been peculiarly obscured by peripheral counterinvasion and destruction. Certainly no later than the Ummayads, the Central frontier advances to the Jaxartes; the Tahirids and Samanids may well have put Transoxania into the Central core, after which it jitters between core, semiperiphery and periphery, tending toward long-term decline, under Karakhanids, Seljuks, Ghuzz, Karakhitai, Khwarizmians, Mongol Khanates, Timurid Emirates and Uzbeks.

The eastward extension of the Muscovite/Russian frontier through Siberia, to the Manchu frontier, enveloping Kazakhs and Uzbeks in Central Asia, becomes the main expansive force of Central civilization in this "northeasterly" direction after the Uzbek conquest of Transoxania. Under Muscovite, Russian and Soviet empires, Central and North Asia become stably semiperipheral, and mostly so remains today, though the Trans-Siberian corridor seems more genuinely "Russian," and so more properly "core" than most of the Asian USSR or RSFSR; again I have so indicated on the final map in the set.

The northward expansion of Central civilization. In the 2nd millennium B.C. the Mitanni and Assyria are Central civilization's marchers; Van and the Medes push the Central frontier northward into the Caucasus. Armenia, the Bosporan kingdom, Colchis, Lazica, Iberia, the Albani, the Abasgians are key players on the frontier, moving it northward only slightly over a long period. The Khazars move it faster; Kievan Russia and its successors complete the northward movement.

The northward movement of Central civilization is notable for its slow pace, and for the degree to which it is embodied less in imperialist conquests of peripheral territory by core states than in the formation of "reaction states" -- states formed by peripheral peoples under pressure from/in admiration of/to defend against/to imitate/to excel their civilizational neighbors. The entry of the northward semiperiphery into the core of Central civilization comes late, with Russian participation in the great wars of the 18th century, but Russia remains in the core, except, perhaps, between the two World Wars of the 20th century.

The northwestward expansion of Central civilization. The Hittites are 2nd millennium members, first of the Mesopotamian civilization's semi-periphery, then of the Central civilization's core. Peripheral Phrygians and Luvians first force the civilization's frontier backward by invasion and conquest, then form reaction states and become members of the Central semiperiphery. Cimmerians push the civilizational frontier back. Lydians advance it again, definitively recruiting (or re-recruiting) the peoples of Aegean civilization to Central, first as semiperipherals.

Persians push the Central semiperiphery into Thrace. Epirus and Macedon remain marchers for a long time. Anabasis and Alexander reflect unsuccessful and successful bids for core status by the Greco-Macedonian semiperipheral peoples on the Central northwest. Rome drives these peoples back to semiperipheral status by the 2nd century BC; some return to the core in the 4th century AD, but lose that status again over the long period of Islamic (Arab/Turk) expansion to local hegemony. The Roman imperial frontiers from Britain to Thrace would then embody the next substantial forward movement of Central civilization's northwest frontier, after the Balkan entry in the 5th-4th centuries BC.[11] The Frankish -- Ostrogothic -- Byzantine frontier represents the next main hesitation and jitter in the continual but discontinuous Central expansion northwestward. The missionary advance of Roman and Eastern Christianity after Charlemagne and Cyril, because it represents enduring political linkage and not simply a change of worldviews, thereafter roughly marks the assimilation of eastern, northern and northwestern Europe into Central civilization. States from this frontier (Frankish, Holy Roman, France, England, Austria, Prussia/Germany, to a lesser degree Holland, Denmark, Sweden) enter the Central core, and by the 17th century largely constitute that core, though always sharing that status with some others, increasingly so in the late 20th century, when core wars perhaps temporarily semiperipheralized Northwest Europe.

The westward expansion of Central civilization. Phrygia and Lydia become the instruments by which Central civilization engulfs Aegean Civilization (by then Greek-dominated). Phoenicians/Carthaginians and westward-moving Greeks bring in the eastern, then the western Mediterranean (and the Atlantic at Cadiz) via colonialism. Etruscans, then Latins/Romans, become reaction-state marchmen, as do Numidians and Mauretanians. Rome brings in the rest of Iberia by straightforward imperialism. The westward expansion then stops at the Atlantic for a millennium and a half.

Rome enters the Central core in the 3rd-2nd centuries BC, leaving it in the 4th-5th centuries AD. Iberia enters the core in the late 15th century, leaves it in the 17th. Italy returns to core status during the Renaissance, and again via nationalistic and imperialist wars in the late 19th and early 20th century. Today the states of this western frontier seek core status, and Italy has perhaps regained it once more, via European integration.

Meanwhile Iberians, and then northwest Europeans, restarting the westward expansion, extend Central civilization to the New World from the late 15th century A.D., in the process reducing Mexican, Peruvian and Chibchan civilizations to semiperipheries of Central civilization. European colonists carry the Central frontier with them beyond the civilizational boundaries of the engulfed New World civilizations: the American frontier is closed in the late 19th century, the Canadian (and Alaskan) in the mid or late 20th. The Amazonian frontier has probably closed by 1990, with the recruitment of the remaining peripheral tribes to semiperipheral subordination and/or resistance. America enters the Central civilizational core by World War I, Canada after World War II; the remainder of the far western (New World) frontier of Central civilization is still semiperipheral today.

The southwestward expansion of Central civilization. The southwestern frontier of Central civilization remains not far from the Nile Valley, blocked by the Sahara, from the mid-2nd millennium B.C. to the mid-2nd millennium A.D. It is then extended by a politico-economic-military envelopment maneuver, the seafaring ventures along the West African coast by Portuguese, Dutch, French and British members of Central civilization, and by trans-Saharan military ventures by Moroccans, which incorporate the West African interior (including the West African civilization) into Central civilization. This encirclement means that the final "southwestward" penetration of Africa is carried out by forces moving **eastward**, and by local opponents forming reaction states in response to pressure from their **west**. The southwestward expansion of Central civilization was completed not later than the 19th century; thus far no areas so penetrated have entered the Central core.

The southward expansion of Central civilization. Nubia is brought into Central civilization by Egyptians in the late 2nd millennium B.C., and is succeeded in the next millennium by Meroe as the south-march (or simply moves its capital upstream from Napata to Meroe?). Axum/Abyssinia takes that marcher role in the first half of the first millennium A.D., carrying Central civilization's frontier to Eritrea and then to Ethiopian plateau. Of these territories, only Napata ever enters the Central core, briefly, under Pi'ankhi (late 8th century BC), before the XXV Dynasty ("Ethiopian") moves its capital to Thebes.

Beyond Axum, the southward expansion of Central civilization quinquefurcates, with different stories for each of the following areas: Ethiopia, Nubia, Sudan, East Africa, Central Africa.

Southward expansion: Ethiopia. The Arab conquest in the 7th century broke Axum's land and sea connections to the Byzantine empire. The Ethiopian link to Central civilization was however maintained -- oppositionally, via Muslim states. The Arab conquests were followed by a continued semiperipherality of the conquered regions, some of which may have become peripheral. Ethiopia was kept connected to Central civilization (1) through

Muslim attacks in the 13th-16th centuries, (2) through Portuguese and Spanish connections in the 16th-17th centuries, and (3) through British and Italian connections in the 19th and 20th centuries, and remains today in the Central semiperiphery.

Southward expansion: Nubia. The outermost Nubian area may have been lost to Central civilization (through deurbanization) when Meroe was destroyed by Ethiopians in the 4th century, and its people moved westward; but a post-Meroitic Nubian civilized area continued downriver near Dongola, linked to Ethiopia and therefore a part of Central civilization. Islamized Egypt maintained this Nubia's Central connection through repeated invasions after the 7th century, infiltration and conversion in the 13th-15th century, Funj rule in the 16th-18th centuries, and Egyptian and British conquests in the 19th century. Contemporary struggles in the state of Sudan represent the pressure of the Arabized northern semiperipheral peoples upon the once peripheral tribal peoples of the south, who are thereby recruited into the Central semiperiphery.

Southward expansion: Sudan. Sudanic states -- from Funj through Kordofan, Darfur, Wadai, Bagirmi, Kanem, Bornu, to the westerly marches of the Hausa states -- arose as a result of westward penetration from Nubia by Arab traders and Islam, and in chain reaction, as an extension (from Nubia) of Central civilization. The 19th century European conquests simply enlarged and redirected the connections of the Sudanic area with Central civilization.

Southward expansion: East Africa. Arab-Islamic penetration established city-states, outposts of the states system of Central civilization, at Mogadisho (contemporary Somalia, c. 900), Malindi (Kenya, 10th century), Mombasa (Kenya, 8th century -- ivory, slaves), Pate (Kenya), Kilwa Kisiwani (Tanzania, by 1200 -- gold, ivory, skins), Sofala (Mozambique after 1000 -- gold, ivory), Cuama (Mozambique, after 1000), Inhambane (Mozambique, after 1000 -- slaves, ivory). Inland, over against the coastal colonies, reaction states formed, e.g., Monomatapa/Mwanamutapa vis-a-vis Sofala c. 1420, and before it, from the 11th century, Great Zimbabwe. Thus civilization in East Africa constituted a semiperiphery of Central civilization well before the 16th century imperialist expansions of the Central states Portugal and Oman rendered East African territories provinces of Central civilization's semiperipheral states.[12]

Southward expansion: Central Africa. State formation was brought to Central Africa by the Cwezi states (in current Uganda) not later than the 14th century, and continued by their Bito successors (Buganda-Bunyoro-Ankole) from around 1500, the Kongo state (in current Angola) in the 14th century, Tutsi states (Rwanda and Burundi) in the 15th, Ndongo (Angola) by the 16th, Luba and Lunda States (Zaire) in the 16th, the Kuba kingdom of the Shongo (Zaire) from the early 17th century. The two extremes (Uganda and Angola) began independently of each other; they were linked up slowly over the next three centuries into a Central African constellation whose states were independent until provincialized through Portuguese (15th century onward), then Zanzibari, British and Belgian (19th century) penetration. When and where urbanization, therefore civilization, occurred among the Central African states, it occurred as a reaction, not only to their penetration by Central-civilization traders, but to the colonial plantation of trading posts, mission stations and city-states on the west and east coasts -- and then to one another's citification. The urbanization of Central Africa accordingly constituted a long and tenuous extension of Central civilization's semi-periphery, and the territories thus recruited to the semiperiphery have remained there, as states, then as imperial colonies or provinces, now once again as states.

The "career" of Central civilization's core. As Central civilization expanded, in all directions, at varying paces, the newly recruited areas generally entered its semiperiphery, where most have remained. Still, the core of Central civilization has certainly both expanded and shifted over time. In the Near Eastern phase the core was at first the line of cities along the Fertile Crescent and the Nile Valley; over time, the core expanded, mostly westward into the Mediterranean littoral, to Asia Minor and to Greece. During the Greco-Roman phase the core area expanded to include Italy, and shifted westward from Mesopotamia. During the Medieval phase the core area once again included Mesopotamia; the core shifted eastward again toward Thrace, Anatolia, Egypt, Syria, Iraq. Italy went out with the decline of Rome and returned to the core with the rise of Venice and other cities of Northern Italy. During the Western phase the whole core of Central civilization shifted north and west to France, Spain, the Low Countries, Germany, Britain. In the global phase the core seems to have expanded greatly, to include America and Russia, and probably Japan. Plausible current candidates for future core status include India and China; Russia (as USSR) shows distinct signs of strain and potential breakup and dropout, but still remains[13] a core state. Many short-term fluctuations and local attainments, disasters and controversies are necessarily passed over in these abbreviated descriptions, which however give the general picture of core enlargement/contraction and shift in language comparable to that employed for the other thirteen civilizations already described.

There is plenty of work to be done debating the dimensions of civilizational movement and mapping core shifts; but it seems beyond much dispute that Central civilization has expanded in space; its core area has expanded in space; its semiperiphery has also expanded in space; its core has shifted over space, with old core areas declining into the semiperiphery and new core areas rising out of same.

These propositions are illustrated in Figures 3 through 11:

Central civilization in 825 BC, 375 BC, 145 BC, AD 737, 1028, 1212, 1478, 1600, and today.[14]

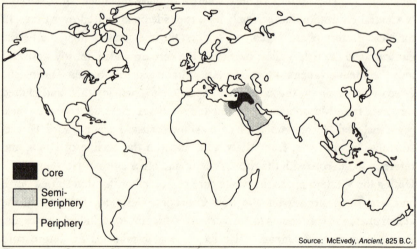

Figure 3.   Central Civilization in 825 B.C.

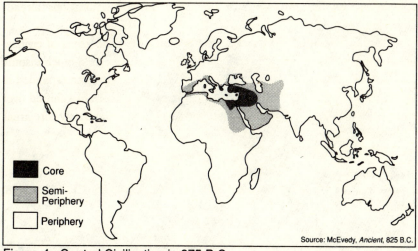

Figure 4. Central Civilization in 375 B.C.

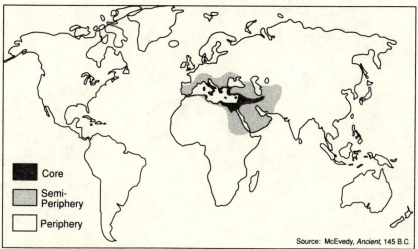

Figure 5. Central Civilization in 145 B.C.

146

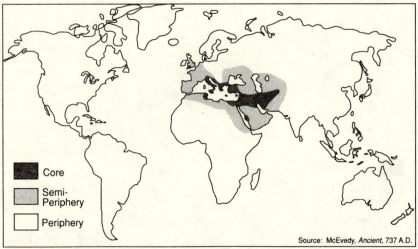

Figure 6. Central Civilization in 737 A.D.

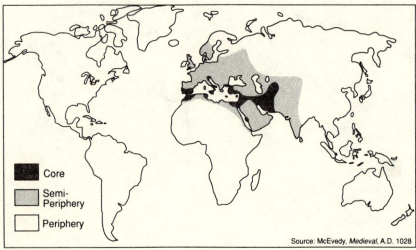

Figure 7. Central Civilization in 1028 A.D.

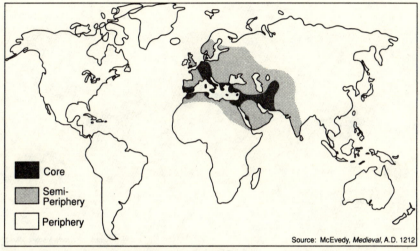

Figure 8. Central Civilization in 1212 A.D.

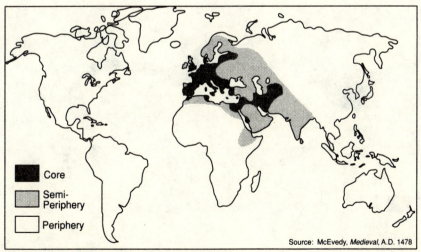

Figure 9. Central Civilization in 1478 A.D.

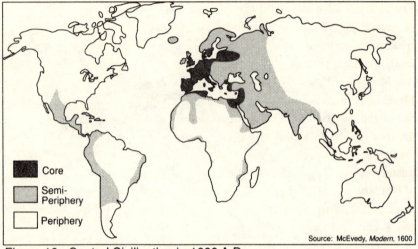

Figure 10. Central Civilization in 1600 A.D.

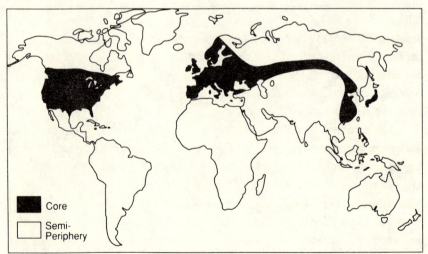

Figure 11. Central Civilization today: mostly semi-periphery.

Core Theoretics

The political form of a civilizational core. A civilization's core may have any of several political forms. It may be a **single state**, as in: Mesopotamian civilization, perhaps, during the (perhaps legendary) 1st Uruk dynasty, c. 2850-2600?; Aegean, perhaps, during the mainland period (Mycenae); Indic during the Maurya rise and fall and the Kushana, Gupta and Kanauj empires; Mexican, perhaps during Oaxacan, Tiahuanaco and Toltec hegemonies and the rise of the Aztecs; Peruvian, perhaps during Chavin, surely during the rise of the Incas; Indonesian, perhaps in the 2nd (Ko-ying), surely in the 15th century (Malacca) and during the rise and fall of Srivijaya and Madjapahit; Far Eastern in late T'ang and northern Sung, and during the rise of Ch'in, the fall of Han, the rise of Sui and of the Mongols; Japanese during Azuchi-Momoyama; Central during the rise and fall of Assyria, the rise of Media and Persia and Rome, and the era of Justinian.

The core may contain **several states, successively hegemonic**: in Mesopotamian civilization, the Sumerian core c. 2500-2360 (Ur, Lagash, Umma). It may constitute **several states simultaneously balanced**, as in: Egyptian during the Intermediate periods; Mesopotamian during the Gutian and Isin-Larsa eras; Aegean during the Anatolian period; Indic between the major empires; Irish throughout -- or at least between hegemonic high kings; "Olmec" Mexican; Huari-Tiahuanaco Peruvian; Chibchan; Indonesian in the 3rd-4th, 7th and 13th century intervals between ascendancies; West African between universal states; Far Eastern in the chaotic Eastern Chou, the Han-Sui interval, and the Ch'in-Southern Sung period; Japanese during the late Ashikaga chaos; Central between universal empires, and for most of the time since the Roman empire's fracturing.

The core may be the **metropolitan region of a universal state**: Egyptian during the kingdoms; Mesopotamian during the empires of Agade, 3rd dynasty Ur, and Babylon; perhaps Aegean, during the Cretan period; Indic during the Maurya empire: Indonesian during the Srivijaya and Madjapahit peaks; West African during the Ghana, Mali and Songhai peaks; Far Eastern during the Western Chou, Later Han, Sui-early T'ang, and Mongol-Ming-Manchu periods; Japanese in the Nara, Heian and Tokugawa periods; Central during the Assyrian, Persian-Macedonian and Roman empires. Or the civilizational core may be a **functionally divided set of areas in a universal state**, as in Far

Eastern civilization in the Ch'in-Former Han and Japanese civilization during the Kamakura period.

The most frequent core forms are: the single dominant or hegemonic state; several competing states; and the universal-empire metropole.

Pulsation of cores. Core areas enlarge and contract. The Egyptian core included part of the Nile valley, then the whole (Dynasties VI-VIII), then part, then all (Dynasties XIII-XVII), then part. The Indic core contracted under the Mauryas, Kushanas, Guptas and Harsha, and reexpanded after the fall of each. The Mexican core expanded between, but contracted during the Teotihuacan, Toltec and Aztec eras; the Peruvian behaved similarly between and during Chavin, Tiahuanaco-Huari, and Inca horizons, the Indonesian between and during Ko-ying, Ho-lo-tan, Kan-to-li, Srivijaya, and Madjapahit-Malacca eras. The Mississippian core expanded from Adena to Hopewell, contracted from Hopewell to Temple Mound. The Far Eastern core expanded in the Three Kingdoms period. The Japanese core expanded in Kamakura and Ashikaga periods, contracted during Azuchi-Momoyama and Tokugawa. Central civilization's core shifts -- westward in the Greco-Roman phase, eastward in the Medieval phase, westward again in the Western phase -- involved expansion at one edge synchronic with contraction at the other; the global phase saw core expansion east and west. Contractions are naturally enough associated with hegemonic struggles and universal-state periods, expansions with all-core epochs; but not perfectly.

Are semiperipheries necessary? Apparently not, since civilizations are often all-core/no-core, i.e. lack a semiperiphery. Egyptian civilization had a semiperiphery during the Kingdoms, did not during the Intermediate periods; Indic did during the empires, not between. Mesopotamian civilization seems always to have had a semiperiphery, Aegean likewise; Irish never did. Mexican civilization had no discernible semiperiphery in the intervals between the Teotihuacan, Toltec and Aztec ascendancies, nor did Peruvian in its Intermediate periods between Horizons. Chibchan may have developed a semiperiphery in Cundirramarca. Indonesian civilization probably had none between the Sumatran, Javan and Malaysian ascendancies, and probably did during those ascendancies. West African civilization probably always had a semiperiphery; Mississippian did at least during Hopewell and Temple Mound. Far Eastern civilization almost always had one, with Eastern Chou and the Han-Sui interregnum notable exceptions. Japanese civilization usually had a semiperiphery, with the Ashikaga period likely the exception. Central civilization has always had a significant semiperipheral area.

Semiperipheries exist more often than not, particularly in universal-empire periods when the metropole is especially favored, but they do not seem necessary features of a civilization: power, wealth, creativity can all be rather widely dispersed, though dispersal usually alternates with concentration.

Directionality of core shift. Cores may move in a single general direction, or oscillate. The Egyptian core shuttled between north and south, the Mesopotamian between Sumer and Akkad. The Aegean core moved north, then east; the Indic core shuttled between west and east, though with an eastward inclination. The Mexican core moved south, then partway north again; so did the Peruvian. The Indonesian core oscillated between Sumatra and Java and then to Malaya. The West African core drifted eastward with a few half-moves back, the Mississippian core drifted westward, the Japanese eastward. The Central core half-moved west, then east, then drifted west and north. No significant patterns are evident.

Reversibility of core decline. Does past experience as a core preclude or assure return to core status? Apparently neither. Let us first take note of, and then set aside all the apparent civilizational-startup first-time cores: the Egyptian south in first unification; Mesopotamian Sumer in the 4th millennium BC; Aegean Crete; Indus basin at the beginning of Indic civilization; all Ireland; Mexican's "Olmec" Gulf and Basin zones; the Peruvian Initial Ceramic complexes; Chibchan Boyaca; Indonesian Sumatra (Ko-ying period); West African Kumbi Saleh; Mississippian (Adena) Ohio; Far Eastern (Shang) Yellow River valley; Japanese Nara; Central civilization's Fertile Crescent + Nile valley.

There are many cases in which a semiperipheral area, never before a core, rose to core status: the Egyptian North in the Old Kingdom; Mesopotamian Akkad in the Kish period; Aegean Greece and Anatolia; Indic (Maurya) Patna, (Kushana) Peshawar, (Harshan) Kanauj; Mexican (Zapotec) Oaxaca; Peruvian (Early Horizon) Chavin, and then (Early Intermediate) most coastal and highland sites; Chibchan Cundirramarca; Indonesian (Ho-lo-tan) Java, (Malaccan) Malaya; West African (Malian) Timbuktu, perhaps Songhai Gao; Mississippian (Hopewell) Illinois; Far Eastern (Western Chou) Wei valley; Japanese (Heian) Kyoto, (Bakufu) Kamakura, and several Ashikaga centers. In Central civilization, such first-time core entrants included Assyria, Persia,

Greece (previously, however, an Aegean core), Macedonia, Rome, Byzantium, Western Europe, America, Russia.

But there are several other cases in which a fallen core area has returned from semiperipheral status, or has regained a solitude it had lost to upstart sharers. In Egyptian civilization: the south in dynasties XI and XVIII, the north in XII. In Mesopotamian civilization: Sumer/Uruk in the Early Dynastic c. 2850-2600; Sumer and Akkad alternatively 2500-1500. In Indic civilization: Patna under the Guptas. In Mexican civilization: the Basin during Teotihuacan, Toltec and Aztec periods. In Peruvian civilization: Cajamarca and Pachacamac in the Late Intermediate, after their eclipse by Huari in the Middle Horizon; Late Intermediate Chimu (replacing Early Intermediate Moche) after the Huari coreship. In Indonesian civilization: Sumatra during Kan-to-li and Srivijaya; Java during Madjapahit. In Far Eastern civilization: the Wei valley under Ch'in. In Central civilization: Abbasid Mesopotamia, and the classic renaissance of Renaissance Italy.

In the transition from semiperiphery to core, history seems somewhat more favorable to naissance than to renaissance, but renaissances do happen.

Within-core differentiation. Different areas may serve as military-political, economic, and cultural-religious cores, and core shifts may occur in these features at different times. The Norse cities were Ireland's economic core, the monasteries its cultural core, the Kingly seats the politico-military core: result, an all-core civilization. Chavin may have been only Peru's cultural center; Tiahuanaco may have been only a cultural, Huari only a military core. The Far Eastern politico-military core long tended to be north and west of the economic-demographic-cultural core. The Japanese religious, politico-military and economic cores drifted apart in Kamakura and Ashikaga and were reunited in Tokugawa days. The most notable discrepancies between Central civilization's economic-technical and politico-military cores are attested by being corrected: the shift from Rome to Constantinople, the Renaissance-ending invasions of Italy, the revolt of the Netherlands, the involvement of British finance and fleets in Continental wars, and the American entry into the World Wars of the 20th century. There is thus some tendency for geographically separated functions to be pulled together; the political-military core may conquer the others (the post-Renaissance invasions of Italy), migrate to them (by a movement of the capital, e.g., to Constantinople or Lo-yang) or usurp them (by taxation and subsidy, e.g., Tokugawa

Edo); or economic cores may invest in politico-military potency (Dutch, British, Americans).

Critique of Core-periphery Theory

In the search for a core-periphery theory, principally a theory of core motion and change, we do not start entirely afresh. Two workers of note, the civilizationist Carroll Quigley and the world-systems analyst Immanuel Wallerstein, have elaborated definite propositions about "cores." Their terminologies differ from that employed here; their propositions are nonetheless of interest.

    Quigley on core and periphery. Quigley's spatial account of civilizations contains the following major propositions bearing on core-periphery issues. (1) Civilizations generally arise on the periphery of previous civilizations, out of cultural mixture. (Quigley, 1961: 78-80.) (2) Since every new civilization has an instrument of expansion, such that within it "inventions begin to be made, surplus begins to be accumulated, and this surplus begins to be used to utilize new inventions," civilizations have early (and sometimes recurring) stages of expansion -- of production, living standards, population, and -- through colonization -- of territory. The expansion process is one half of the major civilizational dynamic. (1961: 80-81.) (3) Expansion produces partition. "As a result of the geographic expansion of the society, it comes to be divided into two areas: the core area, which the civilization occupied [originally], and the peripheral area into which it expanded during [its stage of expansion]" (1961: 81-82.). Here is our first terminological difference: I would agree that civilizations expand into their periphery, but would then restyle the area expanded into as "semiperiphery." This term, of which so far as I know Quigley is the originator, he twice employs (1961:85); but more often he speaks of "more peripheral" and "less peripheral" areas (1966:85-87).

    (4) All civilizational instruments of expansion tend to become corrupted, "institutionalized," non-expansive. The slowdown of expansion is the other half of the major dynamic of civilizational change. (5) The slowdown of expansion is geographically partitioned. "When expansion begins to slow up in the core areas, as a result of the instrument of expansion becoming institutionalized, and the core area becomes increasingly static and legalistic, the peripheral areas continue to expand...." Furthermore, as latecomers they

can often imitate core successes while avoiding time-wasting blind alleys explored by core innovators; so the "peripheral areas...frequently short-cut many of the developments experienced by the core area. As a result, by the latter half of [the civilization's stage of expansion], the peripheral areas are tending to become wealthier and more powerful than the core areas. Another way of saying this is that the core area tends to pass from [a stage of expansion] to [a stage of crisis and conflict] earlier than do the peripheral areas." (1961: 81-82.) (6) The slowdown of expansion produces, among other effects, tension and class conflict.

(7) Because the crisis of expansion is geographically partitioned, it is particularly acute in the civilization's core area. (8) The crisis of expansion also produces imperialist wars intended to continue the local expansion of parts of the civilization, now at the expense of other parts. (9) The core suffers these wars first. (10) The imperialist wars lead to conquests that reduce the number of states in the civilization, eventually to one. (11) The core is unified first: a core empire precedes a universal empire. (1961: 82-85). (12) "In the imperialist wars of [the stage of conflict] of a civilization the more peripheral states are consistently victorious over less peripheral states." Core empires are created by semiperipheral states, universal empires by fully peripheral states (1961: 85). Quigley's terminology is such that power for him can move, leaving the core behind; I would speak of the same phenomenon as the movement of the core into formerly semiperipheral areas.

(13) What are the reasons for the habitual victory of more peripheral states over less peripheral states during the stage of conflict of any civilization? One is the general rule that "material culture diffuses more easily than nonmaterial culture, so that peripheral areas tend to become more materialistic than less peripheral areas; while the latter spend much of their time, wealth, energy, and attention on religion, philosophy, art, or literature, the former spend a much greater proportion of these resources on military, political, and economic matters. Therefore, peripheral areas are more likely to win victories" (1961: 86-87). (14) A second reason "arises from the fact that the process of evolution is slightly earlier in more central areas than in peripheral ones," so that while more peripheral areas are still in a stage of expansion, more central ones, in a later stage of development, "are more harassed by class conflicts and are more paralyzed by the inertia and obstruction of institutions," and generally have undergone and been weakened by a longer period of imperialist wars.

Wallerstein on core and periphery. Immanuel Wallerstein presents a distinctive idea of core and periphery. Cores and peripheries are features of multistate capitalist politico-economic structures ("world-economies") rather than of past one-state "world-empires," in that a world-economy has a geographical as well as a functional division of labor. "World-economies...are divided into core states and peripheral areas." Core states are advantaged, have weak or nonexistent indigenous states (1974: 349). Core and periphery are features of capitalism: "world-empires had joined their 'edges' to the center by the collection of tribute, otherwise leaving relatively intact the production systems over which they had 'suzerainty', whereas the capitalist world-economy 'peripheralized' areas economically by incorporating them into the division of labor." (Hopkins, Wallerstein *et al.*, 1982: 55.)

Why is there regional polarization in capitalist world-economies? Wallerstein's various answers include definitional or functional requisiteness, geoeconomic regionalism (core-likeness) and force (unequal exchange). 1. **Requisiteness.** "[W]ithin a capitalist world-economy, all states cannot 'develop' simultaneously *by definition*, since the system functions by virtue of having unequal core and peripheral regions." (Wallerstein, 1975: 23.) 2. **Geography.** Production processes are linked in complex commodity chains (1983: 16). These chains have a directionality, raw-to-finished. Commodity chains have been geographically convergent: "they have tended to move from the peripheries of the capitalist world-economy to the centres or cores" (1983: 30). The more easily monopolized processes are concentrated in core areas, the less skilled, more extensive manpower processes in "peripheral" areas (1984: 4-5). What "makes a production process core-like or periphery-like is the degree to which it incorporates labor-value, is mechanized, and is highly profitable" (1984: 16). There are core states and periphery states because there "tend to be geographical localizations of productive activities such that core-like production activities and periphery-like production activities tend each to be spatially grouped together" (1984: 15). 3. **Unequal exchange.** "The exchange of products containing unequal amounts of social labor we may call the core-periphery relationship" (1984: 15). There is a parallel political polarization between strong core states and weaker peripheral states, "the 'political' process of 'imperialism' being what makes possible the 'economic' process of 'unequal exchange'" (1984:5). Unequal exchange "means, ultimately, the transfer of some of the surplus of any one area to a receiver of surplus in another" as "consequence of the fact that more labor power has gone into producing the value exchanged in one area than in the other." (1982: 94) Unequal exchange exists when commodities moving one way incarnate more "real input (cost)" than equally-priced commodities moving the other way (1983: 31). Unequal exchange existed pre-capitalism when one party to a market transaction used force to improve his price (1983: 30-31). Core zones are those which gain profit or surplus by unequal-exchange transactions (1983: 31-32). In capitalism, unequal exchange has been concealed by the fact that commodity chains cross state frontiers (1983: 31). Strong core state-machines keep peripheral state-structures weaker, their economies lower on the commodity chain, their wage-rates lower (1983: 32). This is done by force -- wars and colonization -- when there are significant political challenges to existing inequalities, otherwise by market supply-and-demand with an enormous apparatus of force latent (1983: 32-33).

While in Quigley's terminology a semiperiphery is geographically intermediate between fully peripheral areas and the core (and thereby advantaged against the core in empire-building, but disadvantaged against the periphery), in Wallerstein's terms a semiperiphery is intermediate in other senses, especially the economic. "There always exist semiperipheral zones" (1984: 15). Seimperipheral states "function as loci of mixed kinds of production activities" (1984: 15), have enterprises engaged in both "corelike" and "peripheral" processes. In moments of expansion of the world-economy, these states "serve to some extent as economic transmission belts and political agents" of some imperial core power. In periods of stagnation and crisis, core powers' hold on these states may be weakened; one or two, which are strong enough, may play among the rivals, erect new quasi-monopolies, displace some falling core power, and impose themselves as new core powers (1984: 7). Semiperipheral areas "are in between the core and the periphery on a series of dimensions, such as the complexity of economic activities, strength of the state machinery, cultural integrity, etc. Some of these areas had been core areas of earlier versions of a given world-economy. Some had been peripheral areas that were later promoted, so to speak, as a result of the changing geopolitics of an expanding world-economy." (1974: 349).

Quigleyan semiperipheries are contingent products of geographic expansion; Wallersteinian semiperipheries are necessary aspects of a particular politico-economic form. "The semiperiphery is a necessary structural element in a world-economy. These areas play a role parallel to that played, *mutatis mutandis*, by middle trading groups in an empire....These middle areas (like middle groups in an empire) partially deflect the political pressures which groups primarily located in peripheral areas might otherwise direct against core states and the groups which operate within and through their state machineries." (1974: 349-350) The middle stratum in world-economies consists of the semiperipheral states. (1979: 23) "The three structural positions in a world economy -- core, periphery, and semiperiphery -- had become stabilized by about 1640." (1979: 18)

In Wallerstein's theory, by contrast with Quigley's, cores move over time (1984: 103; 1974: 350; 1979: 33). New technologies render different commodities "high profit, high-wage" at different moments: "At first, wheat was exchanged against textiles; later textiles against steel; today steel against computers and wheat" (1984: 103).

Quigley vs. Wallerstein. Quigley seems right to treat cores and peripheries as features of all civilizations, not simply of states-system periods or capitalist instruments of expansion. Universal empires certainly have metropolitan cores. Quigley also seems correct to treat core-semiperiphery-periphery as always having primarily a spatial interpretation.

But Wallerstein seems right to assert that cores move in space over time; this can be seem as a different way of perceiving what is implied in Quigley's contention that at least some semiperipheral and peripheral states have eventually succeeded in conquering their civilizations. If we adopt mobile-core language, Quigley's contention can then be translated into the assertion that, simultaneously as states systems are displaced by universal empires, civilizational cores move long distances onto latecomer territories, which, once peripheral, then incorporated into the semiperiphery, finally attain core status as the imperial metropole.

Quigley seems right again to treat core-semiperiphery distinctions as growing in the first instance from a fact about motion in space over time (rather than from the statics of "capitalism"), in that expansion of civilizations in space over time necessarily means that some regions will enter a civilization later than others. Quigley's causal mechanism, geographic expansion over time, seems sufficient to account for the **origin** of core-semiperiphery distinctions.

Wallerstein's ideas again seem useful in accounting for the **stability** of core-periphery distinctions, over the time in which they do remain stable. Wallerstein's theory must however be generalized beyond capitalism and states-systems, since universal empires show persistence of their metropoles and capitals at century-plus timescales. The enormously uneven concentration of particular natural and social "endowments" (ores, soils, climates, water; ports, trade routes, crossroads, strongpoints) across the globe and each of its regions may combine with a prevalent technology (which renders such endowments "resources" during a particular epoch), with the inequality of the distribution of human populations, and with the self-interested power of the core states/imperial metropoles to monopolize such endowments, to account for the long persistence of cores. But this needs comparative-empirical examination.

The views of Quigley and Wallerstein on the question of the balance of advantage in economic expansion seem to differ. Quigley sees it as lying with the latecomers (because of delayed corruption, developmental short-cuts, and preferential diffusion of material culture); Wallerstein as clearly sees it lying with the core states (greater force, stronger state-machines, unequal exchange). However, if we accept that cores do move, but only slowly, and are stable for significant periods, the apparent differences can be reconciled: Quigley's cited forces may operate at longer timescales than Wallerstein's, and in the opposite direction. The additional variables of technological stagnation (Quigley) or change (Wallerstein), at least if surprising or uncontrolled, and, more effectively and inescapably, core wars (Quigley), may help to account for core declines. Again comparative-historical study seems called for.

It is not clear that the Wallersteinian concept of "unequal" exchange is viable as a description -- it seems to entail some variant of the problematic labor theory of value -- or as an explanation -- it seems to conflate force, which would plausibly explain involuntary transfers of surplus, with technological inequality, which would plausibly explain voluntary exchanges of high-labor-output for low-input commodities. The degree to which goods transports are characterized by **either** vs. **both** those mechanisms would seem to be an intriguing but empirical question. Once we accept that world systems as such -- not just capitalist world-economies -- have cores, it would seem to make sense that it is the politico-military predominance of the core that accounts for the core's ability to drain the semiperiphery: loot, tribute, taxes, price controls, confiscations, trade route closures, and enforced monopolies are politico-military ventures, though for economic objectives. At the same time, it also seems clear that urbanization, and eventually core status, has tended to move slowly toward major semiperipheral supply sources, whose local populations have then perhaps managed to extract maximum monopolistic advantage by establishing political control over their commodities' flows and prices; why they should be able to do so, and at what time scales, remain to be explored by students of the political manipulation of economic exchange. Again we need comparative studies, of core drainage and semiperipheral resistance.

From semiperiphery to universal empire? In support of his proposition that universal empires are commonly the product of peripheral (in our terms, semiperipheral) states, Quigley offers numerous cases. While some of these do not conform to our criteria because they involve only one culture-area within a larger (i.e. Central) civilization, seven of Quigley's cases seem to offer support for his proposition even within our civilizational definitions.

These seven cases are as follows. (1) Mesopotamian civilization: old core states like Uruk, Kish, Ur, Nippur, and Lagash were conquered by (preserving Quigley's terms) more peripheral states like Agade and Babylon, these by more peripheral Assyria, and the whole of western Asia by fully peripheral Persia. (2) In Minoan (Aegean) civilization the core area of Crete itself seems to have been conquered by peripheral Mycenae. (3) In Classical civilization (for us, in Central civilization, which is larger than "Classical"), peripheral Macedonia and more peripheral Rome rise to empire. (4) In Mesoamerica the Mayan core (seen by Quigley) is overcome by the semi-peripheral Toltecs and these, in turn, by the fully peripheral Aztecs. (5) In the Andes, the coastal and northern highlands core are submerged by several more peripheral cultures, notably Tiahuanaco from the southern highlands, and the whole Andean civilization was conquered by the "fully peripheral" Incas from the "forbidding" central highlands. (6) In Far Eastern civilization, which Quigley divides into Sinic and Chinese, Chou, Ch'in and Han are seen as semiperipheral or peripheral conquerors of the Huang Ho core, Mongols as remote, Ming and Manchu as peripheral. (7) In Indic civilization, divided by Quigley into Indic and Hindu, Harappa is suggested as a peripheral Punjab conqueror of a lower-valley (Sind) Chandu-Daro core, while Maurya is acknowledged a "local," i.e. core, dynasty. (1961:85-86.)

Do these cases represent a general rule? If so, what? If we attend to the conquering peoples rather than their base areas, it does seem that many of those cited by Quigley were, a few centuries before their conquests, peripheral or semiperipheral to the civilization they ultimately united, while peoples they conquered in their careers of empire were already in the core. Mycenae, Macedonia, Rome, Toltecs, Aztecs, Chou, Ch'in, Han, Mongols, perhaps Ming, Manchus, all seem to fit this mold. If we rephrase Quigley's proposition accordingly -- the conquering peoples of universal empires are in general recently promoted from semiperiphery and periphery rather than veteran or renascent members of the core -- is it correct?

In Egypt: for the Old Kingdom, uncertain; for the Middle Kingdom, false; for the New Kingdom, false. In Mesopotamia: for Agade, uncertain; for Ur, false; for Babylon, uncertain. In Aegean: for Minoan, uncertain, probably not applicable; there seems not to have been a Mycenean universal empire, but if there had been, true for that. In Indic: for Harappa, uncertain; for Maurya, uncertain. In Mexican: if there had been a Toltec universal empire, true for that; for the Aztec universal empire, true. In Peruvian: if there had been either a Huari or a Tiahuanaco universal empire, true for it; for the Inca universal empire, true. Indonesian: for Srivijaya and Madjapahit, uncertain. West African: for Ghana, uncertain; for Mali, true; for Songhai, true. Far Eastern: for Ch'in-Han, true; for Sui-T'ang, true; for Mongol-Min-Manchu, true. Japanese: for Yamato uncertain; for Hideyoshi-Tokugawa probably true, if we refer to "clans" rather than "peoples." Central: for Assyrian, true; for Persian-Macedonian, true; for Roman, true. If we were to speak of **areas** rather than **peoples**, the proposition would be false for Agade, Babylon and the Aztecs, Srivijaya and Madjapahit. It is often the case, then, that the builders of a civilization's universal empire are relative latecomers, to its network and to its core; less often, but still frequently, they begin their empire-building from a more recently incorporated territory than those they ultimately conquer. Whatever comparative advantages recent recruits may have in the imperialist drama seem likely to be both conditional and complex.

CONCLUSION

Civilizational cores may take any of several political forms, most frequently being: a single dominant or hegemonic state; several competing states; and the metropolitan region of a universal empire. Core areas expand and contract, the latter especially during hegemonic and universal-state epochs. Civilizations usually have a semiperiphery, especially during such periods, but need not, and during states-system periods sometimes do not. Cores may move in a single prevailing direction, or shuttle. Old cores return, and new areas rise, to core status; history shows no marked favoritism to either process.

Different areas may serve a civilization as its political-military, economic and cultural cores, though there is some tendency for the functions to go together or to drift together when parted. Recent arrivals to core status have some advantages in competitions to destroy states systems, but they are not overwhelming nor entirely self-evident.

"Coreness" and "semiperipherality" are multidimensional phenomena, but certainly have politico-military, economic, technological, demographic, religious and cultural components. Politico-military driving variables seem more obvious and accessible to analysis than others, but are unlikely to function alone. Forces need to be posited to explain both the motions and changes of cores -- formations, expansions, pulsations, shuttles, drifts, evaporations -- and core persistence and stability.

Interesting speculative questions about core-periphery include: can an all-core/no-core global society evolve? Would it require a states system? Does the end of the periphery increase the chances for an all-core/no-core society? or a freezing of current core-semiperiphery boundaries? or a speedup in core shift? or a narrowing of the core to a single hegemonic state or imperial metropole?

NOTES

1. My usage of the term "world system" is no doubt a result of having long ago read, doubted, and set aside to wonder over a passage from Frederick L. Schuman's *International Politics*: "As great territorial States developed and fought with one another for dominance, a State System evolved. All early State Systems ultimately gave way to great empires....The 'World State' became the end-point of political evolution, and with its establishment international relations and war came to an end." (2nd ed. New York: McGraw Hill, 1937, p. 5.) For me, "world system" has naturally meant that society whose alternative political forms Schuman labelled State System and World State. Accordingly, I define "world systems" as militarily closed social-transactional networks with an autonomous political history.

2. Before Europe's conquest of the world, trade did not "follow the flag" but far outran it -- trade ties connected much larger areas than did politico-military ties. I prefer to label a trade-connected area an "oikumene" or "ecumene." Rome and China were parts of an Old World ecumene, Aztec Mexico and Inca Peru of a New World ecumene; but Rome and China were not parts of the same civilization/world system, nor were Mexico and Peru.

3. These usages are extensions of the core-semiperiphery-periphery concepts of the civilizationist Carroll Quigley (1961:85-87).

4. It is easiest to get at core-periphery relations by observing cores: they document themselves. Central civilization has also well-documented its periphery, in penetrating, exploring and semiperipheralizing it.

5. Semiperipheryless; a condition in which the geographic regions within the civilization do not display marked inequality of status. We can speak of such a condition as "no-core," in that the historian or archaeologist who searches for a dominant region simply fails to find one. "All-core" might be the slightly better label, however, in that, until this century, civilizations have always possessed peripheries, of but not within them, surrounding them, materially poorer, indeed, yet so weakly connected as not to be subordinated to, dominated by, even meaningfully "unequal" to, the cores. The abolition of any such area in this century creates a problem of nomenclature (among others); if today's global civilization were to abolish its semiperiphery as well (by equalizing it, through levelling up or down), another such problem would arise.

6. I use "Agade" to denote the city cithin the region of "Akkad."

7. It is usual to assert a collapse of one civilization ("Harappan" or "Indus") around 1800-1700 B.C. and the emergence of another ("Ganges" or "Vedic") around the 6th-7th century B.C. Because the "Indus" civilization in fact extended to the upper Ganges (Alamgirpur site, in the Doab) and to the Gulf of Cambay (Lothal, Bhagatrav); because the Aryans seem to have taken perhaps a millennium to roll from Swat to the Deccan; because the early Vedas imply that broken cities retained populations; and because the date of the destruction of Hastinapur implies a temporal, and its upper-Gangetic location a physical, civilizational interpolation between the "two" Indic civilizations, I strongly doubt that there were two. I suggest as an alternative that a core collapse and dispersal, and subsequent core shift, has been mistaken for a civilizational collapse. This is an empirical hypothesis, which Upper Gangetic archaeology will in due course substantiate (or rebut). It will be verified when, and only when, the habitation chronologies of Bhagatrav, Lothal, Ujjain, Rupar, Panipat, Hastinapur, Alamgirpur, Delhi, Mathura, Ayodhya, Kausambi, Rajghat, Vaisali, and Patna are shown to overlap sufficiently to support the proposition that "after c. 2500 B.C. there was always at least one functioning city in India." Nevertheless it has a foundation in first principles of social physics. The Aryan penetration of India was on a millennium timescale, of the order of a mile or two per annum: this is (physically) a diffusional velocity, implying small-band infiltration rather than massive catastrophic conquest. A. Iberall and I have elsewhere demonstrated some of the implications of this human social process rate (Iberall and Wilkinson, 1984a, 1984b). Accordingly, even while presenting my alternative

as a hypothesis for experimental test, I propose, pending such fact, to assume its truth rather then its falsity -- since for taxonomic purposes I cannot avoid going one way or the other.

8. States within states systems are characteristically unequal in power, the ability to advance their interests, implement their designs, impose their will, dominate one another, defend themselves against such domination. Characteristically also the strongest are few, noticeable, alert, meddlesome. They are the states system's Great Powers, or Superpowers, of the moment.

9. An alternative interpretation would be that the Muslim invasions only temporarily and sporadically linked India with Central civilization, while the definitive eastward connection was made only by the Portuguese, English-British, and French penetrations, with the 18th-century Anglo-French wars then providing the latest plausible date for the attachment of India to Central civilization.

10. This instance may help make it clear how my usage of the "semi-periphery" and "periphery" differs in application from that of the Waller-steinian world-system perspective. For me the European colonies in Southeast Asia would be archetypical "semiperipheries" because dominated politically by a core state. For the same reasons, and because they produce raw materials for export to the core using coerced labor, they are archetypic "peripheries" to the world-system perspective.

11. The comparative-historical study of civilizational frontier movement and process will create a wonderland of research topics. A fine recent prototype is Dyson, 1985.

12. An alternative interpretation, to which however I prefer that in the text, would attest that Zimbabwe was the center of an autonomous African civilization from the 3rd to the 5th-6th centuries, and again from the 9th century. If this is so, than this Southern African civilization was linked to the East African city states only after five centuries, via the Monomatapa empire, as a core to a shared semiperiphery -- shared with Central civilization--and the Zimbabwean core may not have been rendered part of the Central semi-periphery until as late as the 16th century Portuguese and Omani penetrations.

13. As of August 20, 1990. As of the same date, Mesopotamia remained outside the core, despite strenuous efforts.

14. Note however that the core area boundaries shown therein are drawn to be consistent with their sources, the most cogent historical atlases available that show large cities, intense trade networks, and major political capitals of major states and empires, while the semiperiphery consists of imperial provinces, conquered states, and poor and dependent areas at the ends of

trade routes. Populous urban regions thereby may on occasion be shown with a higher rank than we have assigned them in the text, which gives greater weight to political power. For instance, Italy in AD 737 and 1600, e.g., and southern Europe and China today, may get more generous treatment in these maps than their political power would warrant.

It would be helpful to the enterprise of core mapping if historical atlases concerned themselves more directly with displaying changing distributions of power in space over time. A contemporary estimate of power-distribution in the states system, which is not mapped but could be, is provided by Cline, 1980.

REFERENCES

Algaze, Guillermo 1989. "The Uruk Expansion." *Current Anthropology* 30:5 (December):571-608.

Barraclough, Geoffrey (ed.) 1984. *The Times Atlas of World History*. Rev. ed. Maplewood, New Jersey: Hammond.

Byrne, Francis John 1973. *Irish Kings and High-Kings*. London: B.T. Batsford.

Chase-Dunn, Christopher 1988. "Comparing World-Systems: Toward a Theory of Semiperipheral Development." *Comparative Civilizations Review* 19(Fall):39-66.

Cline, Ray S. 1980. *World Power Trends and U.S. Foreign Policy for the 1980's*. Boulder, Colorado: Westview.

Daniel, Glyn (ed.) 1977. *The Illustrated Encyclopedia of Archeology*. New York: Thomas Y. Crowell.

de Paor, Maire and Liam 1960. *Early Christian Ireland*. 2nd ed. rev. London: Thames and Hudson.

Dyson, Stephen 1985. *The Creation of the Roman Frontier*. Princeton University Press.

Ekholm, Kajsa, and Jonathan Friedman 1982. "'Capital' Imperialism and Exploitation: Ancient World-Systems." *Review* 4:1(Summer):87-109.

Hawkes, Jacquetta 1976. *The Atlas of Early Man*. New York: St. Martin's.

Hopkins, Terence K., Immanuel Wallerstein, *et al.* 1982. "Patterns of Development in the Modern World-System." Pp. 42-82 in Terence K. Hopkins, Immanuel Wallerstein, *et al. World-Systems Analysis: Theory and Methodology*. Beverly Hills: Sage.

Iberall, Arthur, and David Wilkinson 1984a. "Human Sociogeophysics--Phase I: Explaining the Macroscopic Patterns of Man on Earth." *GeoJournal* 8:2:171-179.

Iberall, Arthur, and David Wilkinson 1984b. "Human Sociogeophysics--Phase II: The Diffusion of Human Ethnicity by Remixing." *GeoJournal* 9:4:387-391.

Kinder, Hermann, and Werner Hilgemann 1975, 1978. *The Anchor Atlas of World History*. 2 volumes. Garden City, New York: Doubleday/Anchor.

Langer, William L 1968. *An Encyclopedia of World History*. Boston: Houghton Mifflin.

Lydon, J.F. 1972. *The Lordship of Ireland in the Middle Ages*. Dublin: Gill and Macmillan.

Mac Airt, Sean, and Gearoid Mac Niocaill, (eds.) 1983. *The Annals of Ulster (to A.D. 1131)*. Dublin Institute for Advanced Studies.

McEvedy, Colin, and Richard Jones 1978. *Atlas of World Population History*. New York: Penguin.

McEvedy, Colin 1961. *Penguin Atlas of Medieval History*. New York: Penguin.

_____ 1967. *Penguin Atlas of Ancient History*. New York: Penguin.

_____ 1972. *Penguin Atlas of Modern History*. New York: Penguin.

_____ 1982. *Penguin Atlas of Recent History*. New York: Penguin.

McNeil, William H. 1963. *The Rise of the West*. University of Chicago Press.

Quigley, Carroll 1961. *The Evolution of Civilizations: An Introduction to Historical Analysis*. New York: Macmillan.

Toynbee, Arnold J. 1934-61. *A Study of History*. 12 volumes. Oxford University Press.

_____ 1961. *Reconsiderations*. Volume XII of *A Study of History*. Oxford University Press.

Ua Clerigh, Arthur n.d. *The History of Ireland to the Coming of Henry V*. Volume 1. London: T. Fisher Unwin.

Wallerstein, Immanuel 1974. *The Modern World-System I: Capitalist Agriculture and the Origins of the European World-Economy in the Sixteenth Century*. New York: Academic Press.

_____ 1975. "The Present State of the Debate on World Inequality." Pp. 9-28 in Immanuel Wallerstein, (ed.) *World Inequality: Origins and Perspectives on the World-System*. Montreal: Black Rose Books.

_____ 1979. *The Capitalist World-Economy*. Cambridge University Press.

_____ 1980. *The Modern World-System II: Mercantilism and the Consolidation of the European World-Economy, 1600-1750*. New York: Academic Press.

_____ 1982. "World-Systems Analysis: Theoretical and Interpretative Issues." Pp 91-103 in Terence K. Hopkins, Immanuel Wallerstein, et al. *World-Systems Analysis: Theory and Methodology*. Beverly Hills: Sage.

_____ 1983. *Historical Capitalism*. London: Verso.

_____ 1984. *The Politics of the World-Economy*. Cambridge University Press.

Wesson, Robert 1978. *State Systems*. New York: Free Press.

Wilkinson, David 1987. "Central Civilization." *Comparative Civilizations Review* (Fall):31-59.

_____ 1988. "Universal Empires: Pathos and Engineering." *Comparative Civilizations Review* (Spring):22-44.

5

The Evolution of Societies
and World-Systems

Stephen K. Sanderson

INTRODUCTION

Evolutionary theories of human social life continue to be much debated in modern social science. Although there are still many advocates of these theories, especially among anthropologists, we are currently in a period in which such theories are unpopular among sociologists. This unpopularity stems from a wide range of criticisms, but clearly one of the most important is the belief that evolutionary theories are unacceptably *endogenist* -- that they view social evolution as a process occurring fundamentally within the bounds of reasonably well-defined societies (cf. Nisbet, 1969; Giddens, 1981, 1984).

As a result of this criticism, many historically inclined sociologists have turned away from the analysis of individual societies and in the direction of larger constellations of societies. Thus the creation by Immanuel Wallerstein in the early 1970s of world-system theory, a type of theory in which individual societies are viewed, not as autonomous, but as inserted into the operation of a larger network. It is this network -- the world-system -- that is then said to be the only proper unit of analysis, with the fate of individual societies being determined principally by their involvement in the world-system as a whole.

Wallerstein's concern has been with the modern capitalist world-economy that he envisages as originating in Europe in the sixteenth century and he has shown very little interest in the precapitalist era. However, the great appeal of his theory has led other social scientists to attempt to apply the concept of a world-system to the entire precapitalist era. It is thus claimed that Wallerstein's basic argument can be generalized backward in time: There were precapitalist world-systems, and the understanding of world history must focus on the operation of these systems rather than on individual societies.

Many world-system enthusiasts see their work as antievolutionary, or at least nonevolutionary, in nature. Since they view evolutionary theories as endogenist theories, they see themselves as setting up an explicitly *exogenist* (and thus nonevolutionary) alternative. However, I hope to show that such a notion is based on a false distinction and a misunderstanding of the nature of social evolutionism. While evolutionary theories have historically given pride of place to endogenous factors, such theories need not be endogenist. They can give equal attention to endogenous and exogenous factors, or even be highly exogenist. Indeed, I shall argue that Wallerstein's world-system theory is a quintessentially evolutionary theory. If I am right -- if one can be a Wallersteinian and an evolutionist at the same time -- then it is quite possible to take an evolutionary approach to understanding precapitalist world-systems. To do so involves demonstrating two fundamental things. It must first be shown that there really were precapitalist world-systems in some meaningful sense of that term. And, if this can be done, one must then try to identify the kind of "evolutionary logic" these systems contained. For, after all, this is exactly what Wallerstein has done for his capitalist world-system -- it is what makes him a type of evolutionist -- and thus if we are to apply his ideas successfully to the precapitalist era it is incumbent upon us to do the same.

Unfortunately, I shall be forced to conclude that this effort to construct an evolutionary analysis of precapitalist world-systems produces, at best, very mixed results. There are some types of precapitalist world-systems, but they differ in some very important respects from the modern capitalist world-economy. Moreover, much of the social evolution that has occurred in the precapitalist era, as well as in the transition to the capitalist era itself, suggests that the proper unit of analysis is not some sort of world-system, but rather something much more akin to the individual society of more traditional evolutionary analyses. Are world-systems or individual societies the proper unit of evolutionary analysis? Which are more important determinants of social evolution, exogenous or endogenous factors? As we shall see, the answers to these questions depend upon the historical period and the type of social system with which we are dealing.

WHAT IS AN EVOLUTIONARY THEORY?

In order to establish the point that there is no inherent antagonism between an evolutionary and a world-system perspective, and that Wallerstein's world-system theory is a type of evolutionism, we first need a proper understanding of what an evolutionary theory actually is. There is, in fact, much misunderstanding on this count, a good deal of which I have reviewed elsewhere (cf. Sanderson, 1990). Because of space limitations, I shall confine myself here to a simple exposition of what I take to be the best definition of an evolutionary theory, that of Erik Olin Wright (1983). Wright suggests that for a theory to be considered evolutionary it must have three features: (1) It must propose a typology of social forms with potential directionality. (2) It must order these social forms in the way it does on the assumption that the probability of remaining at the same stage in the typology is greater than the probability of regressing. (3) It must assert a probability of transition from one stage of the typology to another. It therefore claims the existence of a tendency toward directionality, no matter how weak, in social change. It is also clear that Wright demands the presence of a mechanism that would explain such a directional tendency. However, this need not be a single universal mechanism that would explain every specific evolutionary transition. He recognizes that "the actual mechanisms which might explain movement between adjacent forms on the typology need not be the same at every stage of the typology" (Wright, 1983:26-27).

As Wright is at pains to point out, his way of identifying an evolutionary theory makes no claim that the typology of social forms represents a teleological unfolding of latent potentialities, something many critics of evolutionism falsely assume to be basic to an evolutionary theory. Nor does it claim that such a typology represents a rigid sequence of stages through which all societies must move. Wright does not even assume that all (or even most) societies necessarily evolve. Regression is entirely permitted, and it is fully acknowledged that in most societies "long-term steady states may be more likely than any systematic tendency for movement" (Wright, 1983:26).

WORLD-SYSTEM THEORY AS SOCIAL EVOLUTIONISM

I believe that Wright has come closer than anyone else to pinpointing the genuinely irreducible features of an evolutionary theory. Using his characterization of an evolutionary theory, it can be shown that Wallerstein's world-system theory is evolutionary in a thoroughgoing way. Of course, this approach to historical change is scarcely thought of as evolutionary, and in fact is often identified as strongly antievolutionary. The painstaking detail with which Wallerstein has, in the three volumes of *The Modern World-System* (1974a, 1980, 1989), analyzed historical events seems strikingly at odds with the works of social evolutionists. Moreover, Wallerstein has frequently cited with approval the basic arguments of Robert Nisbet's *Social Change and History* (1969), no doubt the leading antievolutionary work written by a sociologist in the past quarter-century. Surely Wallerstein cannot be an evolutionist.

In fact, though, he is, and very decidedly so. What has thrown people off the track about Wallerstein involves his condemnation of the sort of evolutionism that reigned supreme in American social science in the 1950s and 1960s. But Wallerstein is opposed only to this particular type of evolutionism and to other versions that share key features in common with it. He is only opposed to what he has called the *developmentalist* perspective, by which he means functionalist evolutionism (and its modernization variant) and certain rigidly unilinearist versions of Marxist evolutionism. As he has said, "What thus distinguishes the developmentalist and the world-system perspective is not liberalism versus Marxism nor evolutionism versus something else (*since both are essentially evolutionary*)" (1979:54; emphasis added).

Careful analysis of Wallerstein's works, especially some of his theoretical essays, clearly reveals that he means what he says when he describes his world-system perspective as a type of evolutionism. Following Wright, an evolutionary theory is minimally one that defines some general directional trend in history. The history Wallerstein is interested in is that of capitalism since the sixteenth century, and for him capitalism most assuredly has an overall directionality to it. It is of course, a directionality of the world-system as a single unit rather than individual societies or nation-states. These latter evolve only as parts of the whole.

Along what lines is the capitalist world-economy evolving? Wallerstein (1984a) tells us that there are three main directional trends involved: increasing mechanization of production, increasing commodification of the factors of production (which includes as a very important element the increasing proletarianization of the labor force), and increasing contractualization of economic relationships. These three trends are part and parcel of a "deepening" of capitalist development, a deepening that derives from the accumulationist motivations of capitalist entrepreneurs. It is this drive for the accumulation of capital that constitutes the "evolutionary logic" of modern capitalism -- the "motor" that drives it from one stage to another.

Furthermore, Wallerstein has not shied away from the identification of specific stages in the evolution of the capitalist world-system (cf. Wallerstein, 1974b). The first stage (approximately 1450-1640) involves the emergence of capitalism from the crisis of feudalism and its initial expansion to cover significant portions of the globe. The second stage (roughly 1640-1750) is a stage of the "consolidation" of the world-system. The third stage (about 1750-1917) marks the eruption of industrial capitalism. It is a period of renewed expansion of the world-system, which by the end of this period covers virtually the entire globe. The fourth stage began with the Russian Revolution and is a stage of the "consolidation" of the industrial capitalist world-economy.

I also think it is very obvious that Wallerstein has retained a great deal of what might be called Marx's "evolutionary eschatology." Like Marx, Wallerstein is convinced that capitalism is essentially evil, that it is rife with contradictions that will tear it apart in the end, and that when it collapses it will lead to something more humane. It is just that all of this occurs on a world rather than a national scale. The gap between core and periphery continues to widen, and this spawns "antisystemic movements" that increasingly threaten the continued viability of the system. Within the next 100-150 years capitalism will disintegrate and will be replaced by, most likely, a socialist world-government. What will this world-government be like? Wallerstein (1984b:157) describes it in terms that are highly evocative of Marx :

> The idea is that on the basis of an advanced technology, capable of providing a rate of global production adequate to meet the total needs of all the world's population, the rate and forms of produc-

tion will be the result of collective decisions made in virtue of these needs. Furthermore, it is believed that the amount of new labor-time to maintain such a level of productivity will be sufficiently low as to permit each individual the time and resources to engage in activities aimed at fulfilling his potential.

The global production required will be attained, not merely because of the technological base, but because the egalitarian collectivity will be interested in realizing the full "potential surplus." This being the case, the social motivations for collective aggressive behavior will have disappeared, even if, in the beginning phases, not all the psychological motivations will have done so. Since collective decisions will be pursued in the common interest, then worldwide ecological balance will follow as an inherent objective.

In short, the socialist mode of production seeks to fulfill the objective of the rational and free society which was the ideological mask of the capitalist world-economy. In such a situation, repressive state machinery will have no function and will over time transform itself into routine administration.

Marx thus turns out in the end to be basically right in his prediction of the evolutionary demise of capitalism. It is just that he had his units of analysis mixed up, and so he failed to gauge accurately the timing of the transition from capitalism to socialism.

It must be recognized that Wallerstein's evolutionism is certainly of a complex sort. Mixed in with his evolutionism is a strong emphasis on economic cycles (Kondratieff waves). But this does not vitiate my claim that Wallerstein's basic framework is evolutionary -- it only qualifies it. There is no incompatibility between an emphasis on cyclical rhythms and an evolutionary perspective, because the cycles occur within (and are basic to) the overall directional trends of the capitalist world-economy.

WERE THERE PRECAPITALIST WORLD-SYSTEMS?

The enormous success of Wallerstein's world-system model quickly led some social scientists to ask whether it might have more general applicability. One of the first to do so was Jane Schneider (chapter 2, this volume; orig. 1977). Schneider claimed that one of the main difficulties with Wallerstein's work was that it "suffers from too narrow an application of its own theory" (1977:20). That is, it sees the capitalist world-economy as having no parallels during the precapitalist era. Schneider went on to argue that one of the reasons for Wallerstein's stance on this matter concerns his distinction between the exchange of fundamental goods and the exchange of preciosities, and his insistence that a world-economy is based on the former rather than the latter. Indeed, for Wallerstein the exchange of preciosities is something that is nonsystemic, or that occurs between a world-economy and its external arena. This leads him to exclude precapitalist Europe from involvement in a world-economy, since its exchanges with other regions were exchanges of luxuries rather than fundamental goods.

Schneider objected to Wallerstein's diminution of the importance of trade in preciosities. She claimed that such a trade is of much greater significance than Wallerstein was willing to grant, and that therefore it is "possible to hypothesize a *precapitalist* world-system, in which core areas accumulated precious metals while exporting manufactures, whereas peripheral areas gave up these metals (and often slaves) against an inflow of finished goods" (1977:25). She saw precapitalist Europe as deeply involved in a larger world-system in which it was peripheral to the better established civilizations of the Levant and Asia. She also saw the existence of such a Eurasian world-system as having significance for the historical transition from feudalism to capitalism in Europe, viewing the transition as a world-system event rather than an endogenous evolution of feudal Europe. Within the Eurasian world-system, she claimed, Europe shifted its position from periphery to core over many centuries, eventually becoming dominant over those areas to which it previously had been subordinated.

Other scholars were soon to follow Schneider's lead. In a long essay, Jonathan Friedman and Michael Rowlands (1978) made the notion of "external relations" central to understanding the original rise of civilization. According to them (1978:271):

The development of the early central civilizations clearly depended
on the productive activity of very large areas, and in order to fully
understand the evolutionary process it is necessary to take account
of these larger systems of reproduction. The transformation of
societies does not occur in a vacuum and the relation between units
in a larger system may determine the conditions of evolution of any
one of them.

This idea has been substantially elaborated by Friedman and Kajsa Ekholm
(Ekholm and Friedman, 1982; Ekholm, 1981). Ekholm and Friedman see
world-systems as very general historical phenomena, and as the basic unit to
which evolutionary analyses should apply. Ekholm denies the relevance of
focusing on individual societies, claiming that "evolution occurs only at the
level of the system as a whole" (1981:245). Like Schneider, Ekholm applies
this idea to understanding the European transition from feudalism to
capitalism: "Thus the development of capitalism in Europe is not the result
of an evolution from feudalism *as a system*, but the result of a shift in
accumulation from east to west in a single system" (Ekholm, 1981:245).

At the moment the scholar most vigorously pursuing a world-system
approach to the development of Western capitalism is Janet Abu-Lughod
(1988, 1989). Abu-Lughod claims that by the middle of the thirteenth century
there existed a world-system centered around long-distance trade that had a
strongly capitalistic character. This system consisted of eight subsystems, and
the "kingpin of the entire system lay at the land bridge between the eastern
Mediterranean and the outlets to the Indian Ocean on the south and between
the Mediterranean and Central Asia" (1988:10). At this time Asia was at least
on a par with, and perhaps in a more favorable position than, Europe. What
happened in the centuries ahead to change all that? Abu-Lughod insists that
to answer this question we should not look, as most Western scholars have,
to the internal features of Europe and Asia to see why the former surpassed
the latter. Rather, we should focus on the interactions among the subsystems
of the entire world-system. She argues that the rise to economic dominance
of northwest Europe resulted from geopolitical shifts in the relations among
crucial subsystems (Abu-Lughod, 1988:11): "When the large system tipped, it
was because the Mediterranean northwestern European links deepened and
diversified while the link between the eastern Mediterranean and the Orient
began to fray in places and was rudely torn in others."

The notion of precapitalist world-systems has continued to find strong proponents. In 1987 an important volume of conference proceedings was published on this topic (Rowlands, Larsen, and Kristiansen, 1987). The authors of the individual essays tried to demonstrate the existence of world-systemic networks in ancient times in such places as the ancient Near East, Scandinavia, and ancient Rome. Perhaps the strongest proponent of the idea of precapitalist world-systems is Christopher Chase-Dunn (1986), who has gone considerably beyond previous work in attempting to develop an elaborate typology of world-systems (see also Chase-Dunn and Hall, chapter 1, this volume). Chase-Dunn suggests six basic types of world-systems: (1) stateless world-systems, in which bands, tribes, and chiefdoms are engaged in various types of economic exchange; (2) primary world-economies, which involve regional systems of core/periphery specialization among the pristine states, but without any imperial political structure; (3) primary world-empires, or the earliest forms of core/periphery specialization to have acquired an imperial political structure; (4) complex secondary world-systems, in which primary world-empires were combined into larger world-empires; (5) commercializing world-systems, or precapitalist world-systems with an unusually high level of commercialization or "premodern capitalism"; (6) the capitalist world-economy, which rose to dominance via a shift of influence within the larger "super world-system" that preceded it.

This typology has much to recommend it, especially in giving us food for thought in dealing with questions of social evolution, but some cautions seem in order. First, the whole notion of stateless world-systems appears questionable. This is not to deny that bands, tribes, and chiefdoms have engaged in significant levels of economic exchange with each other, nor is it to deny that these exchanges may have influenced the evolutionary trajectories of the individual societies. The problem is that, in order for us to use the concept of world-system at all meaningfully, there must be more than just a larger system of economic exchanges in which individual societies figure as elements. At the very least there must be some sort of core/periphery structure, and this structure must have a hierarchical organization such that at least some minimal degree of "development of underdevelopment" occurs. This implies some sort of dominance of the core and an exploitative relationship between the core and the periphery. It seems very dubious that the relations among stateless societies can be characterized in such a way, at least as a regular and systematic feature. What I think we are dealing with here are what might be called **world-networks**: loose exchange relationships in which the parts of the whole maintain great autonomy.[1]

When we turn to the other types of world-systems Chase-Dunn proposes, I think we also have to exercise caution. I agree that there were world-economies and world-empires throughout the precapitalist era after the rise of civilization and the state, and I agree that these world-systems may well have had a core/periphery kind of structure and at least something that could be described as the development of underdevelopment. Yet I am concerned about pushing this idea too far, for the parallels between the modern capitalist world-system and earlier world-systems may be rather limited. As Phil Kohl has remarked in an attempt to apply a world-system model to the Bronze Age Near East (1987:16):

> There is little reason to doubt that patterns of dependency or, perhaps better, interdependency were established as a result of intercultural exchange in the Bronze Age world-system. . . . Dependency could lead to exploitation, and . . . the more powerful urban societies could dictate the terms of the exchange. But the relations between ancient cores and peripheries were not structurally analogous to those which underdevelopment theorists postulate are characteristic of First-Third World relations today. Unless conquered (i.e., incorporated into a larger polity), ancient peripheries could have followed one of several options ranging from withdrawal from the exchange network to substitutions of one core partner for another. Archaeological and historical evidence converge to suggest that most intercultural exchange systems in antiquity were fragile, lasting at most a few generations before collapsing. This inherent instability is related to the relative weakness of the bonds of dependency that existed between core and peripheral partners.

Even in the case of world-empires, it remains to be shown that dependency and the development of underdevelopment closely corresponded to what prevails in our modern world-system.

THE EVOLUTIONARY LOGICS OF WORLD-SYSTEMS

Although Chase-Dunn's work on world-systems is at this point substantially typological, he has not failed to ask about the dynamics of these systems. He has suggested that different types of world-systems have different dynamics, or what might be called "evolutionary logics," built into them. We already know what the evolutionary logic of the modern capitalist world-economy is: the ceaseless drive for the accumulation of capital. And we know that this evolutionary logic was basically absent, or at least not well developed, in precapitalist world-systems. On what kind of evolutionary logics, then, did the different precapitalist world-systems depend? In the remainder of this paper I want to sketch the beginnings of an answer to this question. It will become clear that, in the process of doing so, I will be making some significant modifications of Chase-Dunn's ideas.

Stateless World-Systems

Again, I want to emphasize that I do not really accept the notion of a stateless world-system. That being the case, I want to argue that the evolution of stateless societies -- bands, tribes, and chiefdoms, as they are commonly known among anthropologists and archaeologists -- is largely a process of endogenous evolution. Exchange relations between stateless societies play only a secondary, and perhaps very minor, role in the evolutionary transformation of such systems. What, then, is the motor of evolution in such societies?

The answer, I believe, has to do with the ecological adaptations of human communities. The two great evolutionary transformations in the precapitalist era were the Neolithic Revolution and the rise of civilization and the state. In recent years many archaeologists have implicated population pressure as a cause of the shift from hunting and gathering to agriculture as a mode of production. This variable has been given greatest prominence by Mark Cohen (1977). Cohen's position is that ancient hunter-gatherers eventually outgrew the capacity of their foraging technologies to support them at an acceptable standard of living. Once this began to occur, they encountered a "food crisis" that could be effectively solved only by the gradual replacement of foraging by cultivation and animal husbandry.

To my mind, the most persuasive theory of the origin of the state is Robert Carneiro's (1970, 1981, 1987) circumscription theory. This theory is too well known to need more than brief summary here. Carneiro holds that the earliest states developed in environments that were highly circumscribed or impacted. These were areas of fertile soil that had definite geographical limits to the expansion of human populations. As population density rose within these regions, warfare was set off as a response to declining land and resource scarcity. Groups conquered and incorporated other groups. Tribes consolidated into chiefdoms, and with further increases in population pressure and warfare chiefdoms consolidated into states.

One of the interesting things about Carneiro's theory from the point of view of this paper is that it is neither a strictly endogenist nor a strictly exogenist theory. Population pressure may be regarded as an endogenous variable, but the warfare it leads to implicates many different societies in each other's fates. Chiefdoms and states arise only as the result of significant intersocietal contact. However, this contact is decidedly different from the kind of contact (economic exchange) that traditional world-system theory has primarily been concerned with, and thus we are not dealing with a world-system phenomenon in any strict sense of that term.

Marvin Harris (1977, 1979) has subsumed these theories and others like them into a general materialist theory of social evolution. For Harris, the motor of social evolution is the need to advance technology against the lowered living standards that inevitably occur as a result of population pressure and environmental degradation. But technological advance is only a temporary solution, for it in turn ultimately exacerbates population pressure and environmental degradation, thus leading to the need for a new and more intensive wave of technological change. Social evolution -- or at least precapitalist social evolution -- is thus primarily a spiraling process of environmental depletion and intensification in which population growth plays a vital role.

For reasons that I have detailed elsewhere (cf. Sanderson, 1988, 1990) and do not have space to discuss here, I believe that Harris's theory is probably our best general theory of social evolution in stateless societies. It is obvious that it gives priority to the productive forces rather than the relations of production as the motor of change, thus putting it at a considerable remove from the arguments that world-system enthusiasts are advocating. But while this may be a strength of Harris's theory at the level of stateless systems, it seems to be a significant weakness when we move to the level of states and world-systems. At this level, the relations of production deserve more consideration than Harris usually gives them.

World-Empires

I shall have little to say about what Chase-Dunn calls the primary world-economies, simply because at this point I have not studied them sufficiently. Basically, it seems that Wallerstein's point that these tended always to evolve into world-empires has little to contradict it. Let me then try to talk about the evolutionary logic of world-empires.

The conventional view of world-empires, shared by Wallerstein, Weber, and many other thinkers of different theoretical and political persuasions, is that they contain strong built-in obstacles to the movement toward some qualitatively different kind of socioeconomic system or mode of production. It is during the era of history dominated by world-empires that we find that a cyclical, rather than an evolutionary, theory of world history seems to be most appropriate. As Owen Lattimore has said in describing the rise and fall of Chinese dynasties (1940:531):

> The brief chronicle of a Chinese dynasty is very simple: a Chinese general or a barbarian conqueror establishes a peace which is usually a peace of exhaustion. There follows a period of gradually increasing prosperity as land is brought back under cultivation, and this passes into a period of apparently unchanging stability. Gradually, however, weak administration and corrupt government choke the flow of trade and taxes. Discontent and poverty spread. The last emperor of the dynasty is often vicious and always weak - - as weak as the founder of the dynasty was ruthless. The great fight each other for power, and the poor turn against all government. The dynasty ends, and after an interval another begins, exactly as the last began, and runs the same course.

The theme of the absence of any real "evolutionary potential" to the historic world-empires has been echoed by Jonathan Friedman. Friedman notes (1982:182; emphasis added)

that while there is clearly an ... evolutionary process of formation
of states and civilizations, there is no obvious continuity of social
evolution after the emergence of civilization. It would appear that
the regional systems of civilizations, with their commercial centers,
peripheral chiefdoms and tribes, and marginal bands, have been
stable organizations until the modern period. While centers of
accumulation have shifted, *there has been no fundamental change*
in form, only differences in dominant economic sectors -- state
versus private -- and the form of exploitation -- peasant, serf, slave,
or wage labor -- that have been prevalent.

Michael Mann (1986) has characterized the view represented by
Lattimore and Friedman as the *negative view of empires*, and suggests that it
is overdrawn. "Although the militarism of imperial states certainly had its
negative side," he argues, "it could lead to general economic development"
(1986:148). Mann argues that the leading example of militarism having a
catalyzing effect on economic development is the Roman Empire. In this
case, militarism contributed to economic development in a number of ways,
but particularly in terms of the consumption needs of the army. These needs
greatly stimulated demand and, hence, production (Mann refers to this as a
sort of "military Keynesianism"). In the end, though, Mann is forced to admit
that militarism led more often to quite different results, and that empires
"contained no development, no true dialectic" (1986:161).

What has been said above about world-empires in general applies just as
well, I think, to what Chase-Dunn has called commercializing world-systems.
These were systems that had an unusual amount of mercantile activity in
them. Chase-Dunn (1986) suggests that China in the eighth century A.D. was
such a system, and that capitalism came close to becoming dominant there at
the time of the Sung dynasty. But was this really the case? Was the situation
here so different from what we find in other world-empires? Certainly the
outcome was basically no different for, as Chase-Dunn himself notes, this
nascent Chinese capitalism was crushed by the state because the economic
interests of private entrepreneurs were a significant threat to the state.

Chase-Dunn also considers as an example -- undoubtedly the leading
example -- of a commercializing world-system the so-called Afro-Eurasian
super world-system. He accepts the argument of Schneider, Ekholm, and

Abu-Lughod that it was the character of this world-system that led to the development of capitalism in Western Europe in the sixteenth century. I would like to suggest, however, that there was no such world-system -- there was at best only a loose world-network of trade in which Europe participated -- and that the transition from feudalism to capitalism had much to do with evolutionary forces that were endogenous to Europe itself. As we shall see, there was an important exogenous dimension to the feudalism-capitalism transition, but this transition cannot be interpreted as a world-systemic phenomenon in any strict sense of that term. This suggests another important limitation to the effort to apply a world-system model to the precapitalist era.

THE EVOLUTIONARY LOGIC OF FEUDAL SYSTEMS

The Transition from Feudalism to Capitalism in Western Europe

Any intelligent analysis of the European transition from feudalism to capitalism must begin with the famous debate between Maurice Dobb and Paul Sweezy that was conducted shortly after the end of the Second World War. In his classic *Studies in the Development of Capitalism* (1963; first edition 1947), Dobb set forth a Marxist theory of the transition that emphasized the internal contradictions of feudalism as a mode of production. What led the feudal system into crisis and ultimately tore it apart, Dobb asserted, was the growing class struggle between landlords and peasants. The intensified exploitation of the peasantry by the landlord class provoked a peasant flight from the land that was the major cause of the crisis and the transition.

Sweezy (1976; orig. 1950) questioned the basic logic of this theory by asserting that it improperly concentrated on endogenous forces. He argued that there were no endogenous forces within feudalism strong enough to transform it and proposed as an alternative a basically exogenist theory. It was the revival, from about the eleventh century, of long-distance trade between Europe and other world regions that he saw as the impetus for the feudal crisis and the move toward capitalism. The revival of this trade caused feudalism to be increasingly involved in a market economy. As towns grew in size and importance, serfs were increasingly attracted to them and they fled the land in large numbers. Moreover, feudal lords themselves were increasingly attracted by the possibilities inherent in the market economy for the generation of large fortunes.

This exogenist interpretation of the rise of capitalism bears considerable resemblance to the recent theory of the capitalist transition being promoted by a number of world-system enthusiasts (i.e., that the transition was a matter of a geopolitical shift from east to west within the Afro-Eurasian super world-system). By itself, it is a highly dubious interpretation. What strikes me most about Sweezy's theory is its highly ethnocentric character. Sweezy seems to assume that the mere existence of a system of production-for-exchange is sufficient to pull feudal lords away from their customary system of production-for-use. Again and again we see him characterizing feudalism as a mode of production inferior to capitalism, and he clearly assumes that feudal lords would have seen it that way too.

I do not think that Sweezy's interpretation is irrelevant to understanding the rise of capitalism, but by itself it does not get us very far. As for Dobb's theory, I believe that it is moving in the right direction by focusing on the internal structure of feudalism as a mode of production. However, what is wrong with this theory is Dobb's failure to offer a convincing explanation for the flight of serfs from the land. He attributes this to increasing exploitation by the landlord class, but he provides no plausible (to me at least) reason why there should have been such an increase in exploitation.

There is, however, another interpretation that can explain the things that Dobb's theory cannot. This theory, also an endogenist theory, is the demographic argument put forward by such scholars as Postan (1972), Wilkinson (1973), North and Thomas (1973), Le Roy Ladurie (1974), and Perry Anderson (1974a). The argument goes something like this. From about the eleventh until the end of the thirteenth century, feudalism was undergoing significant demographic expansion. As population grew, new and more marginal lands were increasingly brought under cultivation until eventually Europe became "filled up." By 1300 a serious state of overpopulation had been reached. The crisis induced by this overpopulation turns out in effect to have led to its own "cure." Increasing famine, malnourishment, and other disease -- especially the Black Death[2] that first swept Europe in 1348-50 -- led to a population decline that continued until around 1450. This population decline led to a severe labor shortage, which caused a dramatic fall in the incomes of the landlord class and shifted the balance of class power in the direction of the peasantry. The landlord class reacted to their markedly changed economic fortunes in a number of ways, but especially by expropriating the peasantry from the land and turning their estates over to the raising of sheep in order to sell their wool on the market. Landlords were moving more in the direction of becoming capitalist farmers. Moreover, many peasants stayed on the land, but not as traditional serfs. They became transformed into wage-earning farmhands who assisted their former landlords in running a capitalist agricultural enterprise. Some peasants even became transformed into capitalists -- yeoman farmers -- themselves.

While all of this was happening, the towns were growing in importance. The power and significance of the merchants were increasing, and the peasants who fled the land were becoming a growing source of labor for the economic activity of the towns. Now to explain all of this I think we need to bring Sweezy's theory back into the picture. As Michael Mann (1986) has asked, why did the demographic and economic crisis of feudalism get resolved in the way it did? Why did the landlord class react to their declining economic fortunes by gradually transforming themselves, and many of their serfs, into capitalists? Why did they not respond to the growing power of the peasants by intensifying their repression and exploitation of the peasantry? Mann offers a plausible answer to these questions (1986:411):

> If the feudal mode of production gave to the lords a monopoly of the means of physical violence, could they not respond with military force at times when relative product and factor values did not favor them? . . . This is not an idle question, for in many other times and places the response of lords to labor shortages has been to increase the dependency of their laborers. . . . The immediate answer to these questions is that the European lords did try repression and they nominally succeeded, but to no avail. Returning to the example of late-fourteenth-century labor shortages, there was a wave of landlord reaction. The lords attempted with violence and legislation to tie the peasantry to the manor and to keep down wages (just as late Roman landlords had). All across Europe the peasantry rose up in rebellion, and everywhere (except Switzerland) they were repressed. But their lords' victory proved hollow. The lords were compelled not by the peasants but by the transformed capitalist market and by opportunities for profit, and threat of loss, within it. The weak state could not implement legislation without

the local cooperation of the lords; it *was* the lords. And individual lords gave in, leased out their demesnes, and converted labor services into money rents. . . . The feudal mode of production was finally broken by the market.

Now that would be a deeply unsatisfying sentence -- if we stopped the explanation there. Neoclassical economists do leave it there, because they assume the existence of a market in the first place. The "market variant" of Marxism (e.g., Sweezy 1976) also leaves it there.

So, in other words, Sweezy's exogenist theory has a contribution to make, but only in the context of the endogenous evolution of feudalism itself. The revival of long-distance trade historically converged with this endogenous evolution, but had it not been for the internally generated crisis of feudalism, the revival of trade and the market could not have transformed feudal society. Feudalism would have changed somewhat, but it still would have been feudalism. Capitalism would never have emerged.

The Transition from Feudalism to Capitalism in Japan

Although I find the interpretation just advanced highly convincing, some will not. For them it may seem, at best, only one of several plausible interpretations. Let me therefore suggest an additional line of evidence that supports my argument for the great significance of endogenous forces in the feudalism-capitalism transition: the approximately parallel case of Japan.

Perry Anderson (1974b) has argued that the feudal mode of production (in the restrictive sense in which he conceives of it) has existed in only one civilization outside Europe. From approximately the fifteenth to the nineteenth centuries a form of feudalism very similar to European feudalism prevailed in Japan.[3] In tracing the historical development of Japanese feudalism, Anderson has shown that it underwent a remarkable degree of commercialization during its evolution. More boldly, one might say that Japanese society underwent its own transition from feudalism to capitalism. From the point of view of the concerns of this paper, the extraordinary thing about this transition was that it was a completely endogenous process. Indeed, it had to be, because Japan sealed itself off from the rest of the world between 1638 and its "opening" in the middle of the nineteenth century. During this time Japan was a highly autonomous society that was not part of any world-system, or even of any much looser world-network of societies. As Jacques Mutel has argued, in Japan "the first accumulation of capital, as contrasted with Europe, owed nothing to a distant overseas trade. This is proof, if one were needed, that one has overestimated, if not the place, at least the necessity of such trade in the birth of modern society" (1988:142).

According to the account given by Perry Anderson, the Japanese feudal epoch was witness to a considerable commercialization of agriculture. In the eighteenth century there had developed a considerable regional specialization, and many crops were being produced directly for the market. "By the end of the [Tokugawa] Shogunate, it is clear that a remarkably high proportion of total agricultural output was commercialized" (Anderson, 1974b:448). Mercantile activity was also becoming much more vigorous, and many large towns developed and grew in importance. Anderson even speaks of a "crisis of Japanese feudalism" that he believes had become apparent by the early nineteenth century.

Jon Halliday (1975) tells much the same story as Anderson. Halliday makes much of the growing importance of urban merchants during the Tokugawa epoch, and he also describes a process of evolution in Japan that is strikingly similar to what Wallerstein has described for Europe: a feudal aristocracy gradually becoming bourgeois. One might conclude from Anderson's and Halliday's analyses that, by the time Commodore Perry arrived in Japan in 1853, Japan remained a society that was socially and politically feudal, but within a framework that was essentially capitalist. The economic order had changed dramatically from the beginning of the Tokugawa Shogunate in 1603.

Now it must be recognized that there were some importance differences between the Japanese transition and the European one, and that these differences were linked to Japanese isolation. As Anderson has commented (1974b:453-454):

These sealed frontiers were henceforward a permanent noose on the development of merchant capital in Japan. One of the fundamental preconditions of primitive accumulation in early modern Europe was the dramatic internationalization of commodity

exchange and exploitation from the epoch of the Discoveries
onwards. . . . The Shogunal policy of seclusion, in effect, precluded
any possibility of a transition to the capitalist mode of production
proper within the Tokugawa framework. Deprived of foreign trade,
commercial capital in Japan was constantly reined in and re-routed
towards parasitic dependence on the feudal nobility and its political
systems.

Yes, the isolation of Japan from international economic exchanges
certainly limited its development, and thus it was only after the opening of
Japan to the West that it really developed into, in Anderson's phraseology, a
"capitalist mode of production proper." But the fact that it had evolved so far
in the direction of that mode of production in such a short time, and that it
had done so in virtual seclusion, suggests that there is something about
feudalism as a mode of production that gives it a fundamental, endogenous
impetus to breakdown and transformation toward a specifically capitalist
system. Most everyone agrees that the highly decentralized character of
feudalism, a character that permits merchants a freedom of economic maneuver that is generally denied in more centralized political systems, is a crucial
aspect of this impetus. In Europe, the demographic and ecological limitations
of feudalism also seemed to play a vital role, as we have seen. Was this also
the case in Japan? Ester Boserup (1965) has suggested that major demographic changes occurred within Tokugawa Japan, but her argument is much
disputed, and in any event our knowledge of Japan in this area is much too
thin to give a definitive answer.

But regardless of whether or not demographic change played a major
role in the Japanese transition from feudalism to capitalism, it seems
undeniable that this transition was a fundamentally endogenous process in its
early phases. If the full emergence of Japanese capitalism was to require the
participation of Japan in the larger Europe-centered world-economy, this only
shows that exogenous factors played a significant role as well. In the end,
then, the evolution of capitalism in both Europe and Japan exemplifies what
Halliday has fittingly called "the dialectic of the internal and the external."

CONCLUSIONS

This essay has been largely devoted to answering a fundamental question: Is the basic unit of social evolution the individual society or some sort of world-system? The answer, of course, is that it is both. But when it is the one, and when the other, depends very much on circumstances. In the case of stateless societies, most social evolution is internal to societies themselves, the most important stimuli to evolutionary change being population pressure and environmental degradation. In the case of the two great feudal civilizations of world history, it would also seem that societies rather than world-systems are the appropriate unit. After all, neither feudal Europe nor feudal Japan constituted world-systems, even in the form of world-economies.[4] In the case of feudal Europe there existed one of the features that Wallerstein has identified as basic to a world-system, viz., a multiplicity of cultures. But although these cultures interacted, they did not do so via the existence of the type of economic specialization -- a core/periphery hierarchy -- that is a crucial defining feature of a world-system.

That still leaves us with a fair amount of room for the application of a world-system perspective to social evolution. Much of what went on in agrarian civilizations of the past no doubt can -- and often must -- be analyzed from the point of view of their involvement in larger world-economies and world-empires (although, again, the impetus to evolutionary transformation is very weak; disintegration, or dynastic cycles, were the rule). Then there is our modern capitalist world-economy. Wallerstein and others have convincingly demonstrated, that to my satisfaction at least, *the modern world-system* is the basic unit of analysis for understanding the evolution of the individual societies that are part of it. This does not mean that factors endogenous to individual societies play no role. It simply means that those factors can exert their effects only within the context of the constraints of the larger system. As Wallerstein (1985:35) has elegantly put it, "It is not that there are no particularities of each acting group. Quite the contrary. It is that the alternatives available for each unit are constrained by the framework of the whole, even while each actor opting for a given alternative in fact alters the framework of the whole."[5]

NOTES

1. Chase-Dunn and Hall (chapter 1, this volume) explicitly state that some world-systems are not characterized by a core/periphery hierarchy. Rather, these world-systems have core/periphery *differentiation* in the absence of relations of domination and exploitation. I question the use of the concept of core/periphery differentiation for two reasons. First, it is not rooted in a clear and consistent conception of "core" and "periphery." Second, as already noted, it seems to stretch the meaning of "world-system" so far that its utility becomes questionable.

2. Abu-Lughod (1989) points out that the Black Death was introduced into Europe by traders coming from the East. This means, obviously, that it was not simply an endogenous phenomenon. However, it occurred in the context of a demographic decline that was already well under way in Europe, a decline that was firmly rooted in endogenous processes.

3. Anderson argues that the defining features of feudalism are vassalage and the fief, which when combined yield a politico-economic system notable for its merging of landownership and political power. The state and the aristocracy are basically fused as one, and the exercise of political power is highly decentralized. The nobility is a hierarchically structured class that specializes in warfare and thus has a highly militarized ideology.

I agree with Anderson that such a system has prevailed only in Medieval Europe and Japan. Many historical scholars (e.g., Coulbourn, 1956) have defined feudalism more generally and have tried to make a case for its widespread occurrence throughout world history. Obviously I reject such a position.

4. Feudal Europe was not, of course, a single "society." It was a civilizational unit composed of many sovereign states whose unity existed only at the ideological level, i.e., via Christianity. The point is that processes internal to this civilizational unit, and to a large extent even within the separate "societies" within this unit, were critical to its evolution and ultimate dissolution.

5. A crucial concern here is what Chase-Dunn calls "the boundary problem." If we are going to claim that world-systems are the units of social evolution, then we have to be able to define the boundaries of these systems, not only theoretically but operationally. I would argue that this is not too difficult in the case of the modern capitalist world-economy, although problems exist here too (see Chase-Dunn [1989] for a discussion of this, and for a different approach to bounding this system from that taken by Wallerstein). In the case of alleged precapitalist world-systems, though, the problem is much more challenging. In the works of those scholars advocating

world-systems as the units of precapitalist social evolution, it is difficult to see how they are defining the boundaries of the systems they propose, or, indeed, whether these systems could conceivably be said to have well-defined boundaries at all. Often what are called precapitalist world-systems appear nothing more than very loose networks. This is one of my major concerns about applying a world-system perspective to precapitalist social evolution.

For a discussion of the boundary problem with respect to world-systems analysis, see Chase-Dunn and Hall (Chapter 1, this volume).

Actually, the boundary problem does not disappear when we are dealing with societies rather than world-systems. Some scholars, Michael Mann (1986) being one of the most notable, claim that societies cannot ordinarily be conceived as having well-defined boundaries, and thus they cannot be a proper unit of social evolution. Mann prefers to talk about what he calls "intersecting power networks" as a proper unit of sociological analysis. Mann may go too far, but he is on to something important and his criticism has not yet been sufficiently answered by social evolutionists. This is obviously a subject that must be pursued in future discussions.

REFERENCES

Abu-Lughod, Janet 1988. "The shape of the world system in the thirteenth century." *Studies in Comparative International Development* 22(4):3-24.

_____ 1989. *Before European Hegemony: The World System A.D. 1250-1350*. New York: Oxford University Press.

Anderson, Perry 1974a. *Passages from Antiquity to Feudalism*. London: New Left Books.

_____ 1974b. *Lineages of the Absolutist State*. London: New Left Books.

Boserup, Ester 1965. *The Conditions of Agricultural Growth*. Chicago: Aldine.

Carneiro, Robert L 1970. "A theory of the origin of the state." *Science* 169:733-738.

_____ 1981. "The chiefdom: precursor of the state." In Grant D. Jones and Robert R. Kautz (eds.) *The Transition to Statehood in the New World*. New York: Cambridge University Press.

_____ 1987. "Further reflections on resource concentration and its role in the rise of the state." In Linda Manzanilla (ed.) *Studies in the Neolithic and Urban Revolutions*. Oxford: British Archaeological Reports, International Series, No. 349.

Chase-Dunn, Christopher 1986. *Rise and Demise: The Transformation of World-Systems*. unpublished manuscript.

_____ 1988. "Comparing world-systems: toward a theory of semiperipheral development." *Comparative Civilizations Review* 19:29-66.

_____ 1989. *Global Formation: Structures of The World-economy*. Oxford: Basil Blackwell.

Cohen, Mark Nathan 1977. *The Food Crisis in Prehistory*. New Haven: Yale University Press.

Coulbourn, Rushton (ed.) 1956. *Feudalism in History*. Princeton: Princeton University Press.

Dobb, Maurice 1963. *Studies in the Development of Capitalism*. Revised edition. New York: International Publishers. (First edition 1947.)

Ekholm, Kajsa 1981. "On the structure and dynamics of global systems." In Joel S. Kahn and Josep R. Llobera (eds.) *The Anthropology of Pre-Capitalist Societies*. London: Macmillan.

_____ and Jonathan Friedman 1982. "'Capital' imperialism and exploitation in ancient world-systems." *Review* 4:87-109.

Friedman, Jonathan 1982. "Catastrophe and continuity in social evolution." In Colin Renfrew, Michael J. Rowlands, and Barbara Abbott Segraves (eds.) *Theory and Explanation in Archaeology*. New York: Academic Press.

_____ and Michael Rowlands 1978. "Notes toward an epigenetic model of the evolution of 'civilization.'" In J. Friedman and M.J. Rowlands (eds.) *The Evolution of Social Systems*. Pittsburgh: University of Pittsburgh Press.

Giddens, Anthony 1981. *A Contemporary Critique of Historical Materialism*. Berkeley: University of California Press.

_____ 1984. *The Constitution of Society*. Berkeley: University of California Press.

Halliday, Jon 1975. *A Political History of Japanese Capitalism*. New York: Monthly Review Press.

Harris, Marvin 1977. *Cannibals and Kings: The Origins of Cultures*. New York: Random House.

_____ 1979. *Cultural Materialism: The Struggle for a Science of Culture*. New York: Random House.

Kohl, Phil 1987. "The ancient economy, transferable technologies and the Bronze Age world-system: a view from the northeastern frontier of the Ancient Near East." In Michael Rowlands, Mogens Larsen, and Kristian Kristiansen (eds.) *Centre and Periphery in the Ancient World*. Cambridge: Cambridge University Press.

Lattimore, Owen 1940. *Inner Asian Frontiers of China*. New York: American Geographical Society.

Le Roy Ladurie, Emmanuel 1974. *The Peasants of Languedoc*. Champaign: University of Illinois Press.

Mann, Michael 1986. *The Sources of Social Power. Volume 1: A History of Power from the Beginning to A.D. 1760*. Cambridge: Cambridge University Press.

Mutel, Jacques 1988. "The modernization of Japan: why has Japan succeeded in its modernization?" In Jean Baechler, John A. Hall, and Michael Mann (eds.) *Europe and the Rise of Capitalism*. Oxford: Basil Blackwell.

Nisbet, Robert A. 1969. *Social Change and History*. New York: Oxford University Press.

North, Douglass C. and Robert Paul Thomas 1973. *The Rise of the Western World: A New Economic History*. New York: Cambridge University Press.

Postan, Michael M. 1972. *The Medieval Economy and Society*. Berkeley: University of California Press.

Rowlands, Michael, Mogens Larsen, and Kristian Kristiansen (eds.) 1987. *Centre and Periphery in the Ancient World*. Cambridge: Cambridge University Press.

Sanderson, Stephen K. 1988. *Macrosociology: An Introduction to Human Societies*. New York: Harper & Row.

_____ 1990. *Social Evolutionism: A Critical History*. Oxford: Basil Blackwell.

Schneider, Jane 1977. "Was there a pre-capitalist world-system?" *Peasant Studies* 6:20-29.

Sweezy, Paul 1976. "A critique." In Rodney Hilton (ed.) *The Transition from Feudalism to Capitalism*. London: New Left Books. (Originally published 1950.)

Wallerstein, Immanuel 1974a. *The Modern World-System: Capitalist Agriculture and the Origins of the European World-Economy in the Sixteenth Century*. New York: Academic Press.

_____ 1974b. "The rise and future demise of the world capitalist system: concepts for comparative analysis." *Comparative Studies in Society and History* 16:387-415.

_____ 1979. "The present state of the debate on world inequality." In Immanuel Wallerstein, *The Capitalist World-Economy*. New York: Cambridge University Press.

_____ 1980. *The Modern World-System II: Mercantilism and the Consolidation of the European World-Economy, 1600-1750*. New York: Academic Press.

_____ 1984a. "Patterns and prospectives of the capitalist world-economy." In Immanuel Wallerstein, *The Politics of the World-Economy*. New York: Cambridge University Press.

_____ 1984b. "The quality of life in different social systems: the model and the reality." In Immanuel Wallerstein, *The Politics of the World-Economy*. New York: Cambridge University Press.

_____ 1985. "The three stages of African involvement in the world-economy." In Peter C.W. Gutkind and Immanuel Wallerstein (eds.) *Political Economy of Contemporary Africa*. Second edition. Beverly Hills, CA: Sage.

_____ 1989. *The Modern World-System III: The Second Era of Great Expansion of the Capitalist World-Economy, 1730-1840s*. San Diego: Academic Press.

Wilkinson, Richard G 1973. *Poverty and Progress: An Ecological Perspective on Economic Development*. New York: Praeger.

Wright, Erik Olin 1983. "Giddens's critique of Marxism." *New Left Review* 138:11-35.

6

Prehistoric Chiefdoms on the American Midcontinent: A World-System Based on Prestige Goods[1]

Peter Peregrine

Cultural evolution in the eastern United States reached its pinnacle with the emergence of Mississippian societies in the major river valleys of the Midwest and Southeast around A.D. 900 (Smith, 1978:480). Mississippian societies were differentiated from their predecessors because of their reliance on maize horticulture for subsistence, the concentration of population at major riverine centers, often palisaded and containing large, flat-topped mounds, and the presence of an elite social strata (Steponaitis, 1986:387-93). Indeed, Mississippian societies represent the first true chiefdoms in eastern North America (Peebles and Kus, 1977).[2]

Some of these Mississippian chiefdoms grew to enormous proportions. It is estimated that Cahokia and its environs, the largest of the Mississippian centers, was inhabited by at least 10,000 people at the height of its occupation (circa A.D. 1150), and perhaps by as many as 40,000 people (Fowler, 1974:25; cf. Milner, 1990). At least 100 mounds were constructed at Cahokia; the largest, Monks Mound, is estimated to contain over 600,000 cubic meters of earth, and is the largest prehistoric structure north of Mexico (Fowler, 1974:6). Other Mississippian centers were built on a smaller scale, but still demonstrate the political power Mississippian chiefs must have possessed in order to procure the labor necessary to build mounds and palisades, and to keep order within these large communities (Reed, 1973; also see DePratter, 1983:162-170).

I suggest that Mississippian societies operated in the framework of a type of precapitalist world-system that I call a "prestige-good system," and that the extraordinary political power of Mississippian chiefs derived largely from their control over the manufacture and trade of prestige-goods (Peregrine, 1990).[3] The concept of prestige-good systems is not new, and is indeed based largely upon the ideas of Claude Meillassoux (particularly 1978). But viewing prestige-good systems as world-systems is a rather different concept, as I will discuss in a moment. Prestige-good systems themselves have been well documented in the ethnographic literature, and can be described in some detail (Ekholm, 1972; Frankenstein and Rowlands, 1978; Friedman, 1982; Friedman and Rowlands, 1977; Peregrine, 1990; Welch, 1986).

Prestige-Good Systems

Political power in prestige-good systems is based upon the control of objects needed by members of the society to pay social debts such as bridewealth, initiation and funerary fees, punitive fines, and the like (Peregrine, 1990:16). Because political leaders in prestige-good systems control these goods, they are able to control individuals' abilities to pay social debts, and in turn, to socially reproduce themselves. This is the most fundamental aspect of prestige-good systems: those with power control the abilities of others to socially reproduce by controlling the means of social reproduction -- prestige-goods.

Prestige-good systems appear to evolve out of lineage-based societies in situations where lineage elders are unable to control the means of production (Peregrine, 1990:116-19).[4] An alternate strategy for these elders to gain political power is to foster the use of lineage symbols they control in ceremonies of social reproduction. In this way, they come to control the means of social reproduction (Meillassoux, 1978:138-39; also see Brumfiel and Earle, 1987:3).

Friedman (1982:184) suggests that all prestige-good systems share four elements in common:

(a) generalized exchange; (b) monopoly over prestige-good imports that are necessary for marriage and other crucial payments, i.e., for the social reproduction of local kin groups; (c) bilineal tendency in the kinship structure (asymmetrical); and (d) tendency to asymmetrical political dualism: religious-political chiefs, original people-new-comers, etc.

Friedman's notions about prestige-good systems are, however, based largely upon theoretical conceptions of how these types of societies may have operated prehistorically (developed by Friedman and Rowlands [1977]), and only marginally on the way extant systems operate. Certainly the first two elements are present in all prestige-good systems -- they are defining elements. The other two may be present in some systems, but not in all; and Friedman leaves out some elements, most importantly the reproduction of the smallest social unit in the political structure and an emphasis on elder/younger relations, which appear to be central features of prestige-good systems I have studied (Peregrine, 1990:24-120).

In order to discuss the basic nature of prestige-good systems in more detail, and I hope with more accuracy, I will compare and contrast three well-documented systems of varying political centralization, subsistence patterns, and geographic location. The first is the Kongo Kingdom of west Africa (Ekholm, 1972). The second is the Tongan chiefdom in extreme western Polynesia between Fiji and Samoa (Gailey, 1987; Gifford, 1929; Goldman, 1970; Kirch, 1984). The third is the Karavaran big-manship located on Karavar Island between New Britain and New Ireland, off the coast of Papua New Guinea (Errington, 1974, 1977).

In all prestige-good systems generalized exchange of prestige-goods occurs.[5] In both Kongo and Tonga foreign trade and the goods that come from it are controlled at the highest level of the political hierarchy (Ekholm, 1972:100-101,133; Kirch, 1984:238,241). These are distributed down the hierarchy in return for service and tribute, but the distribution is certainly general and not reciprocal. In Karavar, although all do have some *divara* (shell "money"), big men control amounts beyond the potential of most individuals (Errington, 1977:36). This *divara* is given out for specific work done, to subordinates in order for them to enter ritual grades, and at funerary rituals such as *matamatam* (Errington, 1977:27). Distribution of *divara* by big men is also generalized -- in most cases all the big men get in return is prestige and the knowledge that they have strengthened their political position.

Monopoly over goods needed for marriage, initiation, and other crucial payments at the highest level of the political hierarchy is also present in all prestige-good systems. In Kongo, shell beads, raffia cloth, and other imported preciosities are needed to make bridewealth payments, and these can only be obtained from the king (although they flow down the political hierarchy so that most individuals get them from local chiefs or lineage heads [Ekholm, 1972:86,111]). In Tonga, red feathers, fine painted cloth and mats, beaded baskets, and other items needed by Tongans to make extravagant marriage payments in order to arrange status-maintaining or enhancing marriages are traded from Fiji by the *Tui's* (pre-eminent chiefs) and are only obtainable from them (although, as in Kongo, these goods flow down the hierarchy, and are obtained by most people through local chiefs [Kirch, 1984:239,241]). Finally, in Karavar, *divara* is needed to enter the ritual grades necessary for a youth to become a man, and to be eligible for marriage. Again, although anyone can acquire *divara*, the amounts necessary to enter the final ritual grades can only be obtained from a sponsor, often a big man (Errington, 1974:91-97).

A bilineal tendency in kinship is also present, to some extent, in all prestige-good systems I have investigated. In Kongo, matrilineal lineages are contrasted with the patrilineal nature of the political structure (Ekholm, 1972:40-51). In Tonga, the matrilineal line carries status, while the patrilineal line carries political power (Goldman, 1970:289-90). In Karavar, society is organized into matrilineal moieties, while the basic political units are men's groups organized around a big man (Errington, 1977:25-26). It is clear that in all these prestige-good systems there is some tendency for bilineal relationships to occur, but those relationships are highly varied between the three. There seems to be no clear-cut bilineal kinship system at work in these three prestige-good systems, and therefore bilineality may not be as important an element of prestige-good systems as Friedman states.

Rather than focusing on bilineal kinship in prestige-good systems, I believe it is more important to consider the reproduction of a society's basic kinship structures in its political hierarchy. Indeed, it may be this tendency to reproduce kinship structures in the political structure that gives rise to the apparent bilineality Friedman perceives. In Kongo, the basic relationship between elder males and younger males within localized matrilineages is reproduced as a hierarchy of chiefs (Ekholm, 1972:25). Each chief is subordinate to an "elder" chief (except, of course, the king), and superordinate to a "younger" chief. These subordinate/superordinate relationships are designated by kinship terms, such as father/son and grandfather/grandson (Ekholm, 1972:50-51). In Tonga, a similar situation is present, with even the taboos placed upon relationships within the lineage being reproduced in relationships within the political hierarchy (Gifford, 1929:18). In Karavar, one can compare big men with fathers: sponsoring younger males as fathers are supposed to if they can; teaching younger males *dukduk* and *tubuan* magic, again as fathers are supposed to do if they can. Indeed, sponsorship often leads to the ritual adoption of a young man (Errington, 1974:92-98). Karavaran big men, in a sense, are a recreation of the father/son relationship in a political form.

This father / son, elder male / younger male emphasis is another important element in the prestige-good systems I have studied. Political power is directly associated with social elders, and the legitimation of political power lies in possessing elder status. Youths are excluded from political power and prestige, and are exploited by elders to enhance their own power and prestige. To reiterate, in both Kongo and Tonga political superiors are considered to be the social elders of their political subordinates (Ekholm, 1972:37-38, 55). These relationships take on the kinship terms for elder/younger such as father/son and grandfather/grandson (Gifford, 1929:28). In Karavar, although there is no political hierarchy, there is a hierarchy of ritual grades. Those who have entered more of the grades are social elders to those who have not, and only the eldest socially (those who have bought a *tubuan*) are eligible to be big men (Errington, 1974:91). In these prestige-good systems, political power is directly linked to, and legitimated by, being eldest socially.

Finally, Friedman's statement that prestige-good systems tend to have asymmetrical political dualism is not well supported in the prestige-good systems I have investigated. Certainly Tonga has asymmetrical political dualism between the *Tui Tonga*, the spiritual/religious head, and the *Tui Kanokupolu*, the social head (Kirch, 1984:224-25), but neither Kongo nor Karavar exhibit this dualism. Indeed, both have leaders who act as combined religious/political heads. The Kongan king is the closest to the ancestors of all Kongans, yet he is also the political leader (Ekholm, 1972:23-24). A defining feature of the Karavaran big man is the control of the *tubuan* spirit

(Errington, 1974:118). Asymmetrical political dualism only occurs in a few of the prestige-good systems I have studied, and may not be an important element of prestige-good systems in general.

Four major elements seem to characterize prestige-good systems: (1) generalized exchange of prestige-goods; (2) monopoly over prestige-goods at the highest political level; (3) the reproduction of basic kinship structures in the political structure; and (4) political power held by the socially eldest members of society.

Prestige-good systems can be viewed as world-systems when there is competition between localized political leaders for access to foreign prestige-goods. As explained by Frankenstein and Rowlands (1978:76):

> The specific economic characteristics of a prestige-good system are dominated by the political advantage gained through exercising control over access to resources that can only be obtained through external trade...Groups are linked to each other through the competitive exchange of wealth objects as gifts and feasting in continuous cycles of status rivalry. Descent groups reproduce themselves in opposition to each other as their leaders compete for dominance through differential access to resources and labour power.

One of the fundamental aspects of world-systems, competition between localized polities for advantageous economic position (Schneider, Chapter 2), is therefore inherent in prestige-good systems. The other major aspect of world-systems, differentiation and division of labor between localized polities (Schneider, Chapter 2), is inherent in the prestige-goods themselves. By definition, prestige-goods must be exotic or of high labor investment. They embody esoteric knowledge about the world outside of the local group or knowledge of special manufacturing techniques (Helms, 1979, 1988). Because prestige-goods are traded from outside the local group or commissioned from artisans with specialized skills, there is an inherent division of labor in prestige-good systems, as Brumfiel and Earle (1987:7) make clear:

> Interacting regional elites can agree to exchange their stores of domestic wealth, each supplying the other with what becomes a stock of exotic wealth. Exotic wealth then supplements or supplants

domestic wealth as the customary means of social payment (since elders control the statuses to which young men aspire, they can define the qualifying criteria as best suits them). Clients come to depend on patrons to supply wealth which they no longer manufacture for themselves.

Prestige-good systems, therefore, appear to be an unusual form of a precapitalist world-system. They are unusual in that they are founded specifically upon a lineage-based social structure which, although modified as the system becomes more politically centralized, maintains its basic lineage form even in the political hierarchy. They are also unusual because they are based upon a division of labor in exotic goods, a division of labor which some world-system theorists might argue has little impact on the societies involved (Wallerstein, 1974:42, 333, also 1989:130-32). The important thing to recognize here, however, is that these exotic goods are not "luxury" items in prestige-good systems, but are necessary for social reproduction.

The Mississippian Prestige-Good System

There is sound evidence to support the idea that Mississippian societies were participants in some form of a prestige-good system. There was extensive interregional trade in exotica in Mississippian societies: such as marine shell from the Gulf coast, copper from Lake Superior, obsidian, bauxite, and minerals from as far west as the Rockies, and various other minerals and cherts from localized sources scattered across the eastern United States (Griffin, 1967:156). During the height of Mississippian centralization, specific design motifs and unusual artifact types of what has been called the "Southeastern Ceremonial Complex" circulated between centers in a truly pan-Mississippian exchange network of exotica (Waring and Holder, 1945; Galloway, 1989).

More importantly, however, the distribution of these exotic raw materials and the objects made from them appears to be consistent with that expected from a prestige-good system. Evidence to support this idea has been presented in detail elsewhere and need not be repeated at length here (Welch, 1986; Peregrine, 1990). A study I conducted recently showed that the distribution of prestige-goods found in Mississippian burials (giving a per-capita measure of their distribution) paralleled that expected from a prestige-good system, both within and between communities (Peregrine, 1990:179-222). In a study that is somewhat the inverse of mine, Welch (1986) tested four models of chiefdom political economy against the material record for the Mississippian chiefdom at Moundville, Alabama, and found that the model most consistent with the archaeological data was that of a prestige-good system (although his conception of prestige-good systems differs somewhat from mine, particularly as it is not based in a world-system framework). In both studies it was clear that the Mississippian societies being analyzed were participants in some form of a prestige-good system.

Viewing Mississippian societies as participants in this unique type of pre-capitalist world-system is not really helpful unless it increases our understanding of their social structures and evolution. I argue this perspective is able to do both. First, because prestige-good systems are rooted in a lineage-based social system (and indeed, foster specific developments in that social system), probable social structures of Mississippian societies can be inferred readily by viewing the archaeological record through this theoretical lens.

In terms of political organization, the implications of the Mississippian prestige-good system should be clear. Political power was based upon the ability to control prestige-goods, legitimated through a lineage structure (Peregrine, 1990:63-69). Since Mississippian societies were apparently organized as chiefdoms (Peebles and Kus, 1977), a hierarchy of chiefs was likely, similar perhaps to Kongo or Tonga, with the pre-eminent chief located at a major center, and lower level chiefs located at minor centers and in outlying hamlets. This hierarchy seems to be reflected in the Mississippian settlement system (Fowler, 1978; cf. Milner, 1990). The hierarchy was probably organized like a lineage, with individuals in each level both superior and socially "elder" to individuals in levels below them (DePratter, 1983:100-110). At the lowest level in the political hierarchy were localized lineages, with elder males as their heads.

Localized lineages would have formed the basic social structure in Mississippian societies as well, and are represented archaeologically in the organization of Mississippian cemeteries (Goldstein, 1980:136-37) Lineage leaders were the "socially" eldest members of the lineage. Social age was likely a dual product of one's ancestry and one's ability to create alliances with elder lineage members from whom one could obtain both the knowledge and the prestige-goods needed to be initiated into various ritual grades (Meillassoux,

1978). There were probably a number of ritual grades in Mississippian societies, some of which were necessary to simply be recognized as an adult or as a member of the society, and some in which membership brought prestige and political power (Hudson, 1976:325-27, 336-40).

In terms of economic organization, localized lineages may have also been the basic production units. Some individuals apparently served as craftsmen for pre-eminent chiefs, manufacturing prestige-goods at chiefdom centers (Welch, 1986:171-72). Although horticulture was practiced in order to produce enough to both support artisans and political leaders and allow them to remain in the same location, there was probably little systematic trade between centers and outlying hamlets in maize or other agricultural products (Welch, 1986:130-32; cf. O'Brien, 1990).[6] The logistics of bulk trade in the Mississippian period would have been formidable, and major centers were located on rich soils, certainly capable of producing enough to support the inhabitants (Peebles, 1978).

Finally, in terms of ideology, ancestry would have been all-important. A "cult of the ancestors" in some form was a probable feature of Mississippian societies, and may be represented in the unique stone figurines, charnel structures, and elaborate burial ceremonialism characteristic of Mississippian culture (DePratter, 1983:111-54). The pre-eminent chief himself was probably both the social and spiritual "father" of the chiefdom. He was seen as a contact between the ancestors and the people, as he was the social elder of the people, and so the closest to the ancestors (DePratter, 1983:68). This reverts to political power, as the pre-eminent chief's closeness to the ancestors probably reinforced his political position (Shils, 1971). Hence power, social structure, and ideology were all intermeshed in the processes of the Mississippian world-system.

Perhaps more importantly, the prestige-good system model provides a unique theory of Mississippian evolution, one that ties the origins of social stratification to processes beginning more than a thousand years earlier (Peregrine, 1990:278-86). During the late Archaic period, burial mounds began to be constructed, apparently to mark territories controlled by corporate lineages (Charles and Buikstra, 1983). At about the same time systematic interregional trade in exotic goods began (Winters, 1968). The implications are that the Archaic period saw the initiation of lineages in the Eastern Woodlands and the beginnings of elder control and manipulation of imported preciosities (Bender, 1985a).

The control and manipulation of exotic goods by lineage elders apparent-ly became more intense during the Woodland period, culminating in the "Hopewell interaction sphere" through which exotic goods from distant sources were moved across midcontinental North America (Struever and Houart, 1972). These goods were apparently being used to arrange marriages between localized groups (Bender, 1985b), and it is likely that lineage elders were fostering the use of prestige-goods in other ceremonies of social reproduction (Brose, 1979). As these goods came to be in greater demand, the lineage elder's power grew in direct proportion (Peregrine, 1990:75-86). Certainly fostered by population growth which increased the demand for prestige-goods during the Woodland period (Buikstra, 1977:76-77, 81), and perhaps spurred further by an apparent re-organization of society at a lower hierarchical level during the Late Woodland period (Tainter, 1975), lineage elders during the formative Mississippian period gained enough power to differentiate them-selves from other lineage members, and became an emergent elite.

Conflict, perhaps over access to advantageous trade routes, may have played a role in the emergence of Mississippian elites. Many Mississippian centers occupy relatively circumscribed riverine environments and are often surrounded by defensive palisades. Larson (1972) and Green (1977) argue that a need to defend these prime riverine locations was critical to the evolution of Mississippian societies. Although conflict has probably never been the sole factor behind the emergence of social stratification (Wenke, 1984:215-18), the need to coordinate labor for defense (or conquest) could have provided lineage elders in the emergent Mississippian period additional control over junior lineage members, and fostered the development of new social forms legitimating increased levels of political power held by specific individuals (Carneiro, 1970; Johnson and Earle, 1987).

In considering the emergence of social stratification, one must also consider the intensification of production necessary to sustain elites. Indeed Renfrew (1982:263) has argued that "all development towards more complex society implies intensification, permitting the support of administrative and other central activities." Intensification for the support of Mississippian elites was apparently accomplished by increasing labor dedicated to maize horticul-ture, which had been present in the prehistoric East since at least Middle Woodland times, but was never heavily relied upon for subsistence (Griffin, 1985:61). Individuals apparently increased production to support their elites in competitive exchanges with others so that they would have more access to prestige-goods, and hence a better opportunity to socially reproduce themselves (Peregrine, 1990:19-20).

As elites competed for exotic goods in the emergent Mississippian prestige-good system, elites located at nodal points on trade routes, and who had a supportive population, were able to control those routes and the goods flowing through them (Peregrine, 1990:247-69). Elites less fortunately located grew dependent on elites controlling trade routes, and may have been undermined by them. Population was attracted to elites who offered greater access to prestige-goods, and hence better opportunities to socially reproduce. In this way Mississippian centers with dense populations emerged in the central riverine valleys of the midcontinent, where riverine trade could be controlled, and where intensified production through maize horticulture was possible (Peregrine, n.d., 1990:269-73).

Beginning about A.D. 1250, Mississippian societies went into a decline that lasted until the coming of Europeans (Tainter, 1988:15-16). The prestige-good system model provides insight into this decline as well, for these systems appear to be relatively unstable (Friedman and Rowlands, 1977:228, 232). The items that constitute prestige-goods are socially defined, and subordinate elites, disgruntled with a particular leader or group of leaders, have the potential to undermine their power base by promoting the use of alternate prestige-goods (Ekholm, 1972:128-44), or by simply no longer recognizing the need for these goods in ceremonies of social reproduction. Since many prestige-goods are obtained through foreign trade, the disruption of trade routes or alliances can also bring about rapid alterations in prestigegood systems. Peebles (1987) argues that one of the major factors correlated with the collapse of the Moundville chiefdom is the sudden suspension of interregional trade in exotic goods. The prestige-good system model, then, has the potential to explain both the rise and decline of Mississippian societies within a unified framework.

The concept of Mississippian social evolution based on the processes of a prestige-good system also avoids some of the problems present in many theories for the evolution of political complexity (Peregrine, 1990:2-8). Chiefs emerge because of their ability to control prestige-goods, and perhaps from personal ambition, but not from some desire or need to manage their society altruistically. Social evolution grows out of the systemic interaction of independent polities within the prestige-good system, not from simple migration or diffusion. Intensified production through agriculture is not a "prime mover" behind social evolution, but emerges out of the evolutionary process itself. Decline, too, is linked to the processes of social interaction and conflict. In addition, this perspective links the evolution of Mississippian societies to the *longue duree* of North American prehistory, providing a unity of theory that has never been possible before.

Conclusions

Regardless of the impact this perspective might have on our understanding of North American prehistory, I think it carries with it some important ramifications for world-systems theory in general. First, it re-emphasizes and indeed expands the point made by Abu-Lughod (1989:364) that "the principles of organization of world-systems can have considerable variability." In the Mississippian case, the world-system's organization is rooted in the kinship structure of the interacting societies, for the basic economic units of prestige-good systems are localized lineages, and political power is legitimated through the lineage hierarchy. The intimate link that exists between political economy and kinship in stateless societies is one that must be incorporated into world-systems theory if we hope to apply the world-system perspective to the study of these societies and how they change.[7] It is perhaps because many world-system theorists lack a thorough grounding in the study of kinship systems and their relation to political economy that they have been slow to apply the world-system perspective to stateless societies; indeed, since most of these theorists come from disciplines outside of anthropology, they may not even recognize that this crucial link exists.

Second, this study demonstrates that in some circumstances world-systems can be based upon the trade and manufacture of exotica. Again, the lack of understanding among many world-system theorists about the important role exotic goods play in the political economy of many stateless societies has made the application of this perspective to the study of stateless societies very difficult. The simple fact is that systematic trade in foodstuffs, clothing, ordinary raw materials, and other "bulk" goods is rare in stateless societies. Trade in exotica, on the other hand, is common, and as this study demonstrates, can have systemic impact on the societies involved.

I hope the reader is left with an awareness of two basic ideas: first, that stateless societies can be studied using a world-system perspective, and that this perspective can increase our understanding of these societies and how they change; and second, that precapitalist world-systems are often quite different than the ones envisioned by Wallerstein, Abu-Lughod, or even Schneider. Many precapitalist world-systems must be studied with an emphasis not only on economic processes, but also on social ones, for the political economies of these world-systems are intimately linked to their social structures; one cannot be understood in the absence of the other.

NOTES

1. An earlier version of this paper was presented at the 1990 meeting of the International Society for the Comparative Study of Civilizations, Champaign, Illinois. The research presented here was partially supported by a David Ross Grant from the Purdue Research Foundation. I am indebted to Richard Blanton, Robert Fry, Christian Johannsen, Jack Waddell, and the editors of this volume, Christopher Chase-Dunn and Thomas Hall, for their comments, suggestions, and criticisms. Their advice was not always heeded, but their efforts are deeply appreciated.

2. I refer to Mississippian societies as chiefdoms throughout the paper by way of convention, for that is how they are perceived by most North American archaeologists (Peebles and Kus, 1977). This is not to discount arguments that some Mississippian groups were states (O'Brien, 1989). Arguing about these categories, however, clouds the variability in societal scale, complexity, and integration exhibited by individual Mississippian groups (DePratter, 1983). In addition, the criteria used to define societies as chiefdoms or states commonly focus on technological and materialistic traits, rather than the system of social relations and reproduction (viewed within a larger world of inter-societal relations) that I believe more accurately reflects a particular society's "level" of development (Friedman and Rowlands, 1977:201-6).

3. Trade and exchange are used interchangeably throughout the paper as generic terms referring to the passage of material goods between two or more parties.

4. Lineages divide societies into groups based upon genealogical descent by sex. In matrilineal societies, relations are traced only through women; that is, one is only considered to be related to those people on one's mother's side of the family, and membership in the lineage can only be passed on through daughters. The opposite is true for patrilineal societies. Our own society is bilineal, as we consider ourselves related to both our mother's and our father's genealogical lines, and both sons and daughters pass on these genealogical relationships. It is important to note that in most lineage-based societies the lineage, rather than the family, makes up the basic economic unit -- the basic

unit of production, consumption, and settlement. Lineage unity is maintained through worship and reverence for ancestors -- the lineage founders. Lineage elders are perceived as being closest to the ancestors, and are often the political leaders in these societies. Since lineages are basic economic units, lineage elders often have broad control over the economy, and particularly over the production labor provided by junior lineage members (see Ember and Ember, 1983; Fox, 1983; Schusky, 1983).

5. Generalized exchange refers to what might be called simply gift-giving. In a situation of generalized exchange the giver expects nothing material in return from the receiver (although he may expect loyalty, favors, labor, or other such things). A simple example is the American family, where parents provide children with food, clothing, housing, and the like, but expect in return only love and respect, not material re-payment. Generalized exchange is often seen in opposition to reciprocal or balanced exchange, where the giver of an item expects to get something of equal value in return from the receiver (see Belshaw, 1965; Sahlins, 1972:Chapter 5).

6. Although O'Brien (1990) argues convincingly that the major Mississippian center at Cahokia must have been supplied with basic foodstuffs and other bulk goods from well outside its immediate environs, she admits that this type of trade is difficult to measure archaeologically. An attempt made by Welch (1986) to measure systematic bulk trade at Moundville found only minor evidence, and that in a very specific circumstance: the provisioning of elites with choice cuts of venison. Hasenstab (1987) and Dincauze and Hasenstab (1989) have taken the idea of Mississippian trade in bulk goods to its extreme, arguing that Cahokia was the core of a midcontinental world-system that extended as far as Iroquoian groups in Ontario and western New York. Milner (1990) has largely countered these notions (and indeed the idea that Mississippian societies were practicing any kind of systematic bulk trade), but I believe that if we view the entire Mississippian region as the core of a world-system, rather than Cahokia itself, and consider the system based upon trade in exotica, rather than bulk goods, then areas peripheral to the Mississippian "core" (such as Iroquoia) could have been influenced by their position in the Mississippian world-system (Peregrine, 1989), although as Chase-Dunn and Hall (Chapter 1, this volume) hypothesize, this influence was likely not continuous or stable.

7. This point cannot be overemphasized: kinship provides the foundation for the development and legitimation of political power in most stateless societies, and it is through kinship ties that political leaders amass and control labor. To understand the political economy of a stateless society, it is vital to first understand how kinship functions to empower leaders, and how leaders use kinship to organize labor. The relationship between political economy and kinship has not received enough attention even in the anthropological

literature, but an excellent discussion is provided by Friedman and Rowlands (1977).

REFERENCES

Abu-Lughod, Janet 1989. *Before European Hegemony: The World-System A.D.1250-1350*. New York: Oxford University Press.

Belshaw, Cyril 1965. *Traditional Exchange and Modern Markets*. Engelwood-Cliffs, NJ: Prentice-Hall.

Bender, Barbara 1985a. "Emergent tribal formations in the American midcontinent." *American Antiquity* 50:52-62.

_____ 1985b. "Prehistoric developments in the American Midcontinent and in Brittany, Northwest France," in T.D. Price and J.A. Brown (eds.) *Prehistoric Hunter-Gatherers: The Emergence of Cultural Complexity*. New York: Academic Press, pp. 21-58.

Brose, David 1979. "A speculative model of the role of exchange in the prehistory of the Eastern Woodlands," in D. Brose and N. Greber (eds.) *Hopewell Archaeology: The Chillicothe Conference*. Kent: Kent State University Press, pp. 3-8.

Brumfiel, Elizabeth and Timothy Earle 1987. "Specialization, exchange, and complex societies: an introduction," in E. Brumfiel and T. Earle (eds.) *Specialization, Exchange, and Complex Societies*. New York: Cambridge University Press, pp. 1-9.

Buikstra, Jane 1977. "Biocultural dimensions of archaeological study: a regional perspective," in R. Blakely (ed.) *Biocultural Adaptation in Prehistoric America*. Athens: University of Georgia Press, pp. 67-84

Carneiro, Robert 1970. "A Theory of the Origin of the State." *Science* 169:733-738.

Charles, Douglas and Jane Buikstra 1983. "Archaic mortuary sites in the central Mississippi drainage: distribution, structure, and behavioral implications," in J. Phillips and J. Brown (eds.) *Archaic Hunters and Gatherers in the American Midwest*. New York: Academic Press, pp. 117-146.

DePratter, Chester 1983. *Late Prehistoric and Early Historic Chiefdoms in the Southeastern United States*. Ph.D. dissertation, University of Georgia.

Dincauze, Dina and Robert Hasenstab 1989. "Explaining the Iroquois: tribalization on a prehistoric periphery," in T. Champion (ed.) *Centre and Periphery*. London: Unwin Hyman, pp. 67-84.

Ekholm, Kajsa 1972. *Power and Prestige: The Rise and Fall of the Kongo Kingdom*. Uppsala: Scriv Service.

Ember, Melvin and Carol Ember 1983. *Marriage, Family, and Kinship*. New Haven: HRAF Press.

Errington, Frederick 1974. *Karavar: Masks and Power in Melanesian Ritual*. Ithaca: Cornell University Press.

Errington, Shelly 1977. "Order and power in Karavar," in R.D. Fogelson and R.N. Adams (eds.) *The Anthropology of Power*. New York: Academic Press, pp. 23-43.

Fowler, Melvin 1974. *Cahokia: Ancient Capitol of the Midwest*. Addison-Wesley Modules in Anthropology 48.

_____ 1978. "Cahokia and the American Bottom: settlement archaeology," in B. Smith (ed.) *Mississippian Settlement Patterns*. New York: Academic Press, pp. 465-478.

Fox, Robin 1983. *Kinship and Marriage*. Cambridge: Cambridge University Press.

Frankenstein, Susan and Michael Rowlands 1978. "The internal structure and regional context of Early Iron Age society in south-western Germany." *Bulletin of the Institute of Archaeology of London* 15:73-112.

Friedman, Jonathan 1982. "Catastrophe and continuity in social evolution," in C. Renfrew, M.J. Rowlands, and B.A. Segraves (eds.) *Theory and Explanation in Archaeology*. New York: Academic Press, pp. 175-196.

Friedman, Jonathan and Michael Rowlands 1977. "Notes towards an epigenetic model of the evolution of 'civilisation,'" in J. Friedman and M. Rowlands (eds.) *The Evolution of Social Systems*. London: Duckworth, pp. 201-275.

Gailey, Christine 1987. *Kinship to Kingship*. Austin: University of Texas Press.

Galloway, Patricia 1989. *The Southeastern Ceremonial Complex*. Lincoln: University of Nebraska Press.

Gifford, E.W. 1929. *Tongan Society*. Bernice P. Bishop Museum Bulletin 61.

Goldman, Irving 1970. *Ancient Polynesian Society*. Chicago: University of Chicago Press.

Goldstein, Lynne 1980. *Mississippian Mortuary Practices: A Case Study of Two Cemeteries in the Lower Illinois Valley*. Northwestern University Archaeology Program, Scientific Papers, Number 4.

Green, Thomas 1977. *Economic Relationships Underlying Mississippian*

Settlement Patterns in Southwestern Indiana and North-Central Kentucky. Ph.D. dissertation, Indiana University.

Griffin, James 1967. "Eastern North American archaeology: a summary." *Science* 156:175-91.

_____ 1985. "Changing concepts of the prehistoric Mississippian cultures of the eastern United States," in R.R. Badger and L.A. Clayton (eds.) *Alabama and the Borderlands.* University: University of Alabama Press, pp. 40-63.

Hasenstab, Robert 1987. "Canoes, caches, and carrying places: territorial boundaries and tribalization in Late Woodland western New York." *Journal of the New York State Archaeological Association* 95:39-49.

Helms, Mary 1979. *Ancient Panama.* Austin: University of Texas Press.

_____ 1988. *Ulysses' Sail.* New York: Cambridge University Press.

Hudson, Charles 1976. *The Southeastern Indians.* Knoxville: University of Tennessee Press.

Johnson, Allen and Timothy Earle 1987. *The Evolution of Human Societies.* Stanford: Stanford University Press.

Kirch, Patrick 1984. *The Evolution of Polynesian Chiefdoms.* New York: Cambridge University Press.

Larson, Lewis 1972. "Functional considerations of warfare in the Southeast during the Mississippian period." *American Antiquity* 37:383-92.

Meillassoux, Claude 1978. "'The economy' in agricultural self-sustaining societies: a preliminary analysis," in D. Seddon (ed.) *Relations of Production.* London: Frank Cass, pp. 127-157.

Milner, George 1990. "The late prehistoric Cahokia cultural system of the Mississippi River valley: foundations, florescence, and fragmentation." *Journal of World Prehistory* 4:1-43.

O'Brien, Patricia 1989. "Cahokia: The political capital of the 'Ramey' state?" *North American Archaeologist* 10:275-92.

_____ 1990. "The 'world-system' of Cahokia within the Middle Mississippian tradition." Paper presented at the annual meeting of the International Society for the Comparative Study of Civilization, Champaign, Illinois.

Peebles, Christopher 1978. "Determinants of settlement size and location in the Moundville phase," in B.D. Smith (ed.) *Mississippian Settlement Patterns.* New York: Academic Press, pp. 369-416.

_____ 1987. "The rise and fall of the Mississippian in western Alabama: the

Moundville and Summerville phases, A.D. 1000 to 1600." *Mississippi Archaeology* 22:1-31.

Peebles, Christopher and Susan Kus 1977. "Some archaeological correlates of ranked societies." *American Antiquity* 42:421-48.

Peregrine, Peter n.d. "A graph theoretic approach to the evolution of Cahokia." *American Antiquity* (in press).

_____ 1989. "Indigenous world-systems in eastern North America: an introduction." Paper presented at the annual meeting of the American Society for Ethnohistory, Chicago, Illinois.

_____ 1990. *The Evolution of Mississippian Societies in the American Midcontinent from a World-System Perspective*. Ph.D. dissertation, Purdue University.

Reed, Nelson 1973. "Monks and other Mississippian mounds," in M. Fowler (ed.) *Explorations into Cahokia Archaeology*. Illinois Archaeological Survey, Bulletin 7, pp. 31-42.

Renfrew, Colin 1982. "Polity and power: interaction, intensification and exploitation," in C. Renfrew and M. Wagstaff (eds.) *An Island Polity: The Archaeology of Exploitation in Melos*. New York: Cambridge University Press, pp. 264-290.

Sahlins, Marshall 1972. *Stone Age Economics*. New York: Aldine.

Schusky, Edward 1983. *Manual for Kinship Analysis*, Second Edition. Lantham, MD: University Press of America.

Shils, Edward 1971. "Tradition." *Comparative Studies in Society and History* 13:122-59.

Smith, Bruce 1978. "Variation in Mississippian settlement patterns," in B. Smith (ed.) *Mississippian Settlement Patterns*. New York: Academic Press, pp. 479-504.

Steponaitis, Vincas 1986. "Prehistoric archaeology in the southeastern United States, 1970-1985." *Annual Review of Anthropology* 15:363-404.

Struever, Stuart and Gail Houart 1972. "An analysis of the Hopewell interaction sphere," in E. Wilmsen (ed.) *Social Exchange and Interaction*. Ann Arbor: University of Michigan, Museum of Anthropology (Anthropological Papers 46), pp. 47-80.

Tainter, Joseph 1975. *The Archaeological Study of Social Change: Woodland Systems in West-Central Illinois*. Ph.D. dissertation, Northwestern University.

_____ 1988. *The Collapse of Complex Societies*. New York: Cambridge University Press.

Wallerstein, Immanuel 1974. *The Modern World-System, Volume I*. New York: Academic Press.

_____ 1989. *The Modern World-System, Volume III*. New York: Academic Press.

Waring, A.J. and Preston Holder 1945. "A prehistoric ceremonial complex in the southeastern United States." *American Anthropologist* 47:1-34.

Welch, Paul 1986. *Models of Chiefdom Economy: Prehistoric Moundville as a Case Study*. Ph.D. dissertation, University of Michigan.

Wenke, Robert 1984. *Patterns in Prehistory, Second Edition*. New York: Oxford University Press.

Winters, Howard 1968. "Value systems and trade cycles of the Late Archaic in the Midwest," in S.R. Binford and L.R. Binford, (eds.) *New Perspectives in Archaeology*. Chicago: Aldine, pp. 175-221.

7

The Role of Nomads
in Core/Periphery Relations

Thomas D. Hall

OVERVIEW

The extension of world-system theory to "precapitalist" settings necessarily raises questions about the distinctiveness of the "modern world-system" with respect to "precapitalist" world-systems (See Chapter 1, and Wallerstein 1974a, 1974b, 1979, 1980, 1984, 1989, 1990; Abu-Lughod 1987, 1989, 1990; Chase-Dunn 1988, 1989, 1990a; Gailey 1985; Gledhill 1988; Hall 1986, 1989; Kohl 1985, 1987a, 1987b, 1988).[1] An examination of the historical evolution[2] of the role of nomads in core/periphery hierarchies is one way to address these questions. Such a study has additional significances. First, it appears that sedentary social organization emerged from an entirely nomadic context (Nissen 1988). Implicitly problematic here is whether it is possible to have a wholly nomadic core/periphery hierarchy. Because of this issue, the following discussion will be restricted to core/periphery hierarchies with sedentary components. I will return to wholly nomadic core/periphery hierarchies in the final section. Second, nomadic groups frequently play complex intermediary roles in the interactions among sedentary groups, especially states and core/periphery hierarchies. The significance of these roles in changes in core/periphery hierarchies needs to be examined.[3] Third, each new world-system or core/periphery hierarchy is "restructured from" the remains of its predecessor(s) (Abu-Lughod 1990). This is one way in which specific historical events shape general patterns. Fourth, following the work of both Janet Abu-Lughod (1989, 1990) and Thomas Barfield (1989), the rise and fall of the Mongol Empire played a major role in the collapse of the eastern circuits of the thirteenth century Eurasian[4] world-system. This collapse, in turn, initiated a restructuring from which the European "modern world-system" emerged.

Based on Chapter 1, some additional comments are in order. First, there is no reason, *a priori*, to require that every core/periphery hierarchy have a semiperiphery, or that it be limited to only one tier between core and periphery. The extent of the hierarchy should remain an empirical problem. Second, the precise boundaries of nonstate societies (especially nomadic societies) are both theoretically and empirically problematic. On the one hand, nonstate societies -- based on both contemporary ethnographic studies and ethnohistory -- do not have precise borders, but tend to "fade away" in decreasingly important kin and other connections (Wolf 1982). On the other hand, just how much and what type of interaction between state and nonstate societies constitutes a significant connection also remains problematic. Trade in vital goods, trade in luxuries,[5] trade in captives, alliances for frontier buffering, recruitment of nomads for armies, or endemic warfare with other nomads probably have different implications for the historical evolution of core/periphery hierarchies. Third, the thing which is evolving is not a self-contained social unit, such as a "tribe," a "state," an "empire," or a "civilization," but a larger unit, which for want of a better term can be labeled a core/periphery hierarchy.

This chapter contributes to a general discussion of the historical evolution of core/periphery hierarchies. I do this by examining a few cases of nomad - sedentary relations. The goal is not to produce definitive conclusions, but to uncover those aspects of nomad - sedentary relations that are especially salient for the study of core/periphery hierarchies. Because of this goal it is useful to review a few other general issues concerning nomad - sedentary relations.

Pristine States, Trade, Nomads, and Technology

It seems reasonably clear that states, and hence civilizations, originated in interaction systems. Kohl argues that this is the case for the origin of the state:

> One purpose of this study of long-distance trade in southwestern Asia was to show that even the earliest "pristine" example of state formation cannot be explained entirely as an internal process of social differentiation but must be viewed partly as the product of a "world-economy" at different levels of development which stretched at least from the Nile Valley and southeastern Europe in the west to Soviet Central Asia and the Indus Valley in the east" (Kohl 1978, p. 489).

The evidence, as is always the case with archaeological materials, is incomplete, and subject to revision based on new discoveries. Nevertheless, the evidence is very persuasive. Trade between lowland Mesopotamia and highland Iranian plateau supplied goods used by state officials to support their claims to authority and legitimacy. The trade induced mutual dependency between the two areas, and constituted a "world-economy."

In a discussion of the contributions of archaeology to understanding the origin of the state, Gledhill also focuses on the interaction system:

> A regional focus seems of crucial importance, since the fixation of many theories with agricultural intensifications has tended to obscure the possible importance of the fact that the environmental settings of 'pristine' state formation cannot be defined purely in terms of aridity and its agricultural implications. The 'nuclear areas' of ancient civilization were also characterized by intense interactions between nomadic and sedentary populations, interactions which linked farms to fishermen, gatherer-hunters and pastoralists" (Gledhill 1988, p. 23).

Kohl (1978) urges archaeologists to make full use of information available in the historical record, using evidence on such things as:

... qualitatively novel developments in transportation, communication, and military technology associated with the domestication of the horse; the appearance of effective chariots; the spread or "democratization" of metal tools and weapons...(Kohl 1988, p. 30)

Anthony (1986) discusses the domestication of horses in the context of state formation and regional interaction systems. A key point in these discussions is that with the domestication of horses, transportation and communication over land are greatly enhanced. Furthermore, simple iron making technology is very portable and easily diffused among nomads (Kohl 1987a, p. 22). Thus, relative "dependency" between nomad and sedentary groups might be reversed: horses might have enabled nomads to dominate sedentary peoples, and/or might have been the impetus among nomadic groups for technological innovations that subsequently spread to sedentary groups.[6]

With these issues and problems in mind it is now appropriate to turn to a brief examination of several different types of nomad - sedentary interactions.

NOMAD - CIVILIZATION RELATIONS

China and Nomads

The importance of nomads in Chinese history is widely acknowledged (Barfield 1989; Eberhard 1965, 1977; Elvin 1973; Kwanten 1979; Lattimore 1951, 1962c, 1980; Szynkiewicz 1989). This account, however, stresses only certain processes, drawing heavily from the work of Owen Lattimore and Thomas Barfield. As Chinese agriculturists spread to the steppe they adopted other styles of making a living (e.g., herding) that were better suited to the local ecology. Thus, pastoralism was not a case of "devolution," but an alternative survival strategy (Lattimore 1980). Those remaining in agricultural areas eventually developed a cavalry to fight nomads. When "China" consisted of separate kingdoms, many built walls as much to mark their own limits as to keep out the nomads.

Since nomads produced little of interest or value to settled Chinese, nomads used threats of force to induce trade: trading and raiding were alternative means to the same ends. Indeed, some studies show that raiding correlated with changing conditions of trade (Szynkiewicz 1989, p. 154) and changing state stability (Barfield 1989). Chinese officials acquiesced to this trade as a way of controlling nomads. The trade was primarily in luxury goods used by nomadic leaders to shore up and symbolize their power. This interaction fueled changes both in China and among nomads. It helped in incorporating new lands. In times of state decline, nomadic leaders sometimes served as protectors of beleaguered areas. In times of state ascendance, unified Chinese response promoted wider unity among nomads. Nomads were as often a source of change as a receiver (Lattimore 1980, Barfield 1989).

Barfield (1989) analyzes the interconnections between the rise and fall of the Chinese empire and various steppe empires (see especially his chart p. 13). The two are intimately connected via the organizational system of the Chinese empire and the varieties of steppe politics and organization. A key feature in Barfield's analysis is the distinction between inner and outer frontier strategies. The outer frontier strategy is the more familiar. In this strategy a dominant steppe leader uses violent attacks to terrify the court of the sedentary empire, alternates war and peace to successively raise tribute payments, and assiduously avoids taking over Chinese lands and the necessarily intendant entanglements in Chinese court politics (p. 49).

The inner strategy is more subtle, and one that develops when a steppe confederation begins to disintegrate. Some contending steppe faction leader, typically of a weaker faction, seeks alliance with Chinese officials against his rivals. The Chinese officials acquiesce, since typically they favor using "barbarians against barbarians." The steppe faction sometimes uses the Chinese military to aid in the defeat of his rivals, and uses favor at Chinese court to sever tribute flow between the Chinese and his rivals. Typically, this leads to success on the part of the Chinese allied faction. Once dominant, the steppe leader can either use the new power base to unify the steppe and return to an outer frontier strategy or leave the steppe politically fragmented and seek to dominate a local region, monopolizing tribute flow (p. 63).

This oscillation explains the rather long cycles of nomad - Chinese relations (Barfield 1989, p. 13). In particular, it explains the correlation of strong steppe polities with a strong Chinese empire. Only when the empire is strong can it be steadily "milked" via an outer frontier strategy. When the empire is weak, steppe leaders tend to favor an inner frontier strategy, making alliances with local "war lords." The Mongols used both strategies, but with their own peculiar twists.

The Mongol Empire

Analysis of the relations between Mongols and sedentary states is doubly difficult. First, the entire Central Asian field of action must be examined (Morgan 1986; Allsen 1987; Barfield 1989; Kwanten 1979). This is a difficult task because of the way records are made and preserved. The interpretation of documents -- nearly always written by and from the point of view of sedentary state officials -- requires detailed knowledge of many local histories. Second, the Mongols were peculiar in many ways as a steppe empire (Barfield 1989). According to Abu-Lughod (1989, 1990) they played a pivotal role in the thirteenth century collapse of the Eurasian[7] world-system and in the consequent rise of the European world-system.

Mongol success can be attributed to factors and processes occurring at different levels simultaneously (Saunders 1971; Morgan 1986; Lindner 1981, 1982). First, the states in western Asia were weak and thus vulnerable to attack and conquest:

> This was the first time that a major nomadic power direct from the Chinese frontier had invaded the sedentary states of the west. The outer frontier strategy of devastation and terror wreaked havoc with the more fragile ecology of the region. China might replace large population losses within a relatively short period, but here the damage was more long lasting. Cities whose populations numbered in the hundreds of thousands were completely destroyed. Irrigation systems were ruined, severely hampering economic recovery. ... Nomads who had previously entered southwestern Asia from the steppe had always attempted, usually successfully, to found new dynasties and become rulers. The Mongols with their heritage from the Chinese frontier refused to take administrative responsibilities (Barfield 1989, pp. 201-202).

This latter, of course, is the familiar outer frontier strategy, but in this case applied against states which were politically weaker and ecologically more precariously positioned than was typical for China.

Second, continual warfare made a client relation with the Mongols an attractive "bargain" given the alternatives:

> Those areas which accepted the new situation (Manchuria, Korea, Uighar oases)... avoided destructive campaigns by the Mongols and retained their own leaders. Those areas which rejected the Mongol peace terms or reneged on previous agreements (Chin China, western Turkestan, and the Tangut kingdom) became the scenes of numerous campaigns that wiped out much of their population and productivity. In Chinggis' lifetime wars of destruction were aimed at leaders who violated previously agreed peace terms. These campaigns were so devastating that they led to the overthrow of the ruling dynasties and, by default, their direct incorporation into the Mongol Empire (p. 200).

One of the peculiarities of the Mongol empire was a direct result of this policy (rooted in Chinggis' fierce demands for loyalty), namely the conquest of China and the founding of a dynasty due to overly vigorous pursuit of an outer frontier strategy of terror. This is one of the ways in which the Mongols differed from all previous Central Asian nomadic groups. They over-pursued the outer frontier strategy. In the west they destroyed some states or were forced to directly incorporate and administer others. In the east they were ultimately trapped by their own vigor and success into founding a new Chinese dynasty.

A third factor in Mongol success was continued presence of pastoral nomads who maintained a flexible tribal/kin social structure which allowed them to recruit first other nomads, later even sedentary groups, into a larger and larger machine for conquest. Fourth was the presence of several leaders who were able to manage astutely the drive for conquest and plunder, with the needs of administration.[8] Specifically, Mongol leaders were able, for some time, to maintain a sufficient volume of plunder and tribute to insure loyalty of tribes that might otherwise be inclined to leave the confederation. In short they perfected the outer frontier strategy of "milking" sedentary states (with some exceptions noted above). Fifth, superior logistic ability of pastoral nomads in communication, transportation, and mobility was key to conquest of large territories, and even of sedentary states. This superiority was rooted in the pastoral way of life: availability of horses, intimate knowledge of geography, and ability to move their entire society (families and their resource base, their herds) with them. This same superiority was also a key to the collapse of the system.

All the great Khans -- if only temporarily -- have been able to put these processes in operation (e.g., Allsen 1987). First, capitalizing on the inclusive nature of pastoral tribes, conquered groups were given an honorable option of joining the group (the alternative was being put to the sword). This worked well with other pastoralist and poorly with sedentary peoples (unless they wanted to become pastoralists). Second, as in modern pyramid schemes, as long as the system kept expanding, new recruits (groups) could gain both status and wealth. Continued expansion also alleviated, if it did not solve completely, the problem of revenue by a constant inflow of booty. As long as this was successful, it distracted conservative elements from social changes which flowed from this strategy, and minimized factional rivalry. Superior communications and mobility were used to amass troops and overcome enemies. However, this strategy was inherently unstable, that is, temporary.

The instability stems from two closely intertwined sources: political and technological. The political problem is the orderly succession of rulers. A "big man" comes to power on the basis of his personal skills, not the least of which is alliance-building. Among Central Asian pastoralists, this is typically based on military prowess. Hence, succession of rulership necessarily entails armed conflict. When there was only one son who had distinguished himself in battle, conflict was merely postponed for a generation until either there was no such son, or there were several. For the Mongols these problems were exacerbated by the competing, and at time conflicting, principles of lateral (older to younger brothers) and lineal (father to son) succession. The lack of clear priorities inevitably led to justification of succession by arms. Institutionalization of succession would have undermined the very basis of leadership. Thus, it is not only that the Mongol Empire did not institutionalize political control as Eisenstadt (1963) argues, but also that Mongols could not institutionalize leadership and remain Mongols. The same problems inhere in political control and revenue garnering.

A key to Mongol success was communication and mobility of men and resources. These technological factors also contributed to instability because they made it impossible for any central leader to monopolize control of strategic resources as a means of coercing compliance. Hence, there was no way to insure that revenue collectors would forward revenue to the leader.[9]

The same features that make tribes inclusive also make them divisive; what can be built quickly can equally quickly disintegrate. The material basis of this situation is the adaptation to plains/steppe environment. This is the underlying limit of pastoralist expansion. They cannot effectively control territory beyond the plains/steppe without giving up their lifestyle, thus the edge of the steppe remains a permanent frontier (Lindner 1982; McNeill 1964).

Conversely, sedentary states could not conquer nomads -- except by sedentarizing them. They could control them by a combination of constructing barriers and employing highly mobile troops, who could essentially beat the pastoralists at their own game -- decisive hit-and-run victories (Lattimore 1962a, p. 485). Thus, Central Asian pastoralists, especially the Mongols, could build huge empires, but could not maintain them. Conversely, the Chinese could manipulate, but never conquer, their nomadic adversaries. According to several writers (Allsen 1987; Barfield 1989; Lattimore 1951, 1962d; Morgan 1986), this accounts for the convoluted quality of Chinese histories of these events. Chroniclers had to warn princes and emperors of the inherent impossibility of conquest, while never admitting that the "son of heaven" was not all powerful -- a task that makes contemporary American "spin doctors" appear to be rank amateurs.

The Ottoman Empire

The formation of the Ottoman empire is of interest because it was built by the transformation of nomadic pastoralists into sedentary farmer-soldiers. According to Lindner (1983), nomads, particularly of the "tribe" of Osman, played a vital role in the founding of the Ottoman Empire. It was precisely the fluid, multi-cultural aspects of tribal organization that made nomadic "tribalism" an effective model for building a state. Once built, the needs of the new state led to the oppression and destruction of nomads by conversion into sedentary peasants.

The erstwhile nomads, now rulers of a large state, were compelled to sedentarize the remaining nomads. This was done by first shifting obligations of support of the state from contributions of manpower in fighting (nomad tradition) to taxes in kind and/or money, and later by levying taxes in early spring immediately after lambing time, counting all animals as adult sheep, and therefore taxable. This contrasts with the Mongol custom which exempted small herds so that they could continue to function (p. 57). In other words, the goal of Ottoman tax policy was to undermine nomad economy.

Two sets of state needs impelled this policy. First, the state rulers sought to avoid the "state within state" arrangement implied in tribal loyalty, in which the local chief administered his tribe with considerable autonomy. This required clear tribal boundaries, but tribal boundaries are highly permeable, membership changing with shifting economic and political conditions.[10]

The second set of reasons behind sedentarization were military. As the nature of warfare changed, especially as gunpowder came into use, the demand for mounted archers decreased, while the demand for infantry increased.[11] Thus, nomads *per se* had less to offer the state in compensation for their political administrative liabilities. Additionally, more people -- and therefore more fighting men -- could be supported on the same amount of territory in a sedentary, agricultural adaptation than by nomadic pastoralism. The volatility of pastoral production due to disease and weather also makes sedentary production more certain.

While the Ottoman Empire had clear nomadic origins, it became and remained a sedentary state which eventually destroyed its own nomadic foundations. In contrast, the Mongol Empire never made a successful transition to a sedentary state. The tribe of Osman did succeed, but only by ceasing to be nomads.

Spain, America, and Los Indios Bárbaros[12]

The comparison of Spanish and American treatments of various nomadic groups inhabiting what is now the American Southwest, what was long the northwest of New Spain, is useful in several ways. First, the region is the same in both cases. Second, the region was a frontier for both states -- a "periphery of a periphery" (Weber 1982). Third, America and Spain contrast a rising capitalist state with the earliest phases of the capitalist world-system, more akin to an empire (Cipollo 1970, Doyle 1986, Eisenstadt 1963, 1967).[13]

Spanish explorers first entered the region sometime in the 1530s, slightly over a decade after Cortéz conquered Mexico. The region was not formally colonized until 1598. That colony collapsed, due to the Pueblo Revolt, in 1680, and was re-established in the early 1690s. Thereafter it remained a tenuous, but relatively thriving colonial outpost whose fortunes waxed and waned with those of New Spain and the Spanish Empire in general. Both before the Pueblo Revolt, and for the half century or so after the reconquest, the region was marked by a state of endemic warfare with surrounding nomadic groups. In the early eighteenth century this warfare became so intense that the sedentary Pueblos, and erstwhile ousters of the Spaniards, formed a symbiotic alliance with them. The late eighteenth century was marked by considerable local population growth and relative prosperity. In 1786 a lasting peace was established with several closely linked bands of Shoshoni speakers who became widely known as Comanches.[14] This peace between Comanches and Spaniards lasted well into the American era. The Mexican interregnum disrupted this pattern and renewed the pattern of conflict with nomads common in the early phases of the colony.

Throughout the Spanish era, warfare with nomadic groups rose and fell with changes in the trade in Indian captives, with the need for local governors to impress the viceroy with their success in subduing "*los indios bárbaros*" or their desire for more money and troops, and with viceregal and crown concerns for protection of the borders of New Spain from rival European powers. It is the latter concerns that were the driving force behind first maintenance, then re-founding of the colony (Bolton 1929). These concerns likewise shaped policies toward nomadic groups, at once a nuisance along the frontiers, yet simultaneously -- especially after the Comanche peace -- a singularly effective "border patrol" for scouting and controlling movement of European rivals.

The Bourbon reforms, instituted in New Spain in the late eighteenth century, were intended to increase state efficiency. These policies led to a general increase in prosperity throughout the Empire (Lang 1975) and in New Mexico. Subsequent Indian policy aimed at: (1) pursuit of peace in order to increase revenues; (2) use of frontier bands as buffers against foreign intrusion; and (3) lowering the cost of administration and defense. These goals gave rise to four strategies to control nomadic groups. First was the use of "gifts" to engender dependency upon Spaniards. Second, divide-and-conquer strategies were used to pit one group against other hostile groups.

Third, nomadic groups were pressed to form more centralized political structures, which gave rise to the "tribes" we know today. Fourth, the frontier provinces were reorganized, a line of forts was constructed, and highly mobile "flying companies" were used to control hostile nomads (Moorhead 1968, 1975; Griffen 1983a, 1983b, 1984, 1985; Thrapp 1967).[15]

American influence in the Southwest dates to the opening of the Santa Fe Trail in 1821. As trade increased, New Mexico became more strongly oriented toward the United States. The Mexican - American war (1846-1848) resulted in the annexation of the northern half of Mexico to the United States in 1848. California and Texas were the major goals of the conquest. New Mexico (which then included modern Arizona) was primarily a "land bridge" between California and Texas. Fighting with nomadic groups increased until the American Civil War (1860-64), spurred by increasing traffic through nomad lands and increased trade or encroachment on hunting territories. After the Civil War the American state began a major effort to control nomadic groups throughout the west (Utley 1984). The Comanche bands became a major internal nuisance instead of a buffer-border patrol. A major effort was mounted to force them, and subsequently the Apache bands, onto very limited reservation territories.

Comanches declined from "Lords of the South Plains" (Wallace and Hoebel 1952) to a handful of reservation dwellers (from between 20,000 and 30,000 in the early nineteenth century to between 1,000 and 2,000 in the late nineteenth century [Hall 1986, 1989]). Their territory shrank from the western half of Texas to a small reservation in Oklahoma (Indian Territory). They had become a barrier to internal trade in the U.S., and their major resource, the buffalo, had become very scarce.

Apache groups fared better. Centuries of a "raiding mode of production" had perfected their survival techniques. Low interest in New Mexico and Arizona led to considerably lower pressure on Apaches. A combination of eastern sentiments for the "vanishing red man," and lucrative contracts to be had for supplying first the army and later reservations, prevented complete genocide.

Thus, the American state succeeded in accomplishing in less than fifty years what Spanish administrators had not been able to accomplish in nearly two hundred and fifty years -- total sedentarization of nomadic groups.

DISCUSSION, CONCLUSIONS, AND SPECULATIONS

What, then do these brief cases suggest about the roles of nomads in the historical evolution of core/periphery hierarchies? I begin with some general remarks, then turn to some more specific conclusions, and end with discussion and speculation about further research.

Nomads, States, and Core/Periphery Hierarchies

While it is clear that I have not sampled the entire range of nomad - sedentary relations (for instance, there is no examination of wholly nomadic settings as a limiting case, nor of very early, pre-horse, nomad - sedentary relations), still, a tentative, schematic account of the role of nomads in the historical evolution of core/periphery hierarchies is discernible. This sketch is not intended as a definitive statement, but as an elaborate working hypothesis useful for guiding further research.

Once states domesticated horses and mastered the production and use of iron, they more commonly took the core role in core/periphery hierarchies, giving rise to other states, and unleashing interstate competition (Chapters 1, 4; Chase-Dunn 1989, 1990a; Wilkinson 1983, 1987, 1988a, 1988b). States also altered the other elements in core/periphery hierarchies. As core states sought to increase their wealth -- not infrequently to maintain and enhance their internal control over subjugated portions of their populations -- they began to expand territorially. Sometimes this expansion was in the direct pursuit of wealth through conquest, other times through enlarging the quantity and types of trade goods they could acquire. Expansion necessarily led to contact with, and frequently incorporation of, new groups into a core/periphery hierarchy.

The incorporation process varies in both speed and intensity, can be reversed to some degree (Hall 1983, 1986, 1989), usually promotes social change among incorporated groups, and typically elicits resistance to incorporation (Hall 1989; Gailey and Patterson 1987, 1988). This type of change is precisely what is meant by the statement that "civilization gave birth to barbarism" (Lattimore 1962d, p. 99, cited in Wallerstein 1974b, p. 98). Typically, but not exclusively, such "barbarians" occupied peripheral or semiperipheral positions in core/periphery hierarchies.[16] For China, they were nomadic pastoralists; for the early Sumerian states they were other states (see Chase-Dunn 1988). Even the preceding brief account of Central Asian nomads indicates that, as with early marcher states, such "barbarians", once engendered by adjacent states, could become relatively autonomous sources of social change.

When the degree of technological difference between nomad and sedentary populations was low, as it was in the early stages of the agrarian era (3,000 to 1,000 B.C., +/- 1,000 years), which group would dominate a core/periphery hierarchy was an open issue. Stationary targets are easier to attack than mobile ones, thus nomads could readily defeat sedentary groups in battle. Furthermore, sedentary agriculturists could either be forced to pay tribute or be moved and used as slaves elsewhere. Nomads, however, are more difficult to defeat. Additionally, their wealth -- usually in the form of animals -- is mobile, and hence they can avoid paying tribute. Conversely, they are inimical to sedentary life and difficult to make into slaves.

However, nomads can be induced into trade relations. Sedentary peoples typically have some surplus agricultural products, but a shortage of meat and/or horses. Nomads typically have a surplus of meat in the form of animals, but a shortage of vegetable resources. Thus, there is opportunity for trade. Where the terms of trade were not suitable, or where sedentary people were unwilling to trade, raiding became an alternative form of exchange. The Mongols perfected the threat (and use) of violence as a tool in trade relations.

Where large distances separated different states or core/periphery hierarchies, nomads could become middlemen in trade based on their superior mobility, and superior knowledge of the "uncivilized" territory, as was the case for Central Asian nomads and for Comanches under the Spanish empire. Where state traders were sufficiently strong they could conduct trade directly, but were subject to raids by nomads, or they could engage nomads as armed protectors. Nomads were strategically and tactically well positioned to extract "protection rent" (Mann, 1986). Even in the case of strong states, nomads could maintain a considerable degree of autonomy -- or even domination -- if they could play one state against the other (Kohl 1987b). The many ways in which state systems deal with nomads, in turn, shape their own administrative, political, and trade systems, as was clearly the case for both China and the Spanish empire.

Conclusions

Several conclusions emerge from this discussion. First, formal systems (bureaucracies, in short, states) have a very difficult time dealing with informal, or acephalous, societies. This is true whether it is the Aztecs dealing with the "Chichimecas" (McGuire 1980, 1986; Mathien and McGuire 1986), the Romans dealing with Gallic and Germanic "tribes" (Luttwak 1976; Dyson 1985), the Chinese dealing with Mongols or Turks, the Byzantine empire dealing with Turks and others (Lindner 1983), the Spanish empire dealing with "*los Indios bárbaros*," or the United States dealing with various Native American "tribes" (Hall 1989; Utley 1984).

Second, nomads occasionally conquer states, but cannot rule them (for long) without becoming sedentarized. Lattimore (1962b, p.508) has described the problem cogently:

> As the Chinese pithily expressed it long ago, an empire could be conquered on horseback, but not ruled from horseback; civil servants more sophisticated than barbarian warriors were needed to extract a regular flow of taxes and tribute from the civilized part of the empire, they could be recruited only among the upper classes of the conquered civilized people, and they and their families had to be protected and allowed to perpetuate themselves. It was therefore impossible to fuse completely the barbarian and the civilized parts of the structure of empire, and impossible also to make the barbarian conquerors as a whole a new upper class imposed on the conquered society.

Comparison of the Chinese, Mongol, and Ottoman empires underscores this argument: empires require a sedentary base. Clearly, pastoral empires or core/periphery hierarchies are ephemeral. The Mongol empire is distinctive precisely because of its success in thwarting this general tendency. Yet, even the Mongol empire built a capital city, Karakorum.

I must add a caution based on Barfield's account. Under special circumstances nomads can extract some tribute from sedentary states. The outer frontier strategy of Central Asian nomads is an example of this. The outer frontier strategy was not a monopoly of the Mongols. Nomadic Indians in the American Southwest, especially Comanches, were also adept at extracting tribute from the Spanish Empire. There is a significant difference, however, between extraction of a minimal "tribute" which constitutes a nuisance and large scale extraction familiar in tributary empires.

Assessment as to whether "gifts" from sedentary rulers to nomadic clients constitutes tribute or "trinkets" is a complicated matter. Relative worth is a significant component of the assessment. What may have been "mere trinkets" to the state, may have been vital prestige goods to the nomads. Evaluation of relative worth is not facilitated by the nearly universal tendency of contemporary writers (almost all from sedentary societies themselves) to gloss such gifts as trinkets, even when the cost of those gifts was bankrupting the state treasury.[17]

A third, yet abstract, conclusion is that comparisons of seemingly similar social forms, such as "nomads," "tribes," or "chiefdoms" that span long periods (centuries or millenia) must be executed with extreme care. The qualities of these types of social groups have shifted through time as core/periphery hierarchical systems have evolved. Frequently, such social structures cannot be understood apart from their place in larger social systems and social processes. Similar manifest forms may belie very different processes of formation, some of which may have a significant role in shaping further changes. Still, ethnohistorical materials, if used with due caution, can shed considerable light on the processes of change, as Kohl (1978, p. 475) suggests.

Fourth, the qualitative aspects of nomad - sedentary relations have shifted through time. The effect of nomads on states has lessened through time, while the effect of states on nomads has strengthened through time. This trend is due, at least in part, to a growing technological gulf between nomadic and sedentary populations. As Kohl (1987b, p. 22-23) puts it:

> Economic development and dependency were not linked phenomena during the Bronze Age in the manner postulated by contemporary critical theory for -- to paraphrase their terminology -- the development of underdevelopment in the Bronze Age was sharply constrained or itself underdeveloped. Critical technologies, such as metal working, could diffuse relatively easily and new means of transportation and sources of power, such as horses, could be raised in peripheral zones and radically restructure this ancient world-system.

Thus, while relative dependency may be problematic for the Bronze Age, it becomes less problematic after the appearance of mounted pastoralists in Central Asia, and entirely clear by the seventeenth century of the Christian era.

Fifth, the preceding conclusions underscore the argument that world-system theory requires considerable elaboration and modification to provide a framework for examining precapitalist core/periphery hierarchies. In doing so, several supposed distinctive features of the modern world-economy must be seen as somewhat different repetitions of older patterns and processes. The perennial problem of changes in intensity shading into qualitative changes remains. One aspect, however, of the "modern world-system" that is clearly distinctive is the capability, through twentieth century technological means, to eliminate nomads as a source of social change.

These conclusions easily give rise to as many questions as they answer, and suggest a number of continuing research problems.

Speculations

First, the preceding evidence and analysis sheds precious little light on the role and significance of wholly nomadic core/periphery hierarchies -- if indeed, such can even be said to exist. Further research, in this case, highly speculative based on archaeological evidence, will be required to discover if anything like a core/periphery hierarchy existed in a wholly nomadic setting. Analysis of such a core/periphery hierarchy would compound and conflate the problems of permeable group boundaries and fluid group memberships with ephemeral geographic boundaries. Since, by definition, the wealth of nomads is portable, wholly nomadic core/periphery hierarchies probably would have been very fragile, and marked by a very shallow gradient of hierarchy. Hence, they would leave little direct physical evidence of their existence.

Since the formation of states so dramatically altered the entire social field, great caution must be used in using any post-state nomadic societies as bases for speculation about pre-state nomadic societies. This is not to say that the task is insurmountable, but that it must be approached with great caution. The evidence for, or against, the existence of wholly nomadic core/periphery hierarchies will be quite thin.

Methodological and evidential problems notwithstanding, this suggests several interesting research questions. Were the forms of states that we know of from the historical record the only solution to these problems? Were there others? Could there have been others if the extant ones had not preempted the field? Do different solutions to the ephemeral quality of wholly nomadic settings give rise to different types of core/periphery hierarchies?

Second, the profound social changes that accompany changes in transportation technology suggest parallels between the nomad - sedentary distinction and the overland - maritime distinction elaborated by Fox (1971), Hochberg (1985), Genovese and Hochberg (1989), Tilly (1989), and Fox (1989). Horses, like sea transport, enhance communication over broad, trackless areas, and as with maritime powers, do not readily facilitate amassing permanent, large armies. Horses and ships do, however, permit sizable temporary amassings for rapid attacks. A key feature of nomadic empires, like maritime states, is their relative fragility and instability as compared with agrarian states and empires, and the typical dependence of the former on the latter -- albeit with many exceptions. The major differences seem to be that horses can be produced on the trackless area, where ships are built on land, while ships facilitate bulk trade, horses (and camels and mules) are better used for (relative) luxury goods. How important were nomads in the diffusion of ideas and technologies? Clearly, they played a vital role in the diffusion of diseases, transmitting the plagues to both Europe and China (McNeill 1976).

Third, the inner and outer frontier strategies can be seen as precapitalist analogues of strategies for advancement used by semiperipheral states in the "modern world-system" -- right-wing, authoritarian regimes in alliance with capitalists and left-wing, class-based anti-systemic rebellions (Chase-Dunn 1990b). In both settings, the semiperipheral players can be either sources of stability, or instability. This parallel warrants further examination. Is the semiperipheral social position always a locus of change? Does the role, or set of possible roles, of the intermediate tiers of a core/periphery hierarchy change systematically with the type of core/periphery hierarchy? Do the roles change with the type of social unit (sedentary, nomad, state, nonstate) occupying the position?

Whatever the answers to these questions, the evidence appears to be compelling that the study of social change must focus on core/periphery hierarchies, or at least the intersocietal context, and should not focus exclusively on various individual components (states, tribes, etc.) of the hierarchy. Within the system or hierarchy, peripheral and especially semi-peripheral units play highly variable roles, which are at times crucial to processes of change. Specifically, nomadic groups have had major influences on the course of social change. The habit of pushing barbarians beyond the pale -- a military and political goal that was seldom achieved by any empire for any significant period of time -- is for intellectual pursuits at best misleading, and potentially disastrous for understanding the processes and variations of historical evolution.

NOTES

1. This extension of world-system theory parallels the general analysis of "center-periphery" relations in geography and political science (Gottmann 1980; Smith 1976, 1987; Strassoldo 1980), yet preserves world-system theory's key feature: the unit of analysis (Bach 1980; Hopkins 1978, 1979; Hopkins and Wallerstein 1981, 1982).

2. I use the term "historical evolution" to denote a process subject to systematic explanation, one that can be explained, not by reference to abstract categories, but by examination of historical processes. I explicitly reject all unilinear analyses.

3. Chase-Dunn (1988, 1990b) has argued that change often originates in the "semiperiphery," in marcher states. Kohl (1987b) makes a similar argument for Bronze Age South Central Asia. Others have made parallel arguments. Service (1975) sees evolution of civilizations coming primarily from outside forces. Teggart (1918, 1925) has argued that major sources of change are contacts between groups. Others have discussed the formation to "secondary states" (Price 1978) and "tribes" (Fried, 1967, 1975) as results of interactions between states and other groups. Champion (1989, p. 10) and Strassoldo (1989, pp. 47-48) trace the insight of new inventions and social changes originating in peripheral areas to Toynbee and Sorokin. All this, of course, suggests that nomads may be especially important in these processes.

4. We use the term Afro-Eurasian because of the longstanding trade links between not only the African shore of the Mediterranean but also sub-Saharan Africa and the other regions (see Moseley reference in Chapter 1).

5. Champion (1989, p. 8) builds on Schneider's critique (1977; reprinted as Chapter 2) of Wallerstein's emphasis on bulk or utilitarian goods as opposed to luxury goods, to argue that there is really a continuum of types of goods. The importance of the trade lies not in the goods themselves, but the

social uses to which they are put. Rowlands (1987) makes a similar argument. McGuire (1989) presents an intriguing case supporting this interpretation. Peter Peregrine (Chapter 6) analyzes the roles of luxury goods in prestige goods economies found in Cahokia.

6. In this light, Lynn White's (1962) discussion of stirrups is illuminating.

7. See note 4 above.

8. According to Allsen (1987), Möngke was able to implement administrative innovations by keeping conservatives occupied in (successful) battles, giving him a free hand in the center. As Lindner (1981, 1983) notes, this is NOT a reversion to "great man theory" of history. Rather, it is a recognition that "tribal" systems are "big man" systems (Sahlins 1961, 1963, 1968), and hence are strongly affected by a "great," "big man"!

9. According to Peregrine's analysis of Cahokia (Chapter 6), prestige goods economies have structurally similar problems with respect to the monopolization of luxury, prestige goods.

10. See Barth (1969) on this, even though his studies are more or less contemporary, it is clear in Lindner (1981, 1982, 1983), Lattimore (1951, 1962c) and others the fluidity of membership and permeability of boundaries are the essences of pastoralism.

11. See Hodgson (1974, Book Five) for a summary of the massive changes brought about by the use of gunpowder throughout Eurasia.

12. Only minimal references for this discussion will given here. Fuller documentation can be found in Hall (1986, 1989).

13. There is an important debate thinly hidden here over the nature and origin of capitalism. Whether capitalism became a dominant mode of production in the sixteenth century as Wallerstein argues, or much later as others argue. This debate is more than terminological, but for present purposes is not germane. Wolf (1982, Chap. 1) and Hall (1989, Chap. 2) summarize the issues and literature.

14. An important sociological point is often masked by writing conventions. When the term, "the Comanches" is used in conveys a sense of a unitary group which is historically false. Hence, in this account, and in Hall (1989) I use the terms, "Comanches" (without the article "the") or "the Comanche bands" to convey a non-unitary political organization. This also applies to "Apaches," who did eventually remain fragmented in to several "tribes."

15. Flying companies are quite old. Luttwak (1976) describes how the Romans used them and Lattimore (1962a, p. 485) discusses their use by the Chinese.

16. See note 3 above.

17. See Jane Schneider's discussion of gifts and tribute for additional comments on this problem (1977, pp. 23-24; reprinted in Chapter 2, pp. 56-57).

REFERENCES

Abu-Lughod, Janet 1987. "The Shape of the World-System in the Thirteenth Century." *Studies in Comparative International Development* 22:4 (Winter):3-25.

_____ 1989. *Before European Hegemony: The World System A.D. 1250-1350*. New York: Oxford University Press.

_____ 1990. "Restructuring the Premodern World-System." *Review* 13:2 (Spring):273-286.

Allsen, Thomas T. 1987. *Mongol Imperialism: The Policies of the Grand Qan Möngke in China, Russia, and the Islamic Lands, 1251-1259*. University of California Press.

Anthony, David W. 1986. "The 'Kurgan Culture,' Indo-European Origins, and the Domestication of the Horse: A Reconsideration." *Current Anthropology* 27:4(Aug.-Oct.):291-314.

Bach, Robert L. 1980. "On the Holism of a World-System Perspective." Pp. 289-318 in *Processes of the World-System*, edited by T.K. Hopkins and I. Wallerstein. Beverly Hills: Sage.

Barfield, Thomas J. 1989. *The Perilous Frontier*. London: Blackwell.

Barth, Frederik 1969. *Ethnic Groups and Boundaries*. Boston: Little Brown.

Bolton, Herbert E. 1929. "Defensive Spanish Expansion and the Significance of the Borderlands." Pp. 1-42 in *The Trans-Mississippi West*, edited by J.F. Willard and C.B. Goodykoontz. Boulder: University of Colorado Press.

Champion, Timothy C. ed. 1989. *Centre and Periphery: Comparative Studies in Archaeology*. London: Unwin Hyman.

Chase-Dunn, Christopher 1988. "Comparing World Systems: Toward a Theory of Semiperipheral Development." *Comparative Civilizations Review* 19(Fall):29-66.

_____ 1989. *Global Formation: Structures of the World-Economy*. New York: Basil Blackwell.

_____ 1990a. "World State Formation: Historical Processes and Emergent Necessity." *Political Geography Quarterly* 9:2(April):108-130.

_____ 1990b. "Resistance to Imperialism: Semiperipheral Actors." *Review* 13:1(Winter):1-31.

Cipolla, Carlo M. ed. 1970. *The Economic Decline of Empires*. London: Methuen.

Doyle, Michael W. 1986. *Empires*. Ithaca: Cornell University Press.

Dyson, Stephen L. 1985. *The Creation of the Roman Frontier*. Princeton: Princeton University Press.

Eberhard, Wolfram 1965. *Conquerors and Rulers: Social Forces in Medieval China*, 2nd ed. Leiden Brill.

_____ 1977. *A History of China*, 4th ed. Berkeley: University of California Press.

Eisenstadt, S. N. 1963. *The Decline of Empires*. Englewood Cliffs, N.J.: Prentice-Hall.

_____ 1967. *The Political Systems of Empire*. New York: Free Press.

Elvin, Mark 1973. *The Pattern of the Chinese Past*. Stanford: Stanford University Press.

Fox, Edward W. 1971. *History in Geographic Perspective: The Other France*. New York: Norton.

_____ 1989. "The Argument; Some Reinforcements and Projections." Pp. 331-342 in *Geographic Perspectives in History*, edited by Eugene D. Genovese and Leonard Hochberg. London: Basil Blackwell.

Fried, Morton 1967. *The Evolution of Political Society*. New York: Random House.

_____ 1975. *The Notion of Tribe*. Menlo Park, CA: Cummings.

Gailey, Christine Ward 1985. "The State of the State in Anthropology." *Dialectical Anthropology* 9:1-4(June):65-89.

Gailey, Christine Ward, and Thomas C. Patterson 1987. "Power Relations and State Formation." Pp. 1-26 in *Power Relations and State Formation*, edited by Christine Ward Gailey and Thomas C. Patterson. Washington, D.C.: American Anthropological Association.

_____ 1988. "State Formation and Uneven Development." Pp. 77-90 in Gledhill *et al.*, 1988.

Galtung, Johann 1971. "A Structural Theory of Imperialism." *Journal of Peace Research* 8:81-117.

Genovese, Eugene D. and Leonard Hochberg 1989. *Geographic Perspectives in History*. London: Basil Blackwell.

Gledhill, John 1988. "Introduction: The Comparative Analysis of Social and Political Transitions." Pp. 2-29 in Gledhill *et al.* 1988.

Gledhill, John, Barbara Bender, and Mogens Trolle Larsen, eds. 1988. *State and Society: The Emergence and Development of Social Hierarchy and Political Centralization*. London: Unwin Hyman.

Gottman, Jean, ed. 1980. *Centre and Periphery: Spatial Variation in Politics*. Beverly Hills: Sage.

Griffen, William B. 1983a. "The Compés: A Chiracahua Apache Family of the Late 18th and Early 19th Centuries." *American Indian Quarterly* VII:2(Spring):21-48.

_____ 1983b. "Spanish Military Administration of Apache Indians: The North Mexican Peace Establishments of the Late Colonial Period." Paper Presented at the Western Social Science Association meeting, Albuquerque, April.

_____ 1984. "The Spanish System of North Mexican Peace Reserves." Paper presented at American Anthropological Association meeting, Denver, CO, November.

_____ 1985. "Apache Indians and the North Mexican Peace Establishments." Pp. 183-95 in *Southwestern Culture History: Collected Papers in Honor of Albert H. Schroeder*, edited by Charles Lange. Archaeological Society of New Mexico No. 10. Santa Fe, NM: Ancient City Press.

Hall, Thomas D. 1983. "Peripheries, Regions of Refuge, and Nonstate Societies: Toward A Theory of Reactive Social Change." *Social Science Quarterly* 64:3(Sept.):582-597.

_____ 1986. "Incorporation in the World-System: Toward A Critique." *American Sociological Review* 51:3(June):390-402.

_____ 1989. *Social Change in the Southwest, 1350-1880*. Lawrence, KS: University Press of Kansas.

Hochberg, Leonard 1985. "'The Question of Boundaries': A Critique of World-System Analysis for a Socio-Geographic Perspective." Paper presented at the Midwest Sociological Society meeting, April, St. Louis, MO.

Hodgson, Marshall G. S. 1974. *The Venture of Islam. Volume 3: The Gunpowder Empires and Modern Times*. Chicago: University of Chicago Press.

Hopkins, Terence K. 1978. "World-System Analysis: Methodological Issues." Pp. 199-217 in *Social Change in the Capitalist World-Economy*, edited by Barbara Hockey Kaplan. Beverly Hills: Sage.

_____ 1979. "The Study of the Capitalist World-Economy: Some Introductory Considerations." Pp. 21-52 in *The World-System of Capitalism: Past and Present*, edited by Walter Goldfrank. Beverly Hills: Sage.

Hopkins, Terence K. and I. Wallerstein 1981. "Structural Transformations of the World-Economy." Pp. 233-261 in *Dynamics of World Development*, edited by Richard Rubinson. Beverly Hills: Sage.

Hopkins, Terence K. and I. Wallerstein, eds. 1982. *World Systems Analysis: Theory and Methodology*. Beverly Hills: Sage.

Kohl, Philip L. 1978. "The Balance of Trade in Southwestern Asia in the Mid-Third Millennium B.C." *Current Anthropology* 19:3(Sept.):463-492.

_____ 1985. "Symbolic Cognitive Archaeology: A New Loss of Innocence." *Dialectical Anthropology* 9:1-4(June):105-117.

_____ 1987a. "The Use and abuse of World Systems Theory: The Case of the Pristine West Asian State." *Advances in Archaeological Method and Theory* 11:1-35.

_____ 1987b. "The Ancient Economy, Transferable Technologies and the Bronze Age World-System: A View from the Northeastern Frontier of the Ancient Near East." Pp. 13-24 in *Centre and Periphery in the Ancient World*, edited by Michael Rowlands, Mogens Larsen and Kristian Kristiansen. Cambridge: Cambridge University Press.

_____ 1988. "State Formation: Useful Concept or Idée Fixe?" Pp. 27-34 in Gailey and Patterson 1988.

Kwanten, Luc 1979. *Imperial Nomads: A History of Central Asia, 500-1500*. Philadelphia: University of Pennsylvania Press.

Lane, Frederic C. 1973. *Venice: A Maritime Republic*. Baltimore, MD: Johns Hopkins University Press.

Lang, James 1975. *Conquest and Commerce: Spain and England in the Americas*. New York: Academic Press.

Lattimore, Owen 1951. *Inner Asian Frontiers*, 2nd ed. Boston: Beacon Press. (Originally [1940]. New York: American Geographical Society).

_____ 1962a. "The Frontier in History." Pp. 469-491 in Lattimore (1962c).

_____ 1962b. "Inner Asian Frontiers: Defensive Empires and Conquest Empires." Pp. 501-513 in Lattimore (1962c).

_____ 1962c. *Studies in Frontier History: Collected Papers, 1928-58.* London: Oxford University Press.

_____ 1962d. "La Civilisation, mère de Barbarie?" *Annales* E.S.C. 17:1(Jan.-Feb.):95-108 (cited in Wallerstein [1974b, p. 98]).

_____ 1980. "The Periphery as Locus of Innovation." Pp. 205-208 in Gottmann 1980.

Lindner, Rudi Paul 1981. "Nomadism, Horses and Huns." *Past & Present* 92(Aug.):3-19.

_____ 1982. "What was a Nomadic Tribe?" *Comparative Studies in Society and History* 24:4(Oct.):689-711.

_____ 1983. *Nomads and Ottomans in Medieval Anatolia.* Vol. 144 Indiana University Uralic and Altaic Series. Bloomington, IN: Research Institute for Inner Asian Studies.

Luttwak, Edward N. 1976. *The Grand Strategy of the Roman Empire: From the First Century A.D. to the Third.* Baltimore: Johns Hopkins University Press.

Mathien, Frances Joan and Randall McGuire, eds. 1986. *Ripples in the Chichimec Sea: Consideration of Southwestern-Mesoamerican Interactions.* Carbondale, IL: Southern Illinois University Press.

McGuire, Randall H. 1980. "The Mesoamerican Connection in the Southwest." *Kiva* 40:3-38.

_____ 1986. "Prestige Economies in the Prehistoric Southwestern Periphery." Pp. 243-269 in Mathien and McGuire (1986).

_____ 1989. "The Greater Southwest as a Periphery of Mesoamerica." Pp. 40-66 in Champion 1989.

McNeill, William H. 1964. *Europe's Steppe Frontier, 1500-1800.* Chicago: University of Chicago Press.

_____ 1976. *Plagues and Peoples.* Garden City, New York: Doubleday.

Moorhead, Max 1968. *The Apache Frontier: Jacobo Ugarte and Spanish-Indian Relations in Northern New Spain, 1769-1791.* Norman: University of Oklahoma Press.

_____ 1975. *The Presidio: Bastion of the Spanish Borderlands.* Norman: University of Oklahoma Press.

Morgan, David 1986. *The Mongols.* London: Blackwell.

Nissen, Hans J. 1988. *The Early History of the Ancient Near East, 9000-2000 B.C.* Chicago: University of Chicago Press.

Price, Barbara 1978. "Secondary State Formation: An Explanatory Model." Pp. 161-186 in Cohen, Ronald and Elman R. Service, eds. *Origins of the State: The Anthropology of Political Evolution*. Philadelphia: ISHI Press.

Rowlands, Michael 1987. "Centre and Periphery: A Review of a Concept." Pp. 1-11 in *Centre and Periphery in the Ancient World*, edited by Michael Rowlands, Mogens Larsen and Kristian Kristiansen. Cambridge: Cambridge University Press.

Sahlins, Marshall D. 1961. "The Segmentary Lineage: An Organization of Predatory Expansion." *American Anthropologist* 63:2(April):322-345.

_____ 1963. "Poor Man, Rich Man, Big-Man, Chief: Political Types in Melanesia and Polynesia." *Comparative Studies in Society and History* 5:3(April):285-303.

_____ 1968. *Tribesmen*. Englewood Cliffs, NJ: Prentice-Hall.

Saunders, J. J. 1971. *The History of the Mongol Conquests*. New York: Barnes & Noble.

Schneider, Jane 1977. "Was There a Pre-Capitalist World-System?" *Peasant Studies* 6:1(Jan.):20-29.

Service, Elman R. 1975. *Origins of the State and Civilization*. New York: Norton.

Smith, Carol A. ed. 1976. *Regional Analysis, I: Economic Systems; II: Social Systems*. New York: Academic.

_____ 1987. "Regional Analysis in World-System Perspective: A Critique of Three Structural Theories of Uneven Development." *Review* X:4(Spring): 597-648.

Strassoldo, Raimondo 1980. "Centre-Periphery and System-Boundary: Culturological Perspectives." Pp. 27-61 in Gottmann 1980.

Szynkiewicz, Slawoj 1989. "Interactions between the Nomadic Cultures of Central Asia and China in the Middle Ages." Pp. 151-158 in Champion 1989.

Teggart, Frederick J. 1918. *The Processes of History*. New Haven: Yale University Press.

_____ 1925. *Theory of History*. New Haven: Yale University Press. (Both reprinted University of California Press 1942, Peter Smith 1972).

Thrapp, Dan L. 1967. *The Conquest of Apacheria*. Norman: University of Oklahoma Press.

Tilly, Charles 1989. "The Geography of European Statemaking and Capitalism Since 1500." Pp. 158-181 in *Geographic Perspectives in History*, edited by Eugene D. Genovese and Leonard Hochberg. London: Basil Blackwell.

Utley, Robert M. 1984. *The Indian Frontier of the American West, 1846-1890*. Albuquerque: University of New Mexico Press.

Wallace, Ernest and E. A. Hoebel 1952. *Lords of the South Plains*. Norman: University of Oklahoma Press.

Wallerstein, Immanuel 1974a. "The Rise and Future Demise of the World Capitalist System: Concepts for Comparative Analysis." *Comparative Studies in Society and History* 16:387-415.

_____ 1974b. *The Modern World-System: Capitalist Agriculture and the Origins of European World-Economy in the Sixteenth Century*. New York: Academic Press.

_____ 1979. *The Capitalist World-Economy*. Cambridge: Cambridge University Press.

_____ 1980. *The Modern World-System: Mercantilism and the Consolidation of the European World-Economy, 1600-1750*. New York: Academic Press.

_____ 1984. *The Politics of the World-Economy: The States, the Movements, and the Civilizations*. New York: Cambridge University Press.

_____ 1989. *The Modern World-System III: The Second Era of Great Expansion of the Capitalist World-Economy, 1730-1840s*. New York: Academic Press.

_____ 1990. "World-System Analysis: The Second Phase." *Review* 13:2 (Spring):287-293.

Weber, David J. 1982. *The Mexican Frontier, 1821-1846*. Albuquerque: University of New Mexico Press.

White, Lynn Jr. 1962. *Medieval Technology and Social Change*. New York: Oxford University Press.

Wilkinson, David 1983. "Civilizations, States Systems and Universal Empires." Paper delivered at the 12th annual meeting of the International Society for the Comparative Study of Civilizations, Buffalo, NY, May 26-28.

_____ 1987. "The Connectedness Criterion and Central Civilization." Pp. 25-29 in Matthew Melko and Leighton R. Scott (eds.) *The Boundaries of Civilizations in Space and Time*. Lanham, MD: University Press of America.

_____ 1988a. "Universal Empires: Pathos and Engineering." *Comparative Civilizations Review* 18(Spring):22-44.

_____ 1988b. "World Economic Theories vs. Central Civilization." Paper presented at ISCSC meeting May, Hampton, VA.

Wolf, Eric R. 1982. *Europe and the People Without History*. Berkeley: University of California Press.

8

The Monte Albán State:
A Diachronic Perspective on
an Ancient Core and Its Periphery

Gary M. Feinman and Linda M. Nicholas

In a review of contemporary archaeology, Trigger (1984:286) wrote that:

> ...what is important is the growing realization that societies are not closed systems with respect to their neighbors any more than with respect to their environment and that the development of a culture or society may be constrained or influenced by the broader social network of which it is a part. There is also increasing recognition that the rules governing these processes are themselves worthy of scientific investigation. The challenge is to extend a systemic analysis to incorporate what used to be called diffusion.

More recently, Schortman and Urban (1987:54) noted that: "(t)he long-dormant debate concerning the relation between external contacts and local social change has been reopened." Both of these statements call attention to the growing theoretical ruminations in archaeology generated by an increasing dissatisfaction with purely endogenous or local models of societal change. These models were swept into vogue two decades ago with a new perspective now referred to as "new archaeology" (e.g., Binford and

Binford, 1968). At the same time, few archaeologists would welcome a return to the trait-based diffusionism that was associated with an earlier era (see Willey and Sabloff, 1980; Trigger, 1984, for general discussions of theoretical developments in archaeology).

In grappling with the organization of a prehispanic Mesoamerican social system at a scale larger than the site or a tightly defined region, it is not our intent to add to or sort through the burgeoning jargon that already includes cluster interactions, boundaries and frontiers, world-systems, and peer-polity interactions. Nor is it our aim to ignore the importance of local environmental conditions for the elucidation of long-term social change. Rather, our principal objective is to contribute to and expand our understanding of how ancient Mesoamerica was organized and interconnected. To do this, we examine the long-term and changing interrelationship between the prehispanic inhabitants of the Ejutla Valley and those immediately to the north in the larger Valley of Oaxaca (Figure 8.1), both located in the Southern Highlands of Mesoamerica. Soon after the beginning of sedentary agricultural settlement in the Valley of Oaxaca around 1500 B.C., the region was the focus for political and demographic centers that were larger than those found in neighboring regions (including the Ejutla Valley). In this paper, we investigate the dynamic interactions between these centers (first San José Mogote and later Monte Albán) and their surrounding hinterlands (both near and far).

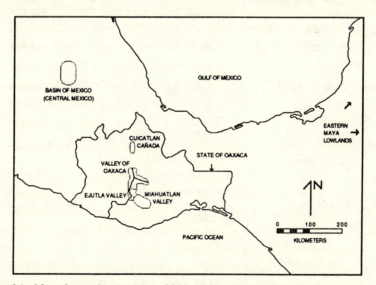

Figure 8.1. Map of central and southern Mexico, with areas mentioned in the text.

In recent years, macro-regional investigations in Mesoamerica have focused primarily on two "text-aided" contexts, the structure of the Late Postclassic Aztec tribute domain (e.g., Smith 1986, 1987; Berdan, 1987), and the relations between the multiple Maya polities that inhabited the eastern lowlands during the Classic period (e.g., Marcus, 1976a; Mathews, 1985; Freidel, 1986; Culbert, 1988) (see Table 8.1). Here, in our long temporal focus on the Southern Highlands, we must depend largely, although not exclusively, on the sketchy outline that can be discerned from the archaeological record (e.g., Marcus, 1976b, 1983; Marcus and Flannery, 1983; Paddock, 1983a).

Table 8.1. Chronological Sequence in Valleys of Ejutla and Oaxaca.

	Ejutla Valley	Valley of Oaxaca	Mesoamerica
1500			
1300			
	Monte Alban V	Monte Alban V	Late Postclassic
1100			
900			
		Monte Alban IV	Early Postclassic
700	Monte Alban IIIB/IV		
		Monte Alban IIIB	Late Classic
500			
	Monte Alban IIIA	Monte Alban IIIA	Early Classic
300			
AD 100	Monte Alban II	Monte Alban II	Terminal Formative
BC 100			
	Monte Alban Late I	Monte Alban Late I	
300			Late Formative
	Monte Alban Early I	Monte Alban Early I	
500			
		Rosario	
700	Rosario		Middle Formative
		Guadalupe	
900			
		San Jose	
1100	Early Formative		Early Formative
1300		Tierras Largas	

In previous studies of precapitalist macro-regional systems, a central concern has been the spatial division of labor (Blanton and Feinman, 1984; McGuire, 1986; Chase-Dunn and Hall, Chapter 1; Schneider, Chapter 2). Thus, in this analysis, a more specific aim is to examine the spatial arrangement of archaeologically discernible economic (craft) specializations in prehispanic Ejutla and Oaxaca, as well as to evaluate both endogenous and macro-regional factors that might account for their distribution. Although these investigations do not yet provide definitive answers, the intent is to give us a better perspective from which to address and assess a series of fundamental issues. Was agricultural tribute the key force behind political expansion? Was the division of labor across the Ejutla-Oaxaca study region uniform, implying only a thin veil of political/elite integration above intraregional self-sufficiency? Can the distribution of craft specialists be accounted for by local agricultural or resource-based considerations? Was macroregional economic interdependence more developed, which by inference would justify at least guarded experimentation with and modification of the fundamental concepts and framework (see Ragin and Chirot, 1984; Abu-Lughod, 1989; Chase-Dunn and Hall, Chapter 1) advanced by Wallerstein (1974).

EMPIRICAL BACKGROUND

Before preceding to a discussion of our empirical foundation, it is important to place the Valley of Oaxaca and Monte Albán in a broader Mesoamerican context. The Valley of Oaxaca has long been recognized as a key region of prehispanic political and demographic importance (Palerm and Wolf, 1957). Soon after the advent of sedentary village life, San José Mogote rose to prominence as one of the largest and architecturally most elaborate centers in Mexico's highlands. Yet, this settlement was neither as monumental as several contemporaneous Gulf Coast lowland communities, nor did it control areas outside the Valley of Oaxaca. By 500 B.C., Monte Albán, a hilltop community located at the hub of the Valley of Oaxaca, was established (see Blanton et al., 1981, for a discussion of the rise of this early center). In size, Monte Albán rapidly eclipsed San José Mogote, and the later site is generally considered to be one of the earliest cities in Mesoamerica. Yet, even at its apogee (after 200 B.C.), Monte Albán appears never to have conquered or controlled areas outside the bounds of the contemporary state of Oaxaca. For most (if not all) of its history, Monte Albán was neither the largest nor the most architecturally monumental site in Mesoamerica (For general discussions of Oaxacan prehistory see Blanton et al., 1981; Flannery and Marcus, 1983). In general, prehispanic Mesoamerica was a world composed of multiple, competing cores and shifting peripheries (see Chase-Dunn and Hall, Chapter 1).

In this analysis, we rely primarily on the findings of the regional archaeological surveys undertaken by the Valley of Oaxaca (Blanton, 1978; Blanton et al., 1982; Kowalewski et al., 1989) and Ejutla Valley (Feinman, 1985; Feinman and Nicholas, 1988) Settlement Pattern Projects. During the last two decades, these large-scale projects have systematically mapped, recorded, and dated archaeological remains over a contiguous 2672 km^2 area (Figure 8.2). Although this large study region certainly does not represent an entire macro-regional system, it does allow for the examination of an area larger than the physiographically defined Valley of Oaxaca (Welte, 1973).

Comparable pedestrian survey procedures were employed over the entire study region. This methodology (see Feinman et al., 1985; Kowalewski et al., 1989:24-38), which was borrowed (with slight modifications) from the archaeological surveys of the highland Basin of Mexico (Sanders, 1965; Parsons, 1971; Blanton, 1972; Sanders, Parsons, and Santley, 1979), entails the systematic coverage of every field, knoll, ridge, arroyo, and street by crews of three to five people walking 50 to 100 m apart (depending on terrain and the visibility of surface artifacts). Site dimensions, environmental variables, earthen or rubble mounds (the remnants of prehispanic platforms and buildings), pottery, chipped stone, ground stone, artifactual indications of craft activities, defensive walls, and all other important or unusual features were recorded. Where possible these features were mapped directly on 1:5000 aerial photographs that each crew carried into the field. Over time, all archaeological remains were recorded on aerial photographs of the region studied. These field procedures were chosen because they yield information on a large corpus of sites across a broadly defined region at an affordable expense in money and time. They provide, at least for the highlands of Mesoamerica, the most systematic means available for producing an inventory of the sizes and distributions of archaeological sites at a spatial scale adequate to study long-term societal change.

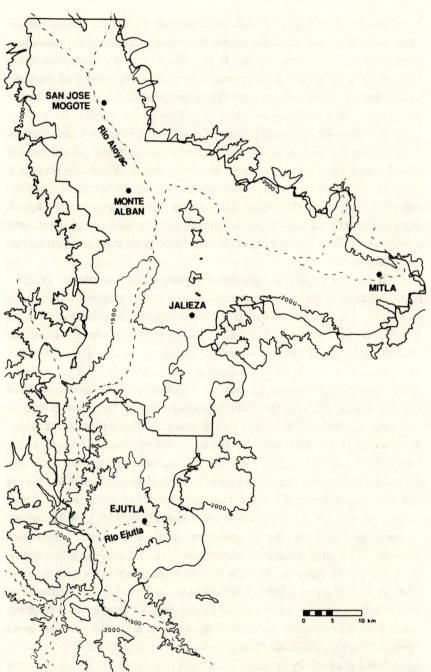

Figure 8.2. Map of the Valleys of Oaxaca and Ejutla, with major sites mentioned in the text.

Population estimates for each occupation were determined as a function of site area, following procedures utilized in previous highland Mesoamerican survey research (Sanders, 1965). Except in those cases where residential features were visible or where surface artifact densities were extraordinarily light or heavy, settlements were calculated as having 10-25 people per hectare of occupied area (see Kowalewski et al., 1989:35, for a fuller discussion). These demographic figures are expressed most appropriately and conservatively as ranges; however, for ease and clarity of presentation (as well as our sanity), we manipulate and refer to mean population values in most of our analyses. Although we recognize the numerous possibilities for error in these estimates, we argue that these data are the closest approximation to a diachronic census of prehispanic settlement that archaeologists can presently achieve--providing relative patterns of population change at broad spatial and temporal scales.

To examine the role of agricultural production and human-land relations in the regional division of labor, data on agricultural strategies and the spatial variability of agrarian resources in ancient Oaxaca was necessary. For this information we rely principally on Anne Kirkby's (1973) landmark, diachronic analysis of the use of land and water resources in the past and present Valley of Oaxaca, Mexico. Kirkby's observations of land quality and productivity, which were supplemented by our own field-by-field observations, were compared with archaeological settlement information for the sequence of prehispanic phases (Table 8.1). Following Kirkby (1973:124-126) and Kowalewski (1980, 1982; see also Feinman and Nicholas, 1987a; Nicholas, 1989), these analyses take into account the increasing productivity of maize during the prehispanic era. We assume that even the region's earliest farmers had the knowledge and the tools to implement the basic water control techniques that can be used locally (Kowalewski, 1982:150). All available archaeological and ethnohistoric evidence suggests that the irrigation and drainage techniques utilized prehispanically were relatively simple (Kirkby, 1973; Lees, 1973; Flannery, 1983), and most of these methods were employed early in the Formative period (Flannery et al., 1967; Drennan and Flannery, 1983). Because we do not know the specific cropping practices and rotations employed prehispanically on each field, we have followed previous investigators (Kirkby, 1973:124-126; Kowalewski, 1982:149-150) in adopting agricultural productivity estimates based entirely on maize (using maize yields as a proxy for total agricultural production). Pre-Conquest maize consump-

tion was presumed (Kowalewski, 1982:158) to correspond to known ethnographic ranges (160-290 kg per person per annum).

In our examination of economic specializations, settlement patterns, and
human-land relationships, we examine three analytical scales smaller than the
entire survey block. To compare the valley's central hub with a southern
edge, we contrast the Valley of Oaxaca Settlement Pattern Project survey area
with the Ejutla region (Figure 8.2). For other analyses, we compare seven
sub-regions, Ejutla and six contiguous segments of the valley that are
internally similar in environment and demographic history (Figure 8.3). For
a finer scale of investigation, we have broken the study region into 229 grid
squares, 4 km on a side (see Figure 8.4 below). The grid square size roughly
corresponds to the amount of land in easy walking distance of sites situated
in each square (see Chisholm, 1968). Use of the grid greatly facilitates spatial
comparisons and cross-phase analyses.

The remainder of the paper is divided into two sections. First, we
approach the question of the spatial division of labor through an examination
of the archaeological evidence for craft activities. In so doing, we evaluate for
Oaxaca-Ejutla several extant models that endeavor to explain the distribution
of non-agricultural production. This discussion of craft activities leads us to
a consideration of prehispanic agricultural production and its spatial arrangement. Second, we review long-term changes in the relationship between the
Ejutla and Oaxaca regions. Through the integration of these empirical
analyses, we gain insight into the macro-regional structure of the ancient
Mesoamerican world as seen through the perspective of the Southern
Highlands of Mexico.

THE SPATIAL DISTRIBUTION OF ECONOMIC SPECIALIZATION

Numerous models have been proposed for the emergence and distribution of
craft specialization. Generally, these models emphasize local factors, which
for prehispanic highland Mesoamerica seem an appropriate starting point
given the limitations of transportation technology. In archaeology, a frequently used model (e.g., Arnold, 1975:192, 1980:147) implies that unpredictable or
inadequate agricultural resources, particularly "population pressures," are likely
to promote non-agricultural production. This expectation is exemplified by

Howard (1981:7), who noted that: "specialization tends to develop as a necessary adaptation to population pressure and poor agricultural land."

An archaeological examination of this proposition is difficult if one wants to extend the test beyond individual specialists and sites. Yet, such scalar expansion clearly is requisite for an adequate evaluation. To gain a broad spatial perspective, dependence on surface remains is necessary, and, as Spence (1983:434) so eloquently recognized, this entails "the imprecision inevitable when working on a regional scale." Furthermore, as Paddock (1983b:433) rightfully has warned, many prehispanic Mesoamerican craft specializations may be invisible to the archaeologist, particularly when reliant on surface remains.

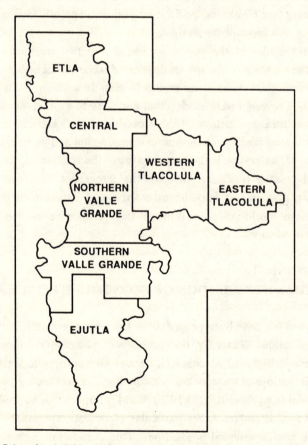

Figure 8.3. Sub-regional divisions of the combined Oaxaca-Ejutla survey block.

Nevertheless, in the combined Oaxaca-Ejutla survey block, we have found 268 occurrences of unusual surface residues of shell, spindle whorls (cloth production), ceramics, obsidian, other chipped stone and ground stone (see Figure 8.4). We are not foolish enough to assert that these sites represent the entire corpus of production locations for these materials; in fact our sample probably is skewed toward larger-scale specialization. Nor do we believe that every identified location was necessarily a locus of non-agricultural production. We also doubt whether even the finest-scale archaeological analysis would be able to distinguish convincingly and repeatedly between seasonal, half-time, three-quarter-time, and full-time specialists. Even workshops may not operate year-round. Who can determine from archaeological or even archival sources what craftsmen did in their off-time or how many hours they worked? Despite the obvious limitations, these 268 locations represent the best regionalscale record for these five economic specializations that we have (or are likely to have in the nearfuture) for the study region.

To examine the proposition advanced by Howard (1981) and others, we worked at the level of the grid square. The 268 locations were located in 94 squares, just under half of the 201 squares that were inhabited at some time in the prehispanic era. At that scale, a previous study (Feinman, 1986) has shown that the distribution of Monte Albán I ceramic production sites in the Valley of Oaxaca was not spatially coterminous with areas in which the estimated population would have exceeded the available agricultural resources under average rainfall conditions (see also Kowalewski and Finsten, 1983:420). Yet, unlike pottery, the other craft specializations are more difficult to date, particularly at sites with more than one occupational episode.

Consequently, to sidestep the problem of chronology, we devised a less demanding, atemporal test of association. For the 201 grid squares, we isolated those squares that had a "dependent population" of at least five people in any one temporal phase (Figure 8.4). By "dependent population," we simply mean a population larger than the number of people that could have been sustained in that particular square by its available land and labor resources. For example, grid square 1206, which includes the site of Monte Albán, could not have provided sufficient maize to feed its occupants during much of the sequence, so it would be included among those squares with "dependent population." By structuring our analysis independent of time, we not only lessened the interpretive demands on the data, but we increased the likelihood of an association, since squares in which population dependence occurred during a different phase than economic specialization would still yield a positive association. Yet, a significant association was not found ($x^2 = .96$, df = 1, not signif. at .05) as only roughly half of the squares with "dependent populations" also had indications of economic specialization.

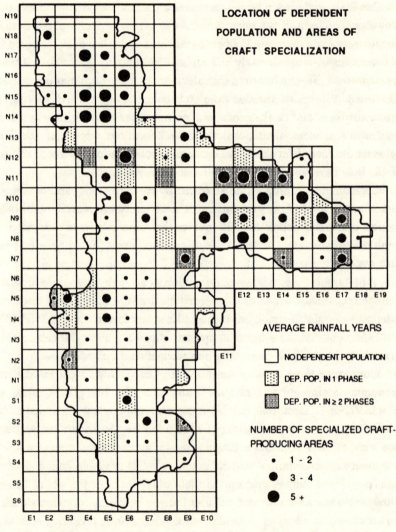

Figure 8.4. Spatial relationship between craft specialization and dependent population in the Valleys of Oaxaca and Ejutla.

Using this grid-based approach, we also found that squares with the least productive agricultural land did not have greater evidence of economic specialization. Here, we limited the analysis to the 129 squares in which 1400 hectares or more had been surveyed (fully surveyed squares have 1600 ha), and then identified the 50 squares with the lowest agricultural potentials. This analysis excluded partially surveyed squares (primarily located in the mountainous zones at the edge of the surveyed area) because a disproportionate number of them would rank among the least productive squares. Most of these edge squares also have little occupation and no evidence of economic specialization. The inclusion of the edge squares in the sample would create an artificially strong negative association between those squares with the least productive land and the presence of economic specialization. Nevertheless, even with the edge squares eliminated, we found no significant association between the loci of economic specialization and poor quality land ($x^2 = 3.49$, df = 1, not signif. at .05). In fact, the opposite tendency was observed. Although the relationship was not statistically significant, economic specialization tended to occur in those squares with better agricultural resources. Evidence for craft specialization was present in only 24 of the 50 least productive squares, yet more than 64% of the remaining squares (79) had such evidence.

Although recent archaeological models of craft production have tended to focus on population pressure or agricultural marginality, a more traditional perspective (e.g., Childe, 1950) viewed subsistence surplus as the trigger for craft specialization. To assess this factor, we first focused on the 50 grid squares in the study block with the most productive agrarian resources. All but fourteen of these squares were spatially coterminous with evidence for economic specialization, hence the association was statistically significant ($x^2 = 16.97$, df = 1, signif. at .01). Yet, clearly this factor cannot explain the relative abundance of economic specialization in the eastern arm of the valley (see Figure 8.4) where agricultural conditions were generally less favorable. A stronger relationship ($x^2 = 30.55$, df = 1, signif. at .01) was found between high population and economic specialization. Here we defined "high population squares" as those ranked in the top 15% (by population) during any prehispanic phase. Although this relationship probably has been strengthened by temporal imprecision, the findings do conform with two sets of theoretical expectations. First, specialists, particularly those producing at a relatively large scale, would tend to situate where there is relatively high demand (e.g., Feinman, Kowalewski, and Blanton, 1984:301). Second, certain specialists may have been "attached" (see Brumfiel and Earle, 1987:5) to particular sponsors, either social elite or civic-ceremonial institutions, concentrated at the major population centers.

Although the spatial arrangement of occupational specialization was partially accounted for by local socio-political and demographic factors, several aspects of the distribution require additional discussion and consideration. For example, evidence for economic specialization was abundant in the eastern or Tlacolula arm, while it is underrepresented at the central core of the valley as well as in distant Ejutla. Tlacolula's agricultural marginality may relate to this apparent density of specialists; however, we already saw that population pressure could not account for the distribution of specialists at the regional scale. Furthermore, the northern arm or Etla had the second-highest concentration of occupational specialization, and it is one of the region's most fertile agricultural areas. Significantly, Tlacolula was densely inhabited in Monte Albán IV and V, and much of the evidence for specialization may pertain to those phases (Finsten, 1983; Kowalewski et al., 1989:348-363). The relative abundance of raw chert sources in both Tlacolula and Etla (Parry, 1987) also may help account for the prevalence of chipped-stone production locations in both of those areas. Yet, pottery and obsidian production locations were abundant in those areas respectively (Figure 8.5), and good clay sources can be found throughout the Valleys of Oaxaca and Ejutla, while no obsidian sources are known in the Central Valleys of Oaxaca.

Specialized stone tool and ceramic production locations were scarce in Ejutla (Figure 8.5), and this relative dearth may be accounted for by the generally lower prehispanic population densities noted in this region as compared to the Valley of Oaxaca (Feinman and Nicholas, 1987b, 1988). In Ejutla, these basically utilitarian goods were more likely to have been made by individual households or at a smaller scale of manufacture. Curiously, the production of higher status goods, like shell and cloth, were more abundant than expected in Ejutla. Shell was recorded at only 20 archaeological locations (out of 2700) in the Valley of Oaxaca; whereas in Ejutla, shell was found at 21 (of 423) sites. Relative to the number of sites in each region, surface shell was between six and seven times more prevalent in Ejutla than Oaxaca. Of the three shell production sites noted in the combined survey area, one was found in Ejutla, while the other two were at San José Mogote and Monte Albán. A fourth shell working area was recorded by Brockington

(1973) and Markman (1981) just south of the Ejutla region in Miahuatlán (Figure 8.1).

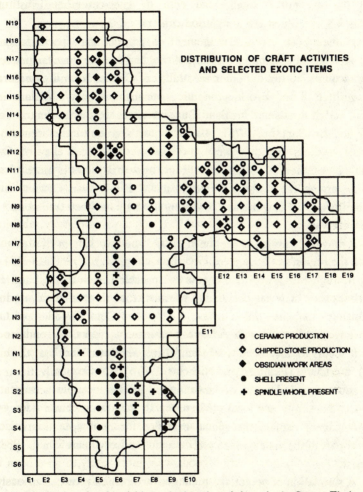

Figure 8.5. Distribution of craft activities and selected exotic items in the Oaxaca-Ejutla survey block. Utilitarian craft activities are represented by the open symbols.

Spindle whorls were rare items in both Ejutla and the Valley of Oaxaca, yet their greater prevalence in Ejutla relative to Oaxaca was even more marked than the differential in the presence of shell. Twice as many spindle whorls were found on the ground surface in Ejutla as in Oaxaca (11 for Ejutla and six for Oaxaca, including Monte Albán), even though Ejutla is only one-fourth the areal size (Feinman and Nicholas, 1987b).

Based on the three important dimensions of hole diameter, total diameter, and weight, nine of the 11 Ejutla spindle whorls would fit neatly into Mary Parsons' (1972) smallest, or Type III, category of Basin of Mexico spindle whorls, which she associates with the spinning of cotton. The other two spindle whorls are similar in size to her larger Type I whorls and may have been used for spinning maguey. According to Late Postclassic ethnohistoric accounts, cotton did enter the Valley of Oaxaca from lowland areas to the south (Ball and Brockington, 1978), probably through Miahuatlán and Ejutla, and at least some highland Oaxacan towns were importing raw cotton (Ball and Brockington, 1978). Some cotton also may have been grown in Ejutla, which is slightly lower in elevation than the Valley of Oaxaca. Spinning, whether of cotton or maguey, apparently was a more prevalent activity among the prehispanic residents of Ejutla than Oaxaca, and the finished product (as with shell ornaments) may have been traded north into the larger valley.

It may be tempting to see the cloth and shell working in Ejutla as simply due to the region's relative proximity to coastal products, yet Oaxaca's eastern arm, through Mitla, provides almost comparable access to shell and cotton. Another exotic material, obsidian (a volcanic stone that was highly desired for its cutting capabilities), could have entered the Central Valleys of Oaxaca from any direction through either the eastern, northern, or southern arms. Yet, it seems to have been worked most frequently in Tlacolula (the eastern arm), not Ejutla (Feinman and Nicholas, 1987b). Consequently, the regional and sub-regional division of labor seems neither entirely accountable to resource proximity nor local environmental conditions. Even demographic factors cannot explain the sparse evidence for craft specialization in the central part of the valley, which often was settled very densely in the prehispanic past.

A simulation of potential agricultural production provides an interesting alternative perspective on this issue (Feinman and Nicholas, 1987a; Nicholas, 1989; Feinman, 1989). For the purposes of this analysis, we define potential production as the quantity of maize that could have been produced at a particular time, if populations farmed only terrain (starting with the best land) within the grid square in which they were located. For each grid, a maximum surplus can then be estimated by subtracting that population's required maize consumption from its potential production. Although in all phases a surplus could have been produced in the majority of squares (or the inhabitants at

least could have fed themselves), a few would have had dependent populations. We also modeled whether these grid square imbalances could have
been evened out within larger sub-regional units. For example, following the
foundation of Monte Albán, the site could not have been supported by the
land available in the grid square in which it was located. One might then ask,
could the site be fed by the immediately surrounding population?

By our figuring, even the potential surpluses produced during average
rainfall years in the squares of the Central sub-region (which includes Monte
Albán) did not compensate for the deficit incurred by the population of Monte
Albán. From Monte Albán Early I through IV, the Central area had to
import maize (see Nicholas, 1989:Figure 14.7). As we saw in the earlier grid
square analysis, we again do not see a strong positive relationship between
population resource imbalance and craft specialization (at the sub-regional
scale). Whereas the population of the Central sub-region seems to have faced
a somewhat recurrent maize deficit, there is very little evidence for prehispanic craft activities in that part of the region. Rather, our alternative
argument follows Blanton's (1985) more general discussion regarding the
spatial structure of prehispanic highland Mesoamerican political-economies.
We argue that the occupants of the Central area, with the exception of the
inhabitants of Monte Albán, were not involved in craft activities because they
were encouraged or coerced to emphasize agricultural production to help feed
the non-producers at the urban center. This hypothesis makes sense given the
high transportation costs for grain (e.g., Lightfoot, 1979, Drennan, 1984a,
1984b).

In earlier works (Nicholas et al., 1986; Feinman and Nicholas, 1987a), we
illustrated that in Oaxaca the potential to produce large local (or grid square)
food surpluses generally was centered around major population centers. This
pattern is significant and would seem to relate to the concentration of
agricultural labor around non-food producers. If we examine sub-regional
surplus from a slightly different angle (one that eliminates from consideration
those grid squares with a population-maize imbalance), the gross agricultural
potential of the rural population of the Central area is illustrated further. The
cumulative surpluses of agricultural production at the gridsquare level (if
those surpluses simply were summed rather than shifted over to feed deficit
squares in the sub-region) were not evenly distributed across the study region.

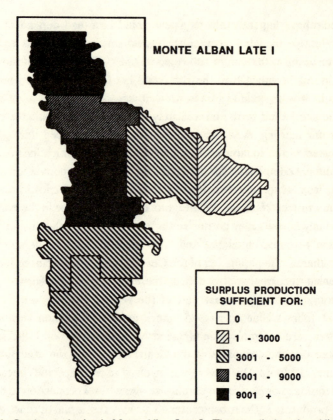

Figure 8.6. Surplus production in Monte Alban Late I. The map displays the additional
population that could be supported by the gross maize surplus of each sub-region
(prior to shifting any produce to squares with food deficits).

For example, in Monte Albán Late I (as in other phases not illustrated here),
the potential surplus of rural producers in the Central area was relatively high
(Figure 8.6), despite the sub-region's comparatively small areal size and
average environmental potential. These food surpluses, which most likely
were consumed by the inhabitants of Monte Albán, clearly were a consequence of the relative abundance of labor in this central portion of Oaxaca.

If we summarize the spatial arrangement of economic specialization in
Oaxaca, what we seem to find is less emphasis on craft specialization at the
valley core, where food imports often were required. Yet, the potential to
produce sizeable local surpluses was present as long as labor was directed
toward agriculture. In contrast, at the edge of the Central Valleys of Oaxaca
in Ejutla, easily transportable, labor intensive, high status goods were

produced more frequently than expected. The craft work of bulkier, heavier, perhaps less costly items (ceramics, obsidian, chipped and ground stone) tended to be concentrated in between. Although, an interpretation of this pattern is highly speculative, it does conform to Blanton's (1985:400-402) scenario in which highland Mesoamerican states encouraged intensive food production near their cores and craft manufacture in the political margins (see also Brumfiel, 1976). A sub-regional division of labor in which statusrelated goods served in part to interdigitate moredistant regions is suggested (Blanton and Feinman, 1984; Schneider, Chapter 2).

The preceding interpretation has glossed over significant temporal variation. For example, a sizeable number of the economic specialization locations in Tlacolula may pertain to the Postclassic period, a time when that sub-region was also a demographic core. The close spatial association between major Postclassic Tlacolula centers, like Mitla, and relatively high rural densities of craftwork may point to another significant organizational difference between Oaxaca during the Postclassic period and earlier (500 B.C.-A.D. 700) when the region was dominated by Monte Albán (see Kowalewski et al., 1983; Kowalewski and Finsten, 1983; Marcus, 1989, for discussions of organizational differences between the Classic and Postclassic periods in Oaxaca).

THE VALLEY OF OAXACA AND THE EJUTLA VALLEY: A DIACHRONIC PERSPECTIVE

We have argued that the character of occupational specialization was different in Ejutla than in the Valley of Oaxaca. In so doing, we have suggested that Ejutla was part of a larger socioeconomic system. In this section, we investigate the long-term interrelationship between these two adjoining valleys. Was the smaller Ejutla Valley simply a microcosm of the larger region, or was its history influenced by its changing ties to the region to the north? How was this relationship structured over time? Was the Ejutla Valley simply an additional source of agricultural tribute for Monte Albán?

In this discussion of the relationship between the Ejutla region and the larger valley to the north, we borrow a conceptual distinction made previously by Strassoldo (1980). He distinguishes "frontiers" as open, sparsely settled, almost "virgin" areas of potential growth from "peripheries," which are dependent, more-closed domains that are distant, yet linked, to more developed cores.

Table 8.2. Prehispanic Occupation by Phase in Ejutla and Oaxaca

Phase	Number of Sites*		Total Site Area†		Total population+	
	Ejutla	Oaxaca	Ejutla	Oaxaca	Ejutla	Oaxaca
Tierras Largas		26		14.8		327
San José	3	41	0.6	104.2	24	1,942
Guadalupe		45		95.8		1,788
Rosario	4	85	1.5	92.1	40	1,835
M.A. Early I	21	261	12.1	819.0	259	14,652
M.A. Late I	63	745	211.7	2,260.3	3,455	50,920
M.A. II	46	519	114.5	1,685.0	2,184	41,319
M.A. IIIA	135	1,077	1,003.1	3,990.3	14,656	115,226
M.A. IIIB		629		3,337.5		78,930
M.A. IV	52	444	153.9	2,788.5	3,029	70,075
M.A. V	362	2,455	1,071.1	7,876.2	19,970	162,557

* Initially defined sites have been grouped for certain analysis.
† In hectares.
+ Mean figure.

The Ejutla region was settled late and rather sparsely compared to the Valley of Oaxaca (Table 8.2). While sedentary settlements were present in the Valley of Oaxaca during the Tierras Largas phase, the earliest ceramics in the Ejutla region resemble valley ceramics of the subsequent San José phase. Such early pottery has been found at only three very small sites in Ejutla, all near the Río Atoyac (Feinman and Nicholas, 1988). In comparison, San José Mogote in the Valley of Oaxaca extended over 79 ha and included civic-ceremonial structures that were built during the San José phase (Flannery and Marcus, 1976; Kowalewski et al., 1989).

The first village settlements in the Ejutla survey region were small pioneering communities that extended down from Oaxaca along the course of the Río Atoyac. At this time, these occupations may have formed a true frontier for the Central Valleys of Oaxaca, as no Early Formative settlements have been discovered in the Miahuatlán Valley directly to the south (Markman, 1981). In the subsequent Rosario phase, the Ejutla region remained a sparsely inhabited frontier, occupied by only four small communities.

The Rosario-Early I transition in the Valley of Oaxaca was characterized by the emergence of Monte Albán, as well as the foundation of a series of smaller centers with nonresidential architecture. Dozens of Early I settlements larger than 2 ha were located in Oaxaca, with at least several of these positioned in each sub-region (Kowalewski et al., 1989). As in the Valley of Oaxaca, the population of Ejutla also increased between the Rosario and Early I phases. Most of the Ejutla settlements still were small farming hamlets located along the Atoyac and its tributaries (Feinman and Nicholas, 1988). Yet in contrast to Oaxaca, none of the Ejutla settlements were larger than 2 ha, and no public architecture could be linked definitively with Ejutla's Early I settlements. The first settlements also were recorded in the Miahuatlán Valley during Monte Albán I (Markman 1981).

Consequently, at this time when the early center of Monte Albán was founded on a hilltop at the center of the larger valley to the north, both Ejutla and Miahuatlán remained sparsely occupied. Even the two valley sub-regions farthest from Monte Albán, the southern Valle Grande and eastern Tlacolula, were settled more than twice as densely as the Ejutla region (Figure 8.7). Since eastern Tlacolula has less fine bottomland and is generally more agriculturally marginal than the Ejutla region, the demographic sparsity of Ejutla relative to Oaxaca seems at least partially a consequence of its spatial position.

The Ejutla region continued to be a lightly settled frontier lacking any archaeological indication of the emergent hierarchical institutions so evident in Oaxaca at this time. The absence of large or civic-ceremonially important Early I centers in both Ejutla and along the southern edge of the Valley of Oaxaca survey region (Kowalewski et al., 1989:103) leads us to suggest that most interactions may have been handled reciprocally by individuals at small, relatively autonomous communities along this southern frontier.

The most rapid episode of prehispanic demographic increase in the Ejutla region occurred between Monte Albán Early I and Late I (Table 8.2). The number of Late I settlements in Ejutla increased three-fold, and these occupations were increasingly differentiated in size and architectural complexity. The population density was roughly similar to what it had been earlier in the Valley of Oaxaca during Monte Albán Early I. Yet based on surface assessments, no Late I settlement in Ejutla was comparable in size or architectural complexity to Late I Monte Albán or for that matter, to Early I Monte Albán, pre-Monte Albán San José Mogote, or even the larger Late I secondary centers in the Valley of Oaxaca.

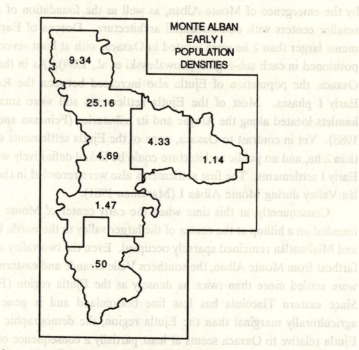

Figure 8.7. Monte Alban Early I population density by sub-region.

In Late I, the Ejutla study area was not dominated by one or two centers as was the Valley of Oaxaca (Kowalewski et al., 1989:113-152). While almost 20% of the Late I Ejutla sites had estimated mean populations greater than 100, none had more than 350 people. Mounds are associated with 16 Late I components; however, most of these sites had no more than four structures, and most of the mounds were very small. Later, larger occupations also were present at the four sites where Late I ceramics were associated with more monumental or more numerous structures, and the larger, more substantial construction almost certainly pertains to these later phases. At four sites where Late I was the sole ceramic phase associated with the structures, the single mounds or plaza groups were low and very small. Pending excavations at several of these sites, we suspect that Late I architectural construction generally was internally similar and simple in plan. The settlements with civic-ceremonial buildings were welldispersed along the region's rivers and tributaries, suggesting that Ejutla was not dominated by one principal settlement.

In Monte Albán II, the number of small hamlets occupied in Ejutla remained roughly constant, yet most of the small Late I Ejutla centers diminished considerably in size or were abandoned entirely. Concurrently, three strategically positioned Late I centers increased in extent and most probably in architectural elaboration. The two smaller and southernmost of these sites grew to their maximum sizes in Monte Albán II. Both were associated with 13 comparatively large structures. Although this construction cannot be placed securely in time, these settlements clearly were much larger in Monte Albán II than they had been earlier.

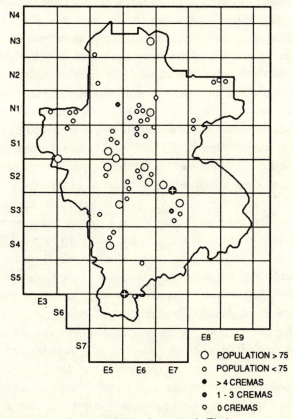

Figure 8.8. Distribution of Monte Alban Late I *cremas* in Ejutla.

The third Monte Albán II center, placed in the middle of the Río Ejutla drainage and positioned underneath the contemporary *distrito* head town of Ejutla (Figure 8.2), grew to roughly twice the size of any prior Ejutla settlement or other contemporaneous community. During two summers of houselot-by-houselot survey, nine very large structures were recorded and measured, and these have a total volume of approximately 80,000 m^3, more than four times the estimated volume of the constructions at the other two large sites. Several of these mounds were built up more than 12 m, and observations of mound fill indicated a Monte Albán II construction date. Earthen platforms of this scale were unprecedented in Ejutla prior to this date.

Other factors also point to a significant Monte Albán II transition in the Ejutla region and a change in the region's interconnection with Oaxaca. The number of small low-lying hamlets in northern Ejutla and the southern Valle Grande decreased, indicating a drop-off in the kinds of open, horizontal communications that are expected along a more open frontier. Instead, for the first time, several Ejutla sites were positioned in defendable locations. However, unlike later defendably situated localities that tended to face outside the valley, the phase II sites were inward looking, positioned over the most direct route between Monte Albán and the Ejutla site. A shift in the nature of interactions between Oaxaca and Ejutla also is suggested by the changing distribution in the latter region of Monte Albán I and II cream paste pottery. These distinctive painted *crema* serving bowls, which were produced (and were recorded) most abundantly in the central and northern parts of the Valley of Oaxaca (Feinman, 1980), were very rare in Ejutla in phase I contexts. The few definitive Monte Albán I *cremas* found were distributed rather randomly in terms of site size and location (Figure 8.8). Yet, the temporally specific and highly decorated Monte Albán II *cremas* were found more frequently and are particularly abundant at the three aforementioned centers (Figure 8.9). Hence, interactions between the two regions may have been handled more directly through elite individuals living at the major centers. Suggestively, prior studies by Spencer (1982) and Redmond (1983) in the Cuicatlán Cañada, a canyon area north of Oaxaca where tropical fruits are grown, document a contemporary episode of local conquest that they relate to Monte Albán expansionism. Marcus' (1980) analysis of the glyphic record on Building 'J,' an arrowhead-shaped structure on the Main Plaza at Monte Albán, led her to a similar hypothesis, that the hilltop center exerted

force against other external domains in the state of Oaxaca during Monte
Albán II.

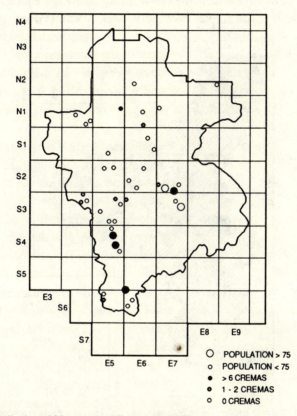

Figure 8.9. Distribution of Monte Alban II *cremas* in Ejutla.

Given the apparent transition of Ejutla from a sparsely settled frontier
to a near periphery of the Valley of Oaxaca, it is worth returning to the
sub-regional modeling of agricultural surplus potential that we discussed
above. Through Monte Albán Early I, the small Ejutla population precluded
the production of any significant maize surplus. Yet, by Late I, a rather large
maize surplus could have been produced, equal to or greater than the surplus
potential of three valley sub-regions, western Tlacolula, eastern Tlacolula, and
the southern Valle Grande (Figure 8.6). Whether the demand for tributary
agrarian surplus was a factor in the southern expansion of the Monte

Albán-centered polity remains unknown; however, our figures suggest that if bulk agricultural surplus was their goal, Monte Albán's incorporation of Ejutla may not have been immediately successful. In Monte Albán II, with the concentration and decline of the sub-regional population, Ejutla's potential for production of maize surplus declined by almost 50% (Figure 8.10).

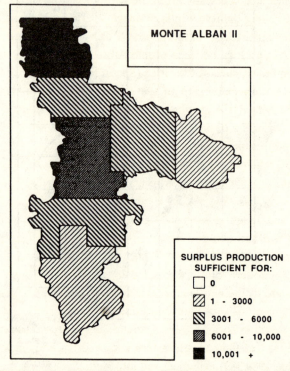

Figure 8.10. Surplus production in Monte Alban II. The map displays the additional population that could be supported by the gross maize surplus of each sub-region (prior to shifting any surplus to squares with food deficits).

Ejutla's potential surplus was roughly comparable to that of eastern Tlacolula, yet the latter sub-region was closer to the valley core, lessening necessary transportation costs. Although some bulk maize could have been sent to Monte Albán from Ejutla in Monte Albán II, the quantities had to have been small. More likely, Ejutla was incorporated as a link to exotic raw materials and craft goods and to solidify defensive and communication networks. In addition, certain tropical plants that could not have been produced in the

Valley of Oaxaca may have been grown with greater success in Ejutla's slightly lower elevations.

During Monte Albán IIIA, the great emphasis on new settlement in the southern arm of the Valley of Oaxaca (Kowalewski et al., 1989:201-250) apparently extended into the Ejutla region, where there was a proliferation of many small hamlets, especially in northern Ejutla and in the central part of the study area along the Río Ejutla drainage. Perhaps this greater exploitation of the southern reaches of the Central Valleys of Oaxaca was interrelated with Monte Albán's loss, between Monte Albán II and IIIA, of more distant northern peripheries, such as Cuicatlán (Spencer 1982). The extension of the demographic patterns observed in the southern Valle Grande into Ejutla during Monte Albán IIIA suggests that the two regions remained interconnected, with perhaps a basic continuation of the core/periphery relationship that developed in Monte Albán II.

In IIIA, much of the Valley of Oaxaca population was concentrated in several large sites, such as Monte Albán, and Jalieza in the Valle Grande, and this pattern also was observed in Ejutla with the establishment of a large center near San Joaquín, in central Ejutla (Feinman and Nicholas, 1987b, 1988). This site had almost four times the population of the next largest contemporary Ejutla settlement. While the old Monte Albán II center, situated under modern Ejutla, increased in extent, it was completely overshadowed in size by the new center 5 km to the northwest (San Joaquín). In Ejutla, the number of sites with nonresidential architecture also increased, and their distribution became more spatially widespread. The ring of hilltop defendable sites that flanked the eastern and southern arms of the Valley of Oaxaca (Elam, 1989:389) extended well into Ejutla. Thus, the incorporation of Ejutla into the Valley of Oaxaca polity appears to have been more complete by Monte Albán IIIA (Feinman and Nicholas, 1987b).

Although several factors point to Ejutla's continuation as an important communication and military link, as well as a source for exotic craft goods in IIIA (Feinman and Nicholas, 1987b), the region could have contributed more than twice the maize surplus of the prior phase. Yet, potential surplus maize was still far less in Ejutla than in any valley sub-region with the exception of eastern Tlacolula (Figure 8.11). For Monte Albán, grain tribute from Ejutla may have been more of an administrative consideration than it was earlier, yet we doubt that the three to four day round-trip movement costs and the

relatively limited potential returns would have made such bulk tribute the
central rationale for continued incorporation.

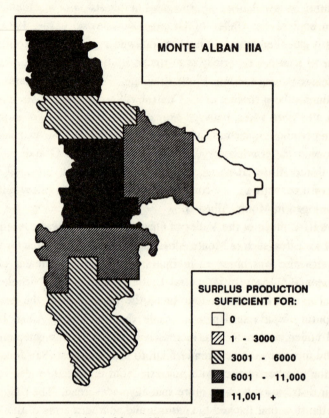

Figure 8.11. Surplus production in Monte Alban IIIA. The map displays the additional
population that could be supported by the gross maize surplus of each sub-region
(prior to shifting any surplus to squares with food deficits).

After IIIA, Monte Albán's hegemony over the Ejutla region began to
wane. By Monte Albán IV, both the Valley of Oaxaca and the Ejutla region
were politically fragmented (Kowalewski et al., 1989:251-305). The population
of Ejutla declined, and no Ejutla settlement was markedly dominant in size or
architectural complexity. Ejutla's population was clustered into several
similarly sized settlement concentrations that were separated by sparsely
settled zones. We found a relative abundance of imitation fine gray and fine
orange pottery at the easternmost Ejutla settlement clusters. These wares,
rare in the Central Valleys of Oaxaca, are thought to signal affiliation with

lowland areas to the south and east. Their relative abundance in Ejutla suggests that the region may have developed its own, more direct ties with Mesoamerican populations situated outside the Oaxacan highlands.

During Monte Albán V, the relative political fragmentation of the Central Valleys of Oaxaca was maintained (Flannery and Marcus, 1983: Chapter 8; Kowalewski et al., 1989:307-366). The Ejutla region contained settlement clusters, perhaps representing semiautonomous petty states, that were roughly comparable in size to smaller settlement concentrations in Oaxaca. In both Oaxaca and Ejutla, these settlement clusters often were separated by unoccupied or sparsely settled shatter zones. The presence of these zones indicates that the entire region was not well integrated politically in this last prehispanic phase, a point borne out in ethnohistoric records (Flannery and Marcus, 1983: Chapter 8; Marcus, 1989). The relative autonomy of the Ejutla population also is suggested by changes in the proportions of obsidian derived from different sources. Ejutla's procurement network for this desirable stone material appears to have been more independent in the Late Postclassic period than it had been during the Early Classic (Feinman and Nicholas, 1987b).

During the Postclassic period, the population densities in Ejutla remained below those in the valley (Feinman and Nicholas, 1987b). Yet, they were closest to the demographic densities observed for the Etla sub-region, an area markedly superior in agricultural potential. However, with Valley of Oaxaca population concentrations now densest in Tlacolula, Etla also was spatially well removed from the areal core (as was Ejutla), suggesting a basis for their relative demographic (as well as architectural) marginality. In sum, in the Late Postclassic, the extent of IIIA political incorporation of Ejutla by Oaxaca was not repeated, and the degree of economic autonomy of the Ejutla region appears to have been somewhat greater.

SUMMARY AND CONCLUSION

This paper has approached the macro-regional organization of the prehispanic Southern Highlands of Mexico from two analytical directions. The first examined the spatial distribution of economic specialization, while the second focused on the diachronic relationship between the Ejutla Valley and the Valley of Oaxaca. Perhaps we should have listened to the old saying that "to do two things at once is to do neither." Yet, the dual examination has afforded us the opportunity to draw together a series of related observations and inferences that may not have emerged from either investigation alone.

We have seen that large-scale differences in economic specialization existed in the Central Valleys of Oaxaca. This diversity and its spatial arrangement could not be explained by either local resource distributions or agricultural conditions alone. Yet these economic divisions may have contributed to the integration and interdependence of the larger socioeconomic system. Clearly, by implication, the notion of relatively uniform, self-sufficient households bound together by a thin political or economic veneer seems much too simple, as does the traditional redistributive model that envisions that the major intercommunity linkages were merely environmentally induced.

The complexity of ancient Oaxaca's regional and macro-regional connections is further implied by the diachronic transitions and transformations that occurred in and between sub-regional cores and margins. Even Ejutla, always demographically marginal to the valley core, underwent major organizational shifts. Episodes of political fragmentation and centralization in Ejutla were roughly concurrent with similar cycles of change in the valley. Yet, at the same time, demographic processes were certainly not coterminous in the two regions.

Luxury goods and craft items apparently had as important a role in the interconnection of the Southern Highland communities and polities as they did in the Central Mexican Aztec world (e.g., Blanton and Feinman, 1984). It seems doubtful that the peripheralization of Ejutla was spurred by Monte Albán's demand for bulk agricultural surplus alone. The food needs of the ancient Oaxacan capital could have been supported from much closer at hand and at much reduced transport costs. Access to shell, cloth, certain varieties of obsidian, and a range of lowland products not presently visible in the archaeological record, as well as to labor to work those goods, and defensive considerations appear more likely factors behind valley expansionism.

In ancient Mesoamerica, the production, exchange, and consumption of ritually important and luxury items should not be divorced entirely from the consideration of more basic necessities. In the pre-Columbian world, where extractive technology was simple and transportation costs high, labor was a critical variable in food production. Yet, symbolically imbued items and non-local products may have played a critical role (through ritual and patron-client transactions) in attracting and integrating the labor necessary to support major centers like Monte Albán. While we would not want to extend these arguments blanketly to other continents and eras, where beasts of burden and wheeled vehicles made grain transport a more efficient proposition, it is our view that systemically significant (as opposed to epiphenomenal) long-distance relations in ancient Mesoamerica were rarely accountable to food and fuel considerations alone.

Although the inhabitants of prehispanic Oaxaca relied on local natural resources, their regional and macro-regional organizations were not simple reflections or consequences of such "natural" factors. Rather, ancient Oaxaca had a much more complex political economy, distinguished by civic-ceremonial cores and peripheries, shifting economic linkages at various scales, uneven demographic change, and a spatial division of labor. As in Colonial and more recent times, inequality, interdependence, and economic differentiation were integral (yet changing) aspects of Oaxaca's archaeological past. In sum, our findings, though tentative, lead us to support Kohl (1987:5) when he argues that "a position that altogether rejects any correspondences between capitalist and precapitalist or western and non-western societies often tends to distort our vision of the present and idealize that of the past."

ACKNOWLEDGMENTS

We are grateful for the National Science Foundation support given to both the Valley of Oaxaca Settlement Pattern Project (GS-28547, GS-388030, BNS-19640 to Richard E. Blanton; BNS-7914124 to Stephen A. Kowalewski) and the Ejutla Valley Settlement Pattern Project (BNS-84-06229, BNS-85-42668 to Gary M. Feinman). The permission and assistance of the Instituto Nacional de Antropología e Historia and the Centro Regional de Oaxaca are recognized with great appreciation. Joaquín García Bárcena and Manuel Esparza have been particularly supportive over the years. We also would like to thank the Rota project and Apple Computer for granting us the equipment on which most of our figures were prepared.

The initial draft of this paper was presented at the 46th International Congress of Americanists in Amsterdam, Holland, in July, 1988. We would like to thank Peter Druijven and Jan Hardeman for the invitation to participate in their stimulating session. Stephen A. Kowalewski, Scott Cook, Richard E. Blanton, and Joseph Whitecotton read earlier versions of this paper, and we thank them for their useful and provocative comments. Christopher Chase-Dunn and Thomas D. Hall offered insightful suggestions that we incorporated into the published manuscript. The final draft of this paper was prepared while the senior author was a resident scholar at the School of American Research. We thank Douglas W. Schwartz and the SAR staff for providing such a wonderful atmosphere for productive research.

REFERENCES

Abu-Lughod, Janet 1989. *Before European Hegemony: The World System A.D. 1250-1350.* New York: Oxford University Press.

Arnold, Dean E. 1975. "Ceramic ecology of the Ayacucho Basin, Peru: implications for prehistory." *Current Anthropology* 16:183-205.

_____ 1980. "Localized exchange: an ethnoarchaeological perspective." Pp. 147-156 in R.E. Fry (ed.) *Models and Methods in Regional Exchange.* Society for American Archaeology, Papers 1.

Ball, Hugh G. and Donald L. Brockington 1978. "Trade and travel in prehispanic Oaxaca." Pp. 107-114 in T.A. Lee, Jr. and C. Navarette (eds.) *Mesoamerican Communication Routes and Cultural Contacts.* New World Archaeological Foundation, Papers 40.

Berdan, Frances, F. 1987. "Cotton in Aztec Mexico: production, distribution and uses." *Mexican Studies/Estudios Mexicanos* 3:235-262.

Binford, Lewis R. and Sally R. Binford (eds.) 1968. *New Perspectives in Archeology.* Chicago: Aldine.

Blanton, Richard E. 1972. *Prehispanic Settlement Patterns of the Ixtapalapa Peninsula Region, Mexico.* University Park: Pennsylvania State University, Department of Anthropology, Occasional Papers 6.

_____ 1978. *Monte Albán: Settlement Patterns at the Ancient Zapotec Capital.* New York: Academic Press.

_____ 1985. "A comparison of early market systems." Pp. 399-416 in S. Plattner (ed.) *Markets and Marketing.* Monographs in Economic Anthropology 4. Lanham, MD: University Press of America.

Blanton, Richard E. and Gary M. Feinman 1984. "The Mesoamerican world-system: a comparative perspective." *American Anthropologist* 86:673-82.

Blanton, Richard E., Stephen A. Kowalewski, Gary M. Feinman, and Jill Appel 1981. *Ancient Mesoamerica: A Comparison of Change in Three Regions*. Cambridge: Cambridge University Press.

_____ 1982. *Monte Albán's Hinterland, Part 1: The Prehispanic Settlement Patterns of the Central and Southern Parts of the Valley of Oaxaca, Mexico*. Ann Arbor: University of Michigan, Museum of Anthropology, Memoir 15.

Brockington, Donald L. 1973. *Archaeological Investigations at Miahuatlán, Oaxaca*. Nashville: Vanderbilt University, Publications in Anthropology 7.

Brumfiel, Elizabeth M. 1976. *Specialization and Exchange at the Late Postclassic (Aztec) Community of Huexotla, Mexico*. Ph.D. Dissertation, Anthropology, University of Michigan.

Brumfiel, Elizabeth M. and Timothy K. Earle 1987. "Specialization, exchange, and complex societies: an introduction." Pp. 1-9 in E.M. Brumfiel and T.K. Earle (eds.) *Specialization, Exchange, and Complex Societies*. Cambridge: Cambridge University Press.

Childe, V. Gordon 1950. "The urban revolution." *The Town Planning Review* 21:3-17.

Chisholm, Michael 1968. *Rural Settlement and Land Use: An Essay in Location*. 2nd ed. London: Hutchinson University Library.

Culbert, T. Patrick 1988. "Political history and the decipherment of Maya glyphs." *Antiquity* 62:135-152.

Drennan, Robert D. 1984a. "Long-distance transport costs in pre-hispanic Mesoamerica." *American Anthropologist* 86:105-112.

_____ 1984b. "Long-distance movement of goods in the Mesoamerican Formative and Classic." *American Antiquity* 49:27-43.

Drennan, Robert D. and Kent V. Flannery 1983. "The growth of site hierarchies in the Valley of Oaxaca: part II." Pp. 65-71 in K.V. Flannery and J. Marcus (eds.) *The Cloud People: Divergent Evolution of the Zapotec and Mixtec Civilizations*. New York: Academic Press.

Elam, J. Michael 1989. "Defensible and fortified sites." Pp. 385-407 in S.A. Kowalewski, G.M. Feinman, L. Finsten, R.E. Blanton, and L.M. Nicholas *Monte Albán's Hinterland, Part II: The Prehispanic Settlement Patterns of Tlacolula, Etla, and Ocotlán, the Valley of Oaxaca, Mexico*. Ann Arbor: University of Michigan, Museum of Anthropology, Memoirs 23.

Feinman, Gary M. 1980. *The Relationship between Administrative Organization and Ceramic Production in the Valley of Oaxaca, Mexico.* Ph.D. Dissertation, Anthropology, City University of New York.

_____ 1985. "Investigations in a near-periphery: regional settlement pattern survey in the Ejutla Valley, Oaxaca, Mexico." *Mexicon* 7:60-68.

_____ 1986. "The emergence of specialized ceramic production in Formative Oaxaca." Pp. 347-373 in B.L. Isaac (ed.) *Economic Aspects of Prehispanic Highland Mexico. Research in Economic Anthropology.* Supplement 2.

_____ 1989. "Demography, surplus, and inequality: early political formations in highland Mesoamerica." Forthcoming in T. Earle (ed.) *Chiefdoms and their Evolutionary Significance.*

Feinman, Gary M., Stephen A. Kowalewski, and Richard E. Blanton 1984. "Modelling ceramic production and organizational change in the pre-hispanic Valley of Oaxaca, Mexico." Pp. 297-333 in S.E. van der Leeuw and A.C. Pritchard (eds.) *The Many Dimensions of Pottery.* Amsterdam: University of Amsterdam.

Feinman, Gary M., Stephen A. Kowalewski, Laura Finsten, Richard E. Blanton, and Linda M. Nicholas 1985. "Long-term demographic change: a perspective from the Valley of Oaxaca, Mexico." *Journal of Field Archaeology* 12:333-362.

Feinman, Gary M. and Linda M. Nicholas 1987a. "Labor, surplus, and production: a regional analysis of Formative Oaxacan socio-economic change." Pp. 27-50 in S. Gaines (ed.) *Coasts, Plains and Deserts: Essays in Honor of Reynold J. Ruppé.* Tempe: Arizona State University, Anthropological Research Papers 38.

_____ 1987b. "Prehispanic interregional interaction in southern Mexico: the Valley of Oaxaca and the Ejutla Valley." Forthcoming in E.M. Schortman and P.A. Urban (eds.) *Resources, Power, and Interregional Interaction.*

_____ 1988. "The prehispanic settlement history of the Ejutla Valley, Mexico: a preliminary perspective." *Mexicon* 10:5-13.

Finsten, Laura 1983. *The Classic-Postclassic Transition in the Valley of Oaxaca, Mexico: A Regional Analysis of the Process of Political Decentralisation in a Prehistoric Complex Society.* Ph.D. Dissertation, Anthropology, Purdue University.

Flannery, Kent V. 1983. "Precolumbian farming in the Valleys of Oaxaca, Nochixtlán, Tehuacán, and Cuicatlán: a comparative study." Pp. 323-339 in K.V. Flannery and J. Marcus (eds.) *The Cloud People: Divergent Evolution of the Zapotec and Mixtec Civilizations*. New York: Academic Press.

Flannery, Kent V., Anne V.T. Kirkby, Michael J. Kirkby, and Aubrey W. Williams, Jr. 1967. "Farming systems and political growth in ancient Oaxaca." *Science* 158:445-453.

Flannery, Kent V. and Joyce Marcus 1976. "Evolution of the public building in Formative Oaxaca." Pp. 205-221 in C.E. Cleland (ed.) *Culture Change and Continuity: Essays in Honor of James Bennett Griffin*. New York: Academic Press.

Flannery, Kent V. and Joyce Marcus (eds.) 1983. *The Cloud People: Divergent Evolution of the Zapotec and Mixtec Civilizations*. New York: Academic Press.

Freidel, David A. 1986. "Maya warfare: an example of peer polity interaction." Pp. 93-108 in C. Renfrew and J.F. Cherry (eds.) *Peer Polity Interaction and Socio-Political Change*. Cambridge: Cambridge University Press.

Howard, Hilary 1981. "In the wake of distribution: towards an integrated approach to ceramic studies in prehistoric Britain." Pp.1-30 in H. Howard and E.L. Morris (eds.) *Production and Distribution: A Ceramic Viewpoint*. British Archaeological Reports, International Series 120.

Kirkby, Anne V.T. 1973. *The Use of Land and Water Resources in the Past and Present Valley of Oaxaca, Mexico*. Ann Arbor: University of Michigan, Museum of Anthropology, Memoirs 5.

Kohl, Philip L. 1987. "The use and abuse of world systems theory: the case of the pristine West Asian state." Pp. 1-35 in M.B. Schiffer (ed.) *Advances in Archaeological Method and Theory*, Volume 11. San Diego: Academic Press.

Kowalewski, Stephen A. 1980. "Population-resource balances in period I of Oaxaca, Mexico." *American Antiquity* 45:151-165.

_____ 1982. "Population and agricultural potential: Early I through V." Pp. 149-180 in R. Blanton, S. Kowalewski, G. Feinman, and J. Appel *Monte Albán's Hinterland, Part I: The Prehispanic Settlement Patterns of the Central and Southern Parts of the Valley of Oaxaca, Mexico*. Ann Arbor: University of Michigan, Museum of Anthropology, Memoirs 15: .

Kowalewski, Stephen A., Richard E. Blanton, Gary M. Feinman, and Laura Finsten 1983. "Boundaries, scale, and internal organization." *Journal of Anthropological Archaeology* 2:32-56.

Kowalewski, Stephen A., Gary M. Feinman, Laura Finsten, Richard E. Blanton, and Linda M. Nicholas 1989. *Monte Albán's Hinterland, Part II: The Prehispanic Settlement Patterns of Tlacolula, Etla, and Ocotlán, the Valley of Oaxaca, Mexico.* Ann Arbor: University of Michigan, Museum of Anthropology, Memoirs 23.

Kowalewski, Stephen A. and Laura Finsten 1983. "The economic systems of ancient Oaxaca: a regional perspective." *Current Anthropology* 24:413-441.

Lees, Susan H. 1973. *Sociopolitical Aspects of Canal Irrigation in the Valley of Oaxaca.* Ann Arbor: University of Michigan, Museum of Anthropology, Memoirs 6.

Lightfoot, Kent G. 1979. "Food redistribution among prehistoric Pueblo groups." *Kiva* 44:319-339.

Marcus, Joyce 1976a. *Emblem and State in the Classic Maya Lowlands: An Epigraphic Approach to Territorial Organization.* Washington, D.C.: Dumbarton Oaks Research Library and Collections.

_____ 1976b. "The iconography of militarism at Monte Albán and neighboring sites in the Valley of Oaxaca." Pp. 123-139 in H.B. Nicholson (ed.) *Origins of Religious Art and Iconography in Pre-Classic Mesoamerica.* Los Angeles: UCLA Latin American Center.

_____ 1980. "Zapotec writing." *Scientific American* 242:50-64.

_____ 1983. "The conquest slabs of Building J, Monte Albán." Pp. 106-108 in K.V. Flannery and J. Marcus (eds.) *The Cloud People: Divergent Evolution of the Zapotec and Mixtec Civilizations.* New York: Academic Press.

_____ 1989. "From centralized systems to city-states: possible models for the Epiclassic." Pp. 201-208 in R.A. Diehl and J.C. Berlo (eds.) *Mesoamerica after the Decline of Teotihuacan A.D. 700-900.* Washington, D.C.: Dumbarton Oaks Research Library and Collections.

Marcus, Joyce and Kent V. Flannery 1983. "The Postclassic balkanization of Oaxaca." Pp. 217-226 in K.V. Flannery and J. Marcus (eds.) *The Cloud People: Divergent Evolution of the Zapotec and Mixtec Civilizations.* New York: Academic Press.

Markman, Charles W. 1981. *Prehispanic Settlement Dynamics in Central Oaxaca, Mexico: A View from the Miahuatlán Valley.* Nashville: Vanderbilt University, Publications in Anthropology 26.

Mathews, Peter 1985. "Maya early Classic monuments and inscriptions." Pp. 5-54 in G.R. Willey and P. Mathews (eds.) *A Consideration of the Early*

Classic Period in the Maya Lowlands. Albany: Institute for Mesoamerican Studies, State University of New York at Albany, No. 10.

McGuire, Randall H. 1986. "Economies and modes of production in the prehistoric southwestern periphery." Pp. 243-269 in F.J. Mathien and R.H. McGuire (eds.) *Ripples in the Chichimec Sea: New Considerations of Southwestern-Mesoamerican Interactions.* Carbondale: Southern Illinois University Press.

Nicholas, Linda M. 1989. "Land use in prehispanic Oaxaca." Pp. 449-505 in S.A. Kowalewski, G.M. Feinman, L. Finsten, R.E. Blanton, and L.M. Nicholas *Monte Albán's Hinterland, Part II: The Prehispanic Settlement Patterns of Tlacolula, Etla, and Ocotlán, the Valley of Oaxaca, Mexico.* Ann Arbor: University of Michigan, Museum of Anthropology, Memoirs 23.

Nicholas, Linda M., Gary M. Feinman, Stephen A. Kowalewski, Richard E. Blanton, and Laura Finsten 1986. "Prehispanic colonization of the Valley of Oaxaca, Mexico." *Human Ecology* 14:131-162.

Paddock, John 1983a. *Lord 5 Flower's Family.* Nashville: Vanderbilt University, Publications in Anthropology 29.

_____ 1983b. "Comment on 'The economic systems of ancient Oaxaca: a regional perspective,' by Stephen A. Kowalewski and Laura Finsten." *Current Anthropology* 24:433.

Palerm, Angel and Eric R. Wolf 1957. "Ecological Potential and Cultural Development in Mesoamerica." *Pan American Union Social Science Monograph* 3:1-37.

Parry, William J. 1987. *Chipped Stone Tools in Formative Oaxaca, Mexico: Their Procurement, Production and Use.* Ann Arbor: University of Michigan, Museum of Anthropology, Memoirs 20.

Parsons, Jeffrey R. 1971. *Prehistoric Settlement Patterns in the Texcoco Region, Mexico.* Ann Arbor: University of Michigan, Museum of Anthropology, Memoirs 3.

Parsons, Mary Hrones 1972. "Spindle whorls from the Teotihuacán Valley, Mexico." Pp. 45-79 in M.W. Spence, J.R. Parsons, and M.H. Parsons *Miscellaneous Studies in Mexican Prehistory.* Ann Arbor: University of Michigan, Museum of Anthropology, Anthropological Papers 45.

Ragin, Charles and Daniel Chirot 1984. "The world system of Immanuel Wallerstein: sociology and politics as history." Pp. 276-312 in T. Skopol (ed.) *Vision and Method in Historical Sociology*. Cambridge: Cambridge University Press.

Redmond, Elsa M. 1983. *A Fuego y Sangre: Early Zapotec Imperialism in the Cuicatlán Cañada, Oaxaca*. Ann Arbor: University of Michigan, Museum of Anthropology, Memoirs 16.

Sanders, William T. 1965. "The cultural ecology of the Teotihuacan Valley." University Park: Department of Sociology and Anthropology, Pennsylvania State University.

Sanders, William T. and Deborah L. Nichols 1988. "Ecological theory and cultural evolution in the Valley of Oaxaca." *Current Anthropology* 29:33-80.

Sanders, William T., Jeffrey R. Parsons, and Robert S. Santley 1979. *The Basin of Mexico: Ecological Processes in the Evolution of a Civilization*. New York: Academic Press.

Schortman, Edward M. and Patricia A. Urban 1987. "Modeling interregional interaction in prehistory." Pp. 37-95 in M.B. Schiffer (ed.) *Advances in Archaeological Method and Theory, Volume 11*. San Diego: Academic Press.

Smith, Michael E. 1986. "The role of social stratification in the Aztec empire: a view from the provinces." *American Anthropologist* 88:70-91.

———— 1987. "Archaeology and the Aztec economy: the social scientific use of archaeological data." *Social Science History* 11:237-259.

Spence, Michael W. 1983. "Comment on 'The economic systems of ancient Oaxaca: a regional perspective,' by Stephen A. Kowalewski and Laura Finsten." *Current Anthropology* 24:433-34.

Spencer, Charles S. 1982. *The Cuicatlán Cañada and Monte Albán*. New York: Academic Press.

Strassoldo, Raimondo 1980. "Centre-periphery and system-boundary: culturological perspectives." Pp. 27-61 in J. Gottmann (ed.) *Centre and Periphery: Spatial Variation in Politics*. London: Sage Publications.

Trigger, Bruce G. 1984. "Archaeology at the crossroads: what's new?" *Annual Review of Anthropology* 13:275-300.

Wallerstein, Immanuel 1974. *The Modern World-System I*. New York: Academic Press.

Welte, Cecil R. 1973. "Ready reference release No. 2." *Oaxaca*.

Willey, Gordon R. and Jeremy A. Sabloff 1980. *A History of American Archaeology*. San Francisco: W.H. Freeman.

EPILOGUE

Christopher Chase-Dunn and Thomas D. Hall

This is our opportunity to review the main issues which have emerged from this collection and to have the last word. There are a number of major controversies, but one conclusion is obvious: the world-systems perspective stimulates new and fruitful approaches to pre-modern socio-economic systems.

Some of the controversies are reflections of old debates within the social sciences:

1. To what extent should we emphasize systemic and evolutionary models *versus* historical conjunctures?

2. What are the important similarities between modern and premodern socio-economic systems and what are the qualitative differences?

3. Have there been major sea changes in the logics of systems (transformations) or have there been only different mixes of logics (or random changes)? How can we measure the extent to which one logic is predominant over another?

4. If there have been major transformations of system logics, how can we theoretically define and empirically measure these logics and how can we explain the transformations?

A second set of issues are more particular to our project as it is constituted in this volume:

1. How to define and bound world-systems?

2. How to define and measure core/periphery hierarchies?

3. Does it make sense to compare stateless intergroup systems with larger state-based systems?

4. Is the comparison of a large number of world-systems theoretically desirable? Is it feasible?

5. Is the study of single world-systems over very long periods of time a more fruitful strategy?

6. Can the scientific study of the transformation of deep structural logics in world-systems provide important clues about how the modern global political economy might become transformed?

Most of these problems are at least implicitly raised in each of the chapters in this collection. We will discuss Chapters 2 through 8 to present our most recent reflections on these matters.

Chapter 2, Jane Schneider's path-breaking discussion, raises many of the issues about the nature and boundaries of world-systems. Schneider argues that prestige goods exchanges are important in reproducing and changing power structures and thus they cannot be considered epiphenomenal. The editors and all of the authors in this volume agree with her. Nevertheless the editors think that Immanuel Wallerstein's emphasis on a division of labor of bulk goods production and exchange should not be abandoned because this is also important to structural reproduction and change. Thus we include both prestige goods networks and bulk goods networks in our definition of world-systems. This creates a boundary problem because the boundaries of these two types of networks are rarely similar. We are most likely to have at least two levels of integration: a number of regional bulk goods networks linked together by a prestige goods network. To complicate things further we also agree with Wilkinson (Chapter 4) that regular political/military competition and cooperation should be used to bound world-systems. This adds an additional degree of fuzziness to the boundaries of world-systems because the networks of political/military interaction do not usually correspond with the networks of prestige goods exchange. This is discussed further below.

The other problem which we need to mention again is the use of modes of production to bound world-systems. Wallerstein uses both modes of production and bulk goods networks, though he sometimes emphasizes one and sometimes the other. As stated in Chapter 1, he argues that the European world-economy and the Ottoman world-empire were separate systems, but he does not argue that they engaged in no trade of bulk goods. Rather he contends that they were different systems because capitalism was dominant in Europe but not in the Ottoman Empire. We have claimed that the use of mode of production criteria to spatially bound world-systems is a theoretical mistake, but this does not leave us in the same camp with Gills and Frank, who argue that there are no transitions between modes of production (accumulation).

We think that capitalism (however defined) did become predominant for the first time in Europe, but that Europe was a subsystem of a larger Afro-eurasian super-system. Europe had not been a separate bulk goods network from the rest of the Mediterranean littoral since at least Roman times and the political/military interactions and prestige goods interactions between Europe and the other areas of the Afro-eurasian super-system have been important at least since the Greeks and Phoenicians moved toward the west. Explanation of the emergent predominance of capitalism in the European subsystem by focussing exclusively on the uniqueness of European feudalism or religion is a myopic exercise which recent work by Abu-Lughod (1989) and others has begun to correct.

Capitalist institutions were neither absent from premodern and non-European systems, nor were they randomly distributed among them. The commodification of land, goods, wealth and labor had been increasing, albeit unevenly, in the Afro-eurasian super-system for thousands of years. The empires of Central Civilization were becoming increasingly commercialized. The Roman and Chinese Empires were perhaps the most capitalist of these, but within them the tributary mode of accumulation remained predominant. Semiperipheral autonomous capitalist city states were important agents of commodification that linked empires to one another and to peripheral regions by marketized trade (Chase-Dunn, 1991). The emphasis on continuities stressed by Gills and Frank is an important antidote to the quaint notion that Europe was unique, but a more valuable approach would study the ways in which commodification emerged and spread within Central Civilization and the other tributary world-systems. Only this kind of approach can sensibly separate the conjunctural aspects of the "rise of the West" from its more evolutionary aspects.[1]

Chapter 3 by Gills and Frank is an outstanding contribution which focusses our attention on the continuities which can be found in *the* world-system. By claiming there has only been one world-system for the last 5000 years they create many difficulties, however. Their own definition belies this. They argue that two regions are in the same system if they importantly affect one another.[2] What about the pre-Columbian systems described by Feinman and Nicholas and by Peregrine? These were certainly not part of *the* world-system. Wilkinson's approach is superior. He is much more specific about how he bounds his civilizations/world-systems and he documents the expansion of *the* world-system (his Central Civilization) without denying the existence of others.

Gills and Frank also raise the issue of the mode of production, which they call "accumulation." Like Ekholm and Friedman (1982), they deny that there is anything unique at the level of the logic of accumulation about the Europe-centered system which distinguishes it from the earlier Eurasian system. As stated above, we do argue that the Europe-centered system was unique in the degree to which capitalist accumulation became predominant. It is possible to acknowledge many of the continuities which Gills and Frank describe while still maintaining that the modern system is qualitatively distinct in fundamental respects.

One major difference between the modern interstate system and the earlier systems of political-military interaction is in the nature of the cycle of political centralization/decentralization. What are the similarities and differences between the rise and fall of empires and the rise and fall of hegemonic core states in the modern world-system? An important specification of the alternation between empires and interstate systems is presented by Wilkinson (see Figure 2 in Chapter 4). The significant difference is that the most successful states in the modern world-system (the hegemons) do not try to create universal empires, but rather act to sustain the multicentric interstate system. In premodern systems the most successful states pursued a strategy of empire-formation by conquest. Our explanation for this difference is the predominance in the modern world-system of an alternative to the tributary strategy of accumulation -- the accumulation of wealth through the production of commodities. Capitalist accumulation thrives on a politically multicentric system, and thus the most successful states, which are now *capitalist* states, act to sustain the interstate system, not to conquer it. [3]

Wilkinson's larger theoretical apparatus and his detailed specification in Chapter 4 are magnificent contributions. They are conceptually explicit and clear. The fund of empirical knowledge which Wilkinson shares with the other civilizationists is detailed and extensive. We have only a few demurs.

Wilkinson is a political scientist of the international relations persuasion and the histories upon which the civilizationists draw are predominantly narratives about the wars of the great men. When Wilkinson says that "diamonds may be forever, but clubs are always trumps" he is both making a witticism and cleaving to a perspective which sees states as the main actors in history. Wilkinson, like Gills and Frank, does not believe in a major sea-change which transformed the logic of the game with the rise of the West. But the game he thinks has continued to be played is different from the one hypothesized by Gills and Frank. They emphasize the interaction between economic exploitation and political domination, while Wilkinson sees political domination as the predominant logic of Central Civilization in all ages.

This state-centric approach is reflected in Wilkinson's use of political/ military interaction as the empirical means to spatially bound world-systems. We agree that conflictual interaction is important, but we expect that the centrality of military conflict varies across different kinds of systems, and we argue that prestige and bulk goods networks are also important forms of interaction. The addition of these other criteria would complicate Wilkinson's spatio-temporal schema. Prestige goods networks are generally larger than regularized political/military interaction nets. China and Rome were linked by prestige goods trade, but not by direct political/military engagement. The mapping of these three network criteria would usually produce regional subsystems of bulk goods exchange within larger systems of political/military interaction within even larger systems of prestige goods exchange.

We propose that: bulk goods networks be called "regional subsystems," political/military interaction networks be labeled "world-systems," and prestige goods networks be termed "supersystems." [4] This sorts out the issues rather clearly, we think, though empirical work will undoubtedly raise many more.

Wilkinson's definition of civilizations/world-systems raises another issue. He uses both "level" and "interconnectedness" criteria. We have already discussed the interconnectedness aspect above in our consideration of definitions and spatial boundaries of world-systems. The "level" criterion is similar to that used by other civilizationists to differentiate between civilizations and precivilizations. Wilkinson requires his systems to have cities, record-keeping, economic surplus and non-producing classes. Gills and Frank also exclude intersocietal systems which existed before the emergence of urbanization and states in Mesopotamia 5000 years ago so they must also believe that some such set of features is essential to a world-system.

Our strategy is quite different. Instead of emphasizing similarities we are searching for differences. In variation we hope to find explanations for the structural characteristics of different kinds of world-systems. Thus we extend the use of the term to classless, stateless systems. This raises many new problems, but we believe that the effort to include these very different kinds of systems will be well worth the trouble. Our distinction at the conceptual level between world-systems and core/periphery hierarchies is helped immensely. Not only do different kinds of world-systems have different kinds of core/periphery hierarchies, but some world-systems do not have them at all.

In terms of the "river system" analogy employed by Gills and Frank to describe how many smaller tributaries joined together to form *the* world-system, we want to study creeks and small streams. We believe that they will be found to have some dynamics which are generally similar to larger systems and yet they differ in important ways. For example, much recent research suggests that there is a process of the rise and fall of chiefdoms which is analytically similar to the cycles of political centralization/decentralization exhibited in the rise and fall of states, empires and hegemonic core powers. We are not claiming that this process is the "same" but rather that the general similarities and the important differences are worthy of investigation.

Does this mean that we are claiming that every kind of human interaction system is a world-system? If everything is inside a category, the category is not useful. We are **not** claiming *a priori* that all human groups live in intergroup systems which importantly determine the conditions of social reproduction and change. Rather we are arguing that whether or not this is true should be examined. We do exclude human interaction spheres in which *all* the groups are extensively nomadic because we believe that territoriality of some kind is fundamentally important to the notion of a world-system.

Another reason to include stateless, classless world-systems in our comparative study is that this allows us to examine what everyone would agree is a fundamental watershed in system logic -- the transformation from the kin-based modes to the state-based modes of production (accumulation). We want to build on the important work of Friedman and Rowlands (1977) and Gailey (1987) to understand the interplay between class formation, gender hierarchy and pristine state formation in the context of these tiny world-systems. For the purposes of the long term goal of building a theory of transformations this provides an additional class of cases to serve as the empirical foundation.

Wilkinson is also pleasantly explicit about his usage of the terms core, periphery and semiperiphery. His definitions differ from ours. We distinguish between core/periphery differentiation and core/periphery domination-exploitation. Our concern is to create concepts which do not carry more baggage from the modern world-system than is desirable, and to allow comparative research to fill in the contents.

Wilkinson's usage more directly focusses on political control or its absence. The semiperiphery, in his usage, is a less developed area which is under core control, while the periphery is in trade or political contact with the core, but not under control. We have already endorsed the notion of the contact periphery, but our periphery also includes areas which are controlled and dominated by the core. We also imagine that an area can be economically exploited without being politically dominated (e.g., neo-colonialism in the modern world-system). Our definitions would produce different zonal boundaries -- most evident in Wilkinson's maps in Figures 10 and 11.[5]

Wilkinson's definition is not incompatible with ours, but it does reflect differences in what he calls "theoretical ancestors" as well as differences in empirical scope. Because we come from a neo-Marxian background we are more likely to stress the importance of economic exploitation. And because we want to examine stateless systems we need to define core/periphery relations broadly enough to be able to capture very different kinds of intersocietal inequalities.

We have already commented on the thoughtful nature of Chapter 5 by Stephen Sanderson. We agree that the world-systems perspective can be thought of as evolutionary once the many pitfalls of prior evolutionism have been exorcised. We do not agree that "internal" factors are generally more important than world-system level factors in premodern systems, but that is a matter for research to determine when hypotheses about the causality of particular outcomes have been specified and operationalized. For now we think that the strong world-system position should be pushed as far as it will go.

Sanderson follows Perry Anderson's claim that European and Japanese feudalism were institutionally unique compared to all the other decentralized tributary systems on Earth, and that this uniqueness accounts for the strong development of European and Japanese capitalism. It is our position that many other regions had experienced the "parcellization of sovereignty," but not in the context of a larger system in which capitalist institutions were so fully developed. This, and the decline of the East described by Abu-Lughod, created an opportunity for semiperipheral Europe to form a new core region in which capitalist-controlled cities were dense and capitalist states became core states for the first time. Earlier states controlled by capitalists -- city states -- had been located in the semiperipheral interstices between empires. It was the formation of a regional subsystem in which an interstate system was dominated by states largely controlled by capitalists which led to the eventual hegemony of the West over a single global system. Europe was simply in the right place at the right time.

Peter Peregrine's study of Cahokia (Chapter 6) is an important contribution because it shows how a complex chiefdom (or pristine state) system can be analyzed as a world-system. The description of this system as based wholly on the monopolization of prestige goods raises questions about the relationship between this sort of control and other forms of power. Friedman and Rowlands (1977) argue that such systems are inherently unstable because those who are dominated by symbolic means can redefine the symbols or change their beliefs. Thus such symbolic power needs to be backed up by military power or by control over less substitutable goods. In support of this, the Cahokia-centered system was unstable. It collapsed almost completely, and perhaps this was due to over-reliance on the monopoly of prestige goods. Even so, the rather hierarchical nature of the system[6] makes us guess that military and bulk goods aspects should be given somewhat more attention than they receive from Peregrine.

Hall's discussion of nomads (Chapter 7) raises many new questions without answering them, but a few conclusions seem relatively solid. First, failure to study the complex roles of nomads in core/periphery hierarchies will distort our understanding of the evolution and transformations of world-systems. Second, the roles of nomads in core/periphery hierarchies are complex, and are, at least in part, understood only in the context of the larger system in which they are embedded. Put another way, frontiers are integral parts of world-systems, even though they are -- by definition -- on the fringe. Third, and more tentatively, the technology of land transportation and communication in combination with changing geopolitical structures accounts for relative changes in the power of nomads within various contexts. Once nomads are contained within a bounded territory, and technology exists to efficiently patrol that territory, nomads cease to play a major role in core/periphery hierarchy processes.

Both Central Asia and Northwest New Spain appear to be unusual in the length of time during which nomads played significant roles in at least regional processes. We say "appear" because nomads have been so seldom studied in this context that we cannot yet realistically assess how unusual these cases are. Regardless, these cases suggest openness and sensitivity to other, more ephemeral yet similar processes, in other locations and other times. In particular, we should examine the roles of nomads -- and others -- as intermediaries between the various levels proposed above: regional subsystems, world-systems, and supersystems. Further empirical examination of these will help refine or concepts and our understanding of general processes.

The contribution by Gary Feinman and Linda Nicholas (Chapter 8) reveals how archaeological data can be used to examine the nature of a regional division of labor. Their interesting finding is that dependency emerges in this region originally not on the basis of food production but on the basis of craft production, probably of prestige goods. This suggests a sequence of core/periphery formation which may also have occured in other early world-systems.

Back to the Future

The comparative study of world-systems poses potentially severe theoretical problems for classical explanations of social change. Most troublesome for Marxists is the possible demotion of class from its central role as the engine of social change. While it is certainly premature to claim this to have been demonstrated, it should be left open as a possibility that Marx was wrong to generalize the centrality of class struggle in early capitalist Europe into the distant past. Class struggle cannot have been the motor of change in classless systems.

On the other hand, the more general Marxist presuppositions employed by several anthropologists (e.g., Wolf, 1982) -- a focus on the way in which social labor is mobilized in connection with the production and reproduction of material life and the institutions which regulate interaction -- may be the most useful theoretical apparatus to employ for developing a new general explanation of historical development which focusses on world-systems and core/periphery hierarchies. The study of production, distribution and accumulation ought to analyze the interaction between intrasocietal class relations and intersocietal core/periphery hierarchies. And, as with the modern system, we should examine the transsocietal aspects of class relations.

The conceptual reformulations of world-systems and core/periphery hierarchies presented in this book knock all the endogenist *versus* exogenist debates into a cocked hat. The issue of the primacy of "internal" *versus* "external" factors is transformed. We now need to explicitly consider the multilevel nature of all world-systems and to study the interactions between levels.

The sorting out of what is external or internal to which context is, of course, complicated by the fuzziness of system boundaries. The designation of bulk goods regional subsystem, political/military world-systems, and prestige goods supersystems (or some other set of terms) clarifies this problem somewhat, but not completely. It is probably more profitable to think in terms of degrees of hierarchy, degrees of interconnectedness, degrees of "systemness," and to study these variables empirically. Stinchcombe's (1985) comment that the early modern world-system was a "ramshackle affair" remains cogent as does John Hall's (1984) dissection of modern world-system holism.

Attention to context within larger networks should also be paid in the comparative study of the processes by which less hierarchical systems become incorporated into more hierarchical ones. Small societies are transformed into ethnic groups in the processes of incorporation, but the nature of these transformations may vary with the type of core/periphery context.[7]

The historical development from small world-systems to the global one has been a process of the emergence of larger and larger levels of organization and the incorporation of less hierarchical systems into more hierarchical ones. The transitions involved in chiefdom formation, state formation, empire formation, the rise and fall of hegemonic core powers (and the possible future emergence of a global state) may be seen as iterations of a general process. It is the shared features in the sequences of political centralization/decentralization, the emergence of larger levels of organization, and the general importance of core/periphery relations in these processes, which are emphasized by Gills and Frank, and Ekholm and Friedman.

But a closer study of these historical patterns will reveal that there have been important **systematic** differences across the iterations. The clarification of these is just beginning. The trick now is to employ a comparative framework which can walk the narrow trail between overly abstract general model-building and overly specific emphasis on uniquenesses and conjunctural circumstances.

Finally, we would like to extend our pluralistic approach to the comparative study of world-systems to include research strategies. Synchronic, diachronic, comparative, and case study strategies are all potentially useful. Synchronic studies need to take into account that contemporaneous world-systems may represent very different types of systems. The degree of independence of cases becomes an increasingly thorny problem through time. Diachronic studies face the same problem in spades. Even in a diachronic case study the context is changing, but if the object of study is a whole world-system this problem should be reduced.[8]

There are at least three broad strategies for dealing with these problems comparatively. The first is to examine a small number of cases synchronically. This is certainly the most feasible approach, and can be most helpful for addressing conceptual issues and for making very general distinctions. It also allows for another important product of case studies -- the consideration of uniquenesses. A second strategy is to make comparisons of trajectories of change, that is to compare long-term case studies -- Chapter 7 uses this strategy. This approach can also be important for formulating concepts and hypotheses about processes of change. The third approach is to make formal comparisons which examine variation across many different world-systems. This approach can only be undertaken after conceptual work has been done and hypotheses about comparative processes have been formulated and operationalized. Though the problems of such formal cross-world-system research are great, it is the only design which can provide strong evidence for or against hypotheses which are derived from contending general theories of historical development. Our effort in Chapter 1 to develop a typology of world-systems is intended to facilitate such comparisons. Hence, not taxonomic completeness, but a preliminary and heuristically useful guide for comparative studies is the goal of our set of types.

Since we began this project we have found many other social scientists who have been working along similar lines and we have managed to convince many others to join the effort. We fancy that this might be the beginning of the shift of social science from multiparadigm childhood to grown-up normal science, but if it is just one more turn in the great sky-wheel which oscillates between historical particularism and evolutionary generalism, so be it. We are not convinced by the current post-modern proclamation that political and scientific progress is always an illusion, though we certainly acknowledge that the ideology of progress has been used as a tool of oppression on many occasions. While we think that the study of less hierarchical societies may be able suggest ways for own very hierarchical world-system to become more humane in the future, we do not follow those who romanticize the "primitive" because they dislike the present. The contemporary involvement of our own global political economy in what almost everyone sees as important restructuring is a further source of inspiration for a new study of the past. A "back to the future" approach to the transformation of the global world-system may turn out to be both politically and scientifically progressive.

NOTES

1. The really big question: was the rise of the West occidental?

2. Walter Goldfrank has commented that this kind of general statement can easily become "one more chorus of the bone song."

3. This idea is discussed in greater detail in Chase-Dunn (1990).

4. If Wallerstein wants to assert property claims over the term "world-system" for bulk goods nets we will drop the hyphen, as have Wilkinson, Gills and Frank.

5. Compare Wilkinson's maps with those in Shannon(1989). Another problem with Wilkinson's maps is their implication that everything on Earth outside of the semiperiphery of Central Civilization is in the periphery. This is contrary to his own definition of a peripheral area, which is defined as in interaction with the core but not politically controlled by it. Surely Tierra del

Fuego was not in the periphery of Mesopotamian civilization. Bounding the contact peripheries may be empirically difficult, but it is not impossible.

6. O'Brien (1990) reports that one of the mounds excavated at Cahokia contained the remains of over 70 young women, apparently sacrificed in a single ritual. The power necessary to produce such an event almost certainly indicates that Cahokia was a state rather than a chiefdom. Prestige goods and ritual monopolies are unlikely to have been the sole basis of such an organization.

7. See T. Hall (1984) for a fuller discussion of this issue.

8. See McMichael (1990) for a detailed strategy and description of how to do this.

REFERENCES

Abu-Lughod, Janet 1989. *Before European Hegemony*. New York: Oxford University Press.

Chase-Dunn, Christopher 1990. "The Limits of Hegemony: Capitalism and Global State Formation." Pp. 213-40 in David P. Rapkin (ed.) *World Leadership and Hegemony*. Boulder, CO.: Lynne Rienner.

Chase-Dunn, Christopher 1991. "The Changing Role of Cities in World-Systems." in Volker Bornschier and Peter Lengyel (eds.) *World Society Studies*, Volume 2. Frankfurt/New York: Campus Verlag.

Ekholm, Kasja and Jonathan Friedman 1982. "'Capital' Imperialism and Exploitation in the Ancient World-Systems." *Review* 6:1:87-110.

Friedman, Jonathan and Michael J. Rowlands 1977. "Notes Toward an Epigenetic Model of the Evolution of 'Civilization.'" Pp. 201-78 in J. Friedman and M.J. Rowlands (eds.) *The Evolution of Social Systems*. London: Duckworth.

Gailey, Christine 1987. *Kinship to Kingship: Gender Hierarchy and State Formation in the Tongan Islands*. Austin: University of Texas Press.

Hall, John R. 1984. "World-System Holism and Colonial Brazilian Agriculture: A Critical Case Analysis." *Latin American Research Review* 19:2:43-69.

Hall, Thomas D. 1984. "Lessons of Long-term Social Change for Comparative and Historical Study of Ethnicity." *Current Perspectives in Social Theory* 5:121-144.

McMichael, Philip. 1990. "Incorporating Comparison Within a World-Historical Perspective: An Alternative Comparative Method." *American Sociological Review* 55:3(June): 385-397.

O'Brien, Patricia J. 1990. "The 'World-System' of Cahokia Within the Middle Mississippian Tradition." A paper presented at the annual meetings of the International Society for the Comparative Study of Civilizations, University of Illinois, May 27.

Shannon, Thomas R. 1989. *An Introduction to the World-System Perspective*. Boulder, CO.: Westview.

Stinchcombe, Arthur. 1985. "Macrosociology is sociology about millions of people." *Contemporary Sociology* 14:5(Sept.):572-575.

INDEX